G.B.B.Hunter

*Studies in the Philosophy
of Thought and Action*

Studies in the Philosophy of Thought and Action

British Academy Lectures by

GILBERT RYLE

STUART HAMPSHIRE

DAVID PEARS

G. E. L. OWEN

BERNARD WILLIAMS

A. J. AYER

P. F. STRAWSON

C. LEWY

P. T. GEACH

G. J. WARNOCK

Selected and Introduced by
P. F. STRAWSON

OXFORD UNIVERSITY PRESS

LONDON   OXFORD   NEW YORK

1968

Oxford University Press

LONDON   OXFORD   NEW YORK
GLASGOW   TORONTO   MELBOURNE   WELLINGTON
CAPE TOWN   SALISBURY   IBADAN   NAIROBI   LUSAKA   ADDIS ABABA
BOMBAY   CALCUTTA   MADRAS   KARACHI   LAHORE   DACCA
KUALA LUMPUR   HONG KONG   TOKYO

SELECTION AND INTRODUCTION
© OXFORD UNIVERSITY PRESS 1968

First published by Oxford University Press, London, as an
Oxford University Press paperback, 1968

PRINTED IN GREAT BRITAIN

Contents

P. F. STRAWSON

Introduction

The lectures included in this volume were all delivered to the British Academy within the space of the last ten years. They have not been selected with a view to illustrating trends. Yet several of them invite a grouping which indicates a major direction of interest in English philosophy in the period. The lectures of Ryle, Ayer, Hampshire, Pears, and Williams, together with my own, may all be brought under the broad heading of *Philosophy of Mind*. The fact that at least two of them could equally well be classified under *Ethics* serves only to show how closely these two areas are linked through the ideas of action and freedom, decision and reason.

Within this group of six lectures there are natural sub-groups. Ryle discusses thinking in general, Williams, specifically, imagination. The concepts are sensitively explored, in each case with a definite clarificatory purpose, the removal of a mystery or the dispelling of an illusion. We can, often easily enough, say what our thoughts were, or are. But if we are asked in exactly what occurrences of inner or mental life the having of those thoughts consisted, the question seems irksome, difficult, and oddly irrelevant to any real concern. Ryle suggests that we can better understand the irksomeness and difficulty of this question when we see that the difficulty of identifying and isolating such thought-vehicle-occurrences is paralleled by the less obvious difficulty of identifying, in isolation, separate and successive thoughts. Thoughts are what they are only because of the places they hold in actual or possible patterns or trains of thought; and thinking itself is not a separate activity, parallel to other human activities, but something essentially continuous with, and involved in, all human activities which are not wholly mechanical or instinctive. Ryle comments on the inadequacy of Plato's 'In thinking the soul is conversing with herself'. Perhaps the origin of the mystery of these elusive inner vehicles which should, it seems, carry our thoughts like passengers through the mind lies in the fact that when we *tell* our thoughts, our *sentences* can be individuated and counted, one by one.

Williams examines, first, the concepts of imagining and visualizing and their objects; second, the logical force and limits of the notion of self-identity. At the point at which these ideas merge— when one is said to imagine oneself as thus-and-so—a certain illusion may be generated or reinforced, unless one has a clear conception of *how* they merge. His lecture subtly and elegantly supplies the necessary clarification.

Ryle's and Williams's lectures are pure essays in the philosophy of mind, without ethical implications. Such implications are very much to the fore in Hampshire's lecture and my own, another natural pair. Hampshire sets out, with force and sympathy, those bold connections which Spinoza made between the ideas of freedom and necessity. Freedom, as ordinarily conceived, is, at least often, an illusion due to inadequate knowledge. But adequate knowledge, in particular knowledge of the universal laws of mental life, promotes freedom. It has the power to liberate us from negative and destructive passions by giving us an objective view of their causes, and thereby makes possible that unillusioned functioning of the mind in which a rational being asserts himself as an individual. Hampshire suggests that we may find in Spinoza the elements of a view of the mind capable, on the one hand, of receiving support from empirical psychology and, on the other, of grounding a more adequate conception of individual and political freedom than the liberal tradition has so far supplied. But freedom of mind, as understood by Spinoza, is admittedly rarely achieved.

My own lecture presents a picture—complementary, rather than opposed, to the above, but somewhat less austere in tendency—of the interconnections of personal feelings, moral sentiments, and social practices; the whole making up a human and social web or network which is capable, certainly, of modification but from which we can hardly imagine ourselves, and perhaps would hardly wish to imagine ourselves, altogether emancipated. A proper understanding of these interconnections offers us, it is suggested, a way between the crudely utilitarian insistence that a belief in the prevalence of natural law poses no threat to moral concepts, and the outraged counter-insistence that such a belief would utterly undermine them.

In the spectrum of topic and treatment, Pears's lecture, 'Predicting and Deciding', is located in the area between these first two sub-groups. Pears begins from the cases where one might be said to predict inductively the decision one will subsequently make without in the meantime losing memory of the prediction or its grounds. The most interesting case is that in which one has reason for thinking that one's desires may change. Decision does not come till the ultimately effective direction of desire is felt. So prediction can outstrip decision because knowledge of desire can outstrip desire. But the deeper interest of this question lies in the light it may cast on a different and more general question about the relations between an agent's *immediate* knowledge of what he will do and why, and a spectator's *inductive* knowledge of what the agent will do and why. How do these two kinds of knowledge fit together? Pears makes an extremely bold and deep-going attempt to explain the fitting together of these two kinds of knowledge by anchoring them both to a firmly 'empiricist' base. In this way the mystery which has come to surround the topic of an agent's self-knowledge may be dispelled. The daring of the argument is matched by its subtlety.

Highly relevant to the topics of Ryle's, Williams's, and Pears's lectures, but more general than any of them, is Ayer's lecture on 'Privacy'. The, or a, distinction between the mental and the physical is often made in terms of mental items being *private* while physical items are *public*. Ayer indicates some of the confusions into which a distinction, so made, may fall. He distinguishes four criteria of privacy of which one alone seems to offer hope of yielding something like the intended distinction. A sub-class of ascriptions to people is such that the subject of those ascriptions is the final authority as to their correctness. In what is thus ascribed, in what is in this sense private, we may perhaps find the central core of the mental, the 'immediate contents of consciousness'. Clearly this question stands at the very centre of the philosophy of mind; and the relating of Ayer's view to the topics previously mentioned is a task which promises both difficulty and reward.

Of the four remaining lectures I have selected, three are in part contributions to the critical history of philosophy. They are not very closely connected with each other or with the six already referred to. Yet there are connections. Reason and virtue were linked in one way by Spinoza. They were linked in a very different way by Kant. Warnock selects, for cool examination, the question why the 'Moral Law' was an object of such peculiar veneration to this latter philosopher. Since Kant's official view is that the source, the end, and the essence of the Moral Law lies in our 'rational nature', his attitude to morality should, it seems, be paralleled by a similar attitude to reason in general. But theoretical reason receives no such awestruck obeisance from him. Does the practical, or moral, employment of reason have the superiority because it commits us, as Kant holds, to the postulates of God, Freedom, and Immortality, which theoretical reason is powerless to establish? But this argument is reversible: one who really venerates reason must hold it an impurity in its moral, or practical, employment that it commits us to the acceptance of propositions which we cannot possibly show to be true. We must suppose, then, that, in spite of his theoretical identification of them, the real object of Kant's veneration is not Reason, but Virtue; and for the explanation of this attitude we must look outside his theory of morals to other and less purely intellectual sources and influences.

G. E. Moore, in his own way, gave as distinctive a turn to moral philosophy as Kant in his. Moore had, too, a distinctive conception of philosophical analysis, perhaps never fully worked out, and certainly not worked out at the time of the publications of *Principia Ethica*. Lewy's lecture casts historical and analytical light on both. He reports on an unpublished and incomplete draft, dating from the early 1920s, of what was designed as a Preface for a second edition of *Principia Ethica*. (The project of a second edition was abandoned for a reason which Moore gives in a note to the 1922 reprinting.) It has often been pointed out that Moore used the expression, 'the naturalistic fallacy', confusedly to stand for a number of different views, all of which he held to be mistaken, but which he failed, in *Principia Ethica*, to distinguish from each other. Lewy's report shows that Moore anticipated his critics: the distinctions are clearly made in the draft Preface. Having reported on Moore's criticism of himself, Lewy proceeds to discuss an argument used in *Principia Ethica* to establish the conclusion that the concept of Good—the distinctive concept, if there is such, with which Moore took himself to be concerned—is not identical with any non-ethical concept; and he shows, much as Moore himself might have done, that this argument too is a confusion of different arguments, one of which he holds to be valid. Its setting out turns on distinguishing the consequences of concept-identity for propositional identity in different cases, and involves reference to that famous crux, the Paradox of Analysis.

Owen's lecture on the Platonism of Aristotle introduces us to an area of scholarly debate where much is uncertain, but one thing is certain, namely that philosophical acumen is a necessary condition of historical accuracy. Owen argues persuasively that the logical and metaphysical strands in Aristotle's thinking must be considered together to appreciate the subtle relationship of Aristotelian development to Platonic doctrine and method.

Geach's lecture, 'Some Problems about Time', has some Aristotelian affinities, but in general stands somewhat apart from the others. It is an essay neither in moral philosophy nor in philosophy of mind nor, though McTaggart receives honourable mention, in philosophical history. Geach edges his common sense with logic to attack some fanciful philosophical theorizing—claiming to derive respectability from physics—which, in place of our ordinary conception of objects undergoing change, advocates thinking of a three-dimensional-object-at-a-time as a 'temporal slice' of a four-dimensional object. He presses his criticisms by urging the lack of analogy, the radical differences, between spatial and temporal order; and concludes with the conjecture that it may prove possible to reduce to modal logic the fundamental rules which govern temporal discourse. Geach's lecture, besides commending itself by its intrinsic power, may stand as the representative of another concern not unknown to recent English philosophy, namely a concern with the connection between logic, broadly conceived, and ontology.

All the lectures are here reproduced, with a few minor corrections, as they were originally printed in the *Proceedings of the British Academy*. The lectures of Hampshire, Owen, Lewy, and Warnock were Dawes Hicks Lectures on the History of Philosophy; the remainder were Henriette Hertz Trust Annual Philosophical Lectures.

GILBERT RYLE

A Puzzling Element in the Notion of Thinking

Usually when we philosophers discuss questions about thinking, we concentrate, for very good reasons, upon what people do or might think; that is, on the opinions that they form, the beliefs that they have, the theories that they construct, the conclusions that they reach and the premisses from which they reach them. In a word, our usual questions are questions about the truths or falsehoods that people do or might accept. Their thoughts, of which we discuss the structures, the implications and the evidential backings, are the results in which their former ponderings and calculations have terminated. For when a person knows or believes that something is the case, his knowledge or belief is something that he now has or possesses, and the pondering which got him there is now over. While he is still wondering and pondering, he is still short of his destination. When he has settled his problem, his task of trying to settle it is finished.

It should not be forgotten that some of the problems that we have to try to settle are not theoretical problems but practical problems. We have to try to decide what to do, as well as try to decide what is the case. The solution of a problem is not always a truth or a falsehood.

We should not assume, either, that all thinking is trying to settle problems, whether theoretical or practical. This would be too restrictive. A person is certainly thinking when he is going over a poem that he knows perfectly, or dwelling on the incidents of yesterday's football match. He has, or need have no problems to solve or results to aim at. Not all of our walks are journeys.

Lastly, we should not assume that all or even most of the truths or falsehoods that are ours are the fruits of our own ponderings. Fortunately and unfortunately, a great part of what we believe and know we have taken over from other people. Most of the things that we know we have not discovered for ourselves, but have been taught. Most of the things that we believe we believe simply because we have been told them. As with worldly goods, so with truths and falsehoods, much of what we possess is inherited or donated.

It is a vexatious fact about the English language that we use the verb 'to think' both for the beliefs or opinions that a man has, and for the pondering and reflecting that a man does; and that we use the noun 'thought'·both for the truth or falsehood that he accepts, and for the activity of reflecting which, perhaps, preceded his acceptance of it. To think, in the sense of 'believe', is not to think, in the sense of 'ponder'. There is only the verbal appearance of a contradiction in saying that while a person is still thinking, he does not yet know what to think; and that when he does know what to think, he has no more thinking to do.

The problems which I wish to discuss are questions not about the propositions that a person does or might believe, but about his activities of pondering, perpending, musing, reflecting, calculating, meditating, and so on. I shall be talking about the thinking which is the travelling and not the being at one's destination; the winnowing and not the grain; the bargaining and not the goods; the work and not the repose.

A person does not have to be advanced in age or highly schooled in order to be able to give satisfactory answers to ordinary interrogations about his thinking. A child who has never heard a word of psychological or philosophical discourse is not in the least embarrassed at being asked what he had been thinking about while sitting in the swing. Indeed, if asked not very long afterwards, he is likely to be quite ready to give a moderately detailed account of the thoughts that he had had, and even perhaps of the rough sequence in which he had had them. The task does not feel to him hugely different from the task of recounting what he had been doing so quietly or so noisily in the nursery or what he had seen and whom he had met during his afternoon walk.

None the less, familiar though we are with the task of recounting our thoughts, we are embarrassed by a quite different task, set to us by the psychologist or the philosopher, the task, namely, of saying what the having of these thoughts had consisted in. I mean this. If during a certain period I had been, say, singing or mending a gate or writing a testimonial, then when recounting afterwards what I had been doing, I could, if required, mention the concrete ingredients of my activity, namely the noises that I had uttered, the hammer-blows that I had struck, and the ink-marks that I had made on the paper. Of course, a mere catalogue of these concrete happenings would not yet amount to an account of what I had been doing. Singing a song is not just uttering one noise after another; the sequence of noises must be a directed sequence. Still, if no noises are made, no song is sung; and if no ink-marks are produced, no testimonial is written. If I recollect singing or writing a testimonial, then I recollect that I made some noises or some ink-marks.

But when I recollect, however clearly, a stretch, however recent, of my musing or pondering, I do not seem to be, in the same way, automatically primed with answers to questions about the concrete ingredients of the thoughts the having of which I have no difficulty in recounting. I tell you, for example, '. . . and then the idea occurred to me that, since it was Sunday, I might not be able to get petrol at the next village'. If now you ask me to say what concrete shape the occurring of this slightly complex idea had taken, I may well be stumped for an answer, so stumped, even, as half to resent the putting of the question.

You might press your irksome question in this way. You say, 'Well, you have just recounted to us in a dozen or more English words the idea that had occurred to you. Did the idea itself occur to you in English words? Does your recollection of the idea occurring to you incorporate the recollection of your saying something to yourself in a dozen or more English words, whether in your head or *sotto voce*? Or, having recently returned from France, did you perhaps say something to the same effect to yourself in a dozen or more French words?' To this very specific question my answer might be, 'Yes; I do now recall saying something to myself in my

head, in English words, to the effect that as it was Sunday there
might be no petrol available in the next village.' But my answer
might be, 'No; I don't recall saying anything to myself at all.' Or
my answer might be, 'Well, I'm not absolutely sure that I did not
just say "Sunday" in my head, but I'm sure that I did not say
anything more.'

Your pertinacity is irritating, since I want to say that it does not
really matter whether I said anything to myself or not. Having the
idea in question did not require my saying anything to myself, in
the way in which singing does require uttering noises and repairing
a gate does require *either* hammering *or* wire-tying *or* bolt-tighten-
ing *or* something of the same concrete sort.

Ignoring my irritation you now press me with another batch of
specific queries. You say, 'If when you had that idea you did not say
anything to yourself in your head or *sotto voce*, then was it that
instead you saw some things in your mind's eye? Was it that you
had mental pictures blurred or sharp, well coloured or ill coloured,
maybe of villagers entering a village church, and of a garage with its
doors closed; so that it was in this concrete shape, or something like
it, that the idea came to you that since it was Sunday you might not
be able to get petrol?' Again I might answer, 'Yes, I did visualize
scenes like this.' But I might answer, 'No, I am sure that I did not
visualize anything.' Or I might answer, 'Well, I do remember seeing
in my mind's eye the duck-pond of the village in question: I usually
do when I think of that village. But this had nothing to do with the
special idea that the garage there might be closed for Sunday.' Once
again I might be irked at the question being pressed at all. Why
should my thinking the thought have gone with either the saying of
something to myself or with the seeing of something in my mind's
eye or with any other proprietary happenings?

There are, however, certain special thinking-activities which
certainly do seem to require our saying things in our heads or *sotto
voce* or aloud, and we need to examine what there is about these
special activities which requires the inward or outward production
of words and phrases.

(*a*) If I have been trying to compose a poem or an after-dinner
speech, then I must indeed have been producing to myself words
and phrases, examining them, cancelling or improving them,

assembling them and rehearsing assemblages of them. That is, if my thinking happens to be a piece of thinking what to say and how to say it, then it must incorporate the tentative, exploratory, and critical saying of things to myself; and then, if asked to recount in retrospect whether I had been saying things to myself in English or in French, I should answer without hesitation. There is here no question of my first thinking out my poem or my speech, and only then, in reply to posthumous interrogations, putting my composition into words. The thinking was itself a piece of word-hunting, phrase-concocting, and sentence-mending. It was thinking *up* words, phrases, and sentences.

(*b*) If I have been doing a slightly complex piece of computation, whether in my head or on paper, like multiplying £13. 12*s*. 4*d*. by 7, then not only must my answer, if I obtain one, be a numerical or worded formula, £95. 6*s*. 4*d*., perhaps, but also the results of the interim multiplying-operations, dividing-operations, and adding-operations will be numbers. What I say to myself in my head, if I do the sum in my head, will parallel the things that I should write down one after another, if I worked the sum out on paper, and these will be numbers of pounds, shillings, or pence. If asked afterwards whether I had, at a certain stage, said to myself 'Seven twelves are eighty-four, plus two, makes eighty-six' or whether I had in my mind's eye seen the corresponding numerals, or both together, I might recollect just which I had done; and I should not feel irked at the suggestion that I must have done one or the other. Certainly, multiplying does not consist merely in saying numbers aloud or in our heads; but we are ready to allow that it requires this, or some alternative, in the same sort of way as singing a song requires, though it does not reduce to, the uttering of noises. Trying to get the correct answer, unlike just making a guess at it, involves trying to establish checkable intermediate steps, in order to make the correct moves from those steps to the right answer; and these steps, to be checkable, must be formulated.

(*c*) Some kinds of problems, like those of advocates, debaters, and philosophers, have something in common with the task of composition and something in common with the task of computation. The thinker has, all the time, both to be trying to find out what to say and how to say it, and also to be trying to establish as true what he says. He wants his hearers—including himself—not only to understand what he says but also to accept it, and to accept it perforce. As his task is, in two dimensions, a forensic task, his thinking involves him in producing and canvassing, in however sketchy a manner, words, phrases, and sentences, conclusions, reasons, and rebuttals of objections.

Now, if, improvidently, we pick on one of these three special varieties of thinking as our universal model, we shall be tempted to say, as Plato said, that 'in thinking the soul is conversing [or perhaps 'debating'] with herself', and so postulate that any piece of meditating or pondering whatsoever has got, so to speak, to run on the wheels of words, phrases, and sentences.

Or, if forced by our own reminiscences to allow that sometimes we have thoughts when no wording of these thoughts takes place, we may then be tempted simply to give to the model one extension and postulate that in thinking the soul is *either* conversing with itself *or else* performing some one specific alternative to conversing, such as visualizing things. In either case we are presupposing that thinking, of whatever sort, must, so to speak, employ a concrete apparatus of some specifiable kind or other, linguistic or pictorial or something else. This general presupposition is sometimes formulated in the following way. Just as an Englishman who has become perfectly familiar with the French language may say that he can now think in French, so, and in the same sense of 'in', he must always think either 'in' his native English or else 'in' some alternative apparatus, like French or visual imagery or algebraical symbols or gestures or something else that he can produce, on demand, from his own resources. The generic term 'symbol' is sometimes used to cover all the postulated vehicles of thinking. It is a psychological necessity, or perhaps even a part of the very concept of thinking, that when thinking occurs, there occur, internally or externally, things or symbols that the thinker thinks in.

It is if we make this presupposition that we are especially embarrassed at being required to tell in retrospect in what symbols (in this awkwardly distended use of the word) we had, for example, the idea that as it was Sunday there might be no petrol available at the next village. For often we cannot recollect any such vehicles being present on the occasion when, as we clearly do recollect, we had that thought.

I want to attack this presupposition. I want to deny that it even makes sense to ask, in the general case, what special sort or sorts of things we think *in*. The very collocation of 'think' with 'in so and so' seems to me factitious, save in our very special case of the Englishman who describes himself as now being able to think in French. So let us clear his case out of the way.

The primary thing that he means when he says that he now thinks in French is that when he has to talk to Frenchmen, he does not any longer have to think out how to say in French what he wants to say. He no longer, for example, has first to say to himself in English what he wants to say, and then to struggle to translate from English into French for the benefit of his French audience. The composition of French remarks is no longer any more difficult for him than the composition of English remarks, that is, it is not difficult at all. But to say that he no longer has to think out how to say things in French has not the slightest tendency to show that all or most of the thoughts that he thinks are now accompanied or 'carried' by the production of French words. It is only to say that *when he is conversing with Frenchmen* he does not have to think about the vehicles of this conversing. When he does have to compose in French he does not have to think *up* French words. But most of the things he thinks about are not matters of French composition, just as most of the things we think about are not matters of English composition. Roughly, he thinks in French when he says what he wants to say in French without any groping or fumbling.

Secondarily, when he says that he now thinks in French, he may also mean that *when* he debates matters with himself he conducts these debates in French without wondering how to put his points in French; and, more generally, that *when* he converses with himself in internal monologue he does this in French without having to consider how to say in French what he wants to say. Even so, to describe him as thinking in French, because what he says to himself he says effortlessly in French, is to put a new strain on the phrase 'thinking in', under which it did not labour in our primary use of the phrase 'to think in French'. One never does ask it, but *could* one ask a friend who has been deliberating what to do whether he had been deliberating in English? If we did ask him this, I suspect that he would reply that while he had said or half-said a lot of things to himself in English, this had not been any part of his deliberating. He had not deliberated *by means of* saying things to himself, any more than the proof-corrector searches for misprints *by means of* putting marks in the margins of the galley-proof.

But anyhow, what is true of his debatings and conversings, whether with Frenchmen or with himself, need not be true of his thinkings which are done when no debating or conversing is done. The phrases 'in French' and 'in English' do attach natively to verbs of saying; it does not follow that they attach to verbs of thinking, unless the thinking happens to be thinking what to say or how to say it.

Strained though it may be, save in the one special context, to speak of a person thinking in French or in English, it is worse than strained to speak of him as thinking in, say, mental pictures. Certainly it is true, not of all people, but of many, when thinking about certain sorts of matters, though not of all, that they see things in their mind's eyes, and even that their ability to solve some of their problems is tied up, somehow, with their ability to visualize clearly. Doubtless, some chess-players can think out chess-problems in their heads, if and only if they can visualize chess-situations clearly and steadily.

Consider this case of the would-be solver of a chess-problem. First let us provide him with a chess-board and the requisite chessmen. He disposes the pieces in their proper places and then, with his eyes fixed on the board and his fingers moving piece after piece, he tries to think out the solution to his problem. Are we to say that the thinking that he is doing is done 'in' pieces of ivory or 'in' the experimental moves that he makes with these pieces of ivory? Clearly, there is no place for the word 'in' here. He is thinking *about* the pieces; he is thinking out what they could and could not do or suffer if moved elsewhere or if kept where they are.

But now suppose that we refuse to provide him with a chessboard, so that he has to tackle his task entirely in his head. The chess-problem itself that he has to solve is exactly the same as before; but he is now confronted with an extra set of tasks which he had not had to cope with before. He has, among other things, to remember, at each given moment, exactly where each of the pieces is, whereas previously he just looked and saw where it was. He is like the hostess who can see which of her guests is sitting next to which until the light fails; then she has to remember their positions. This remembering may be preceded by the labour of trying to remember; or she may not have to try. She may just remember. Now if the chess-player has to struggle to remember the positions of his pieces, this struggling could obviously not be described as involving the employment of mental pictures of their positions. He struggles because he cannot yet remember and therefore cannot yet see in his mind's eye how the pieces had been disposed. If in the course of this struggling alternative possible dispositions are pictured, still these, if wrong, have to be scrapped. They are not the vehicles but the boss-shots of the thinking. Conversely, when, after struggling to remember the positions of the pieces, the chess-player does remember, then his seeing them in his mind's eye, if he does do this, is not something by means of which he gets himself to remember. It is the goal, not a vehicle of his struggle to remember. *A fortiori*, if he remembers without having to try to remember, then his mental picture of the positions of the pieces is not something that he thought *in* or *with* or *on*, since he did not have to think at all.

Certainly this chess-player has to *use his memory* in trying to solve the chess-problem in his head, where he had not had to use his memory when he had had the board in front of him. But this is not at all the same thing as to say that he *uses his memory-images* in trying to solve the problem in his head. If we hanker still to reserve some special sense for the phrase 'using images', this will be very different from the sense of the verb in which we speak of someone using such and such French words when speaking to Frenchmen. That we cannot talk French without using French words is a dull truism; that some people cannot solve chess-problems in their heads without, in some sense, using mental pictures may be true, but it is not a logician's truism.

So now we seem to be further off than ever from achieving what we thought that we wanted, namely to nominate some reasonably concrete stuff to be the peculiar apparatus of all of our thinkings.

No singing without noises, no testimonial-writing without ink-marks, no thinking without . . ., but we can nominate no proprietary things or sets of things to fill this gap. Indeed, we have, I hope, become suspicious of the very attempt to assimilate in this way thinking with these other special activities, which do possess their own proprietary implements or materials.

We may be tempted to postpone the evil day by suggesting that thinking differs from singing and testimonial-writing just because its proprietary stuff is a very peculiar stuff, more transparent and more shapeless than jelly-fishes, more scentless than the most scentless gases, and more uncapturable than rainbows. Perhaps its stuff is the stuff that dreams are made of, mental or spiritual stuff, and that is why it slips through our retrospective sieves. But we are soon brought to our senses if we remind ourselves that our own neighbours' very ordinary children, Tommy and Clara, make no more bones about recounting the thoughts that they have had than in recounting the games that they have played or the incidents that they have witnessed. They seem to need no esoteric instructions in order to be able to tell us of the ideas that have come to them or the thinking that they have done. In a way these are the most domestic and everyday sorts of things that there could be. The seeming mysteriousness of thinking derives from some sophisticated theoretical presuppositions, presuppositions which induce us, though only when theorizing, to try to squeeze out of our reminiscences or our introspections some evasive but pervasive drop of something, some psychic trace-element the presence of which, in bafflingly minute doses, is required if thinking is to occur. Yet Tommy and Clara, who were never told of any such psychic trace-element, describe their thinkings in ways which we understand perfectly; nor, when we tell them of the thoughts that crossed Cinderella's mind as she sat among the ashes, do we employ a strange para-chemical vocabulary.

Now let us drop, for the time being, the attempt to find a filling or a set of alternative fillings for the gap in the slogan 'No thinking without such and such' and consider a different, though connected, problem.

When a person, who has been for a short or a long time musing or pondering, is asked what he had been thinking about, he can usually, though not quite always, give a seemingly complete and definite answer. All sorts of answers are allowable; for example, that he had been thinking about his father, or about the next General

Election, or about the possibility of getting his annual holiday early, or about yesterday's football match, or how to answer a letter. What he has been thinking about may or may not be, or contain, a problem. We can ask him whether he had decided how to answer the letter and if so what his decision was. But his thoughts about yesterday's football match may have been entirely uninterrogative. He was thinking it over, but not trying to think anything out. His thinking terminated in no results; it aimed at none. Now though, normally, the thinker can give a seemingly complete and definite answer to the question What had he been thinking about?, he can very often be brought to acknowledge that he had had in mind things which, at the start, it had not occurred to him to mention. To take a simple instance. A rowing-enthusiast says that he had been thinking about the Oxford University crew; and if asked bluntly, would deny that he had at that moment been thinking about the Cambridge crew. Yet it might transpire that his thought about the Oxford crew was, or included, the thought that though it was progressing, it was not progressing fast enough. 'Not fast enough for what?' we ask. 'Not fast enough to beat Cambridge next Saturday.' So he had been thinking about the Cambridge crew, only thinking about it in a sort of threshold way. Or I ask a tired visitor from London what he has been thinking about. He says, 'Just about the extraordinary peacefulness of your garden.' If asked, 'Than what do you find it so much more peaceful?' he replies, 'Oh, London, of course.' So in a way he was thinking not only of my garden but of London, though he would not, without special prompting, have said for himself that he had had London in mind at all. Or my visitor says, 'How lovely your roses are', and then sighs. Why does he sigh? May he not, in a marginal way, be thinking of his dead wife who had been particularly fond of roses?—though he himself would have said, if asked, that he was only thinking about my roses. He does not say to me or to himself, 'Roses—her favourite flower.' But roses are, for him, her favourite flower. The thought of them is an incipient thought of her.

Take one more case. I ask the schoolboy what he is thinking about, and he says that he had been trying to think what 8×17 makes. On further questioning it turns out that his total task is to multiply £9. 17s. 4d. by 8; and that at that particular moment he had got to the 17s. So I ask him whether he had forgotten the 2s. 8d. that he had got when multiplying the 4d. by 8; and now he says that he had not forgotten this; indeed he was keeping the 2s. in mind ready to add to his shillings column. So, in a way, his thought was not totally filled by the problem of multiplying 17 × 8. The thought of the total multiplication task was, in a controlling though background way, built into his interim, but foreground task of multiplying 17 × 8. For it was not just 17, but the seventeen shillings of the £9. 17s. 4d. that he was then engaged in multiplying by 8. He would have gone on from the shillings to the pounds if I had not interrupted.

It was not that my widowed visitor just *forgot* and had to be reminded that he had been thinking about his wife as well as about the roses, but that his task of telling just what he had had in mind was in some important ways totally unlike the task of trying to recall, say, just how many telephone calls he had made during the morning. The difference between merely thinking how fine these roses are and thinking how she would have admired them is not like the difference between having made eleven and having made twelve telephone calls, namely a difference in the number of happenings to be recorded. Recounting one's thoughts is not like turning back to an earlier page and trying to give an exhaustive inventory of the items one rediscovers there. The question whether or not the Cambridge crew had been in the rowing-enthusiast's mind was not one that he could settle by racking his brains to recollect a bygone fleeting something. In our example it was settled in quite a different way, namely by asking him what the rate of progress of the Oxford crew had seemed to him inadequate for. When he acknowledges that he had been, in a threshold way, thinking of the Cambridge crew, one thing that he does not say is 'Ah yes, your question *reminds* me that the Cambridge crew was in my thoughts after all.' He had not been reminded of a forgotten item but shown how his account of his thought had been an incomplete account. He had failed to indicate part of its internal tenor.

Reporting one's thoughts is not a matter of merely chronicling the items of a procession of quick-fading internal phenomena. If we can pick out any such phenomena and record them, our record of them is not yet a statement of the drift or content of a piece of thinking. The way in which the widower's thinking of the roses was, in a way, thinking about his wife is not that during the time that he was thinking about the roses there occurred one or two very fleeting wafts of recollections of his wife. Such wafts do occur, but it was not them that he was acknowledging when he acknowledged that in thinking of the roses he had been incipiently thinking of his wife. Rather, he had thought of the roses *as* her favourite flower; in the way in which the rowing-enthusiast had thought of the progress of the Oxford crew *as* insufficient to beat Cambridge; or in the way in which the schoolboy had thought of the 17 that he was multiplying by 8 *as* the 17s. to be dealt with after the 4*d*. and before the £9.

What, then, is the virtue of this 'as', which makes a young man's thought of next Thursday *as* his 21st birthday different from his mother's thought of next Thursday *as* early-closing day for Oxford shops?

We can approach at least a part of the answer in this way. Sometimes we deliberately advise people to think of something *as* so and so. For instance, when giving a child his very first explanation of what a map is, we might tell him to think of the map of Berkshire *as* a photograph taken from an aeroplane very high up over the middle of Berkshire. This may already lead him to expect to find big things showing on the map, like towns, rivers, highroads, and railways, but not very small things like people, motor-cars, or bushes. A little later he inquires, in perplexity, what the contour-lines are which wriggle so conspicuously along and around the Berkshire Downs. We tell him to think of them *as* high-water marks left by the sea, which had risen to drown even the highest parts of the county. This flood, he is to suppose, subsided exactly 50 feet every night, leaving a high-water mark each time. So a person walking along one high-water mark would remain all the time at the same height above the normal level of the sea; and he would all the time be 100 feet higher than someone else who was following the next high-water mark but one below him. Quite likely the child could now work out for himself why the contour-lines are closely packed on the side of steep hill and widely separated on a gradual incline.

Getting him to think of the map as a photograph taken from very high up, and of the contour-lines as high-water marks makes it natural or at least quite easy for him to think further thoughts for himself. It is to implant the germs of these further thoughts into his initially sterile thoughts about the map. If there was no follow-up, however embryonic and whether in the desired direction or any other, then he had not thought of the map as a photograph or of the contours as high-water marks. To describe someone as thinking of something as so and so is to say of him, at least *inter alia*, that it would be natural or easy for him to follow up this thought in some particular direction. His thinking had those prospects, that trend in it. It should be noticed that what thinking of something as so and so leads naturally or easily into may be subsequent thinkings, but it may equally well be subsequent doings. The golf-professional who tells me to think of my driver not as a sledge-hammer but as a rope with a weight on the end, expects me to cease to bang at the ball and to begin to sweep smoothly through the ball. The parent who gets his child to think of policemen not as enemies but as friends gets him not only to think certain consequential thoughts but also to go to policemen for help when lost.

A person who thinks of something as something is, *ipso facto*, primed to think and do some particular further things; and this particular possible future that his thinking paves the way for needs to be mentioned in the description of the particular content of that thinking—somewhat as the mention of where the canal goes to has to be incorporated in our account of what this adjacent canal-stretch is. Roughly, a thought comprises what it is incipiently, namely what it is the natural vanguard of. Its burthen embodies its natural or easy sequel.

There are other things as well which are, in partly similar ways, constitutionally inceptive. To lather one's chin is to prepare to wield one's razor. Here the vanguard act is an intentional or even deliberate preparation for the future act. We had to learn thus to pave the way for shaving. To brace oneself is to get ready to jump or resist at the next moment; but this inceptive movement is not normally intentional or the result of training; it is instinctive. The tenors that our thoughts possess are similarly sometimes the products of training; but often not. In all cases alike, however, the description of an inceptive act requires the prospective specification of its due or natural sequel. Notice that its due or natural sequel may not actually come about. Having lathered my chin, I may be called to the telephone; and the dog, having braced himself, may be reassured or shot. We must employ the future tense in our description of the inceptive act, but we must hedge this future tense with some 'unlesses'.

At first sight we may suspect the presence of a circularity in the description of something as essentially the foreshadowing of its own succession. But this feature, without any air of circularity, belongs also to our descriptions of promises, precautions, threats, and betrothals, and even of nightfalls, thaws, and germinations. There could be no complete description of such things which was not proleptic. However, our special case seems to be in a worse plight since I am saying that a piece of thinking of something as something is natively inceptive of, *inter alia*, subsequent thinkings in a way in which a thaw is not the inception of another thaw, or a nightfall the beginning of another nightfall.

So here we are reminded, if not of circles, at least of the verse:

> Big fleas have little fleas upon their backs to bite 'em,
> Little fleas have lesser fleas and so *ad infinitum*.

But is this reminder disconcerting? Were we not already aware in our bones of just such a feature of thinking, namely that any attempt to catch a particular thought tends to develop into an attempt to catch up with something further? Our story of a particular piece of thinking seems in the nature of the case to terminate in nothing stronger than a semicolon. It is not incidental to thoughts that they belong to trains of thought.

Now maybe we can begin to see the shape of the answers to both of our two dominant questions. We can begin to see why it is that the narrative of a piece of my thinking cannot be merely the chronicling of actual, monitored happenings 'in my head'. For the content of the thinking comprised its tenor and to describe its particular tenor is prospectively to mention its natural or easy sequels.

But also we can begin to see why we cannot, and do not in our hearts of hearts wish to reserve for our thinkings any peculiar concrete stuff, apparatus, or medium, X, such that we can say, 'As no singing without noises, so no thinking without X.' For adverting to anything whatsoever can be what puts a person, at a particular moment, in mind of something or other. The motorist in the last village but one before home may think of the petrol-station alongside of him *as* being possibly the last place for buying petrol on a Sunday. The widower thinks of my roses that he is gazing at as being of the sort of which she was so fond. The schoolboy thinks of the number 17 that his eye is on as the 17*s*. in the total of £9. 17*s*. 4*d*. that he has to multiply by 8. The poet thinks of the word 'annihilating' that crops up in a conversation as a candidate for the gap in his half-composed couplet. The housewife thinks of next Thursday as the day when she will not be able to shop in Oxford after lunch, while her son thinks of it as the day when he comes of age. We could stretch our slogan, if we hanker for a slogan, to read 'No thinking without adverting to something or other, no matter what', but then it would be as empty as the slogans 'no eating without food', 'no building without materials' and 'no purchases without commodities'.

However, the very vacuousness of our new slogan 'no thinking without adverting to something or other, no matter what' has a certain tension-relieving effect. From the start we felt, I hope, a gnawing uneasiness at the very programme of treating thinking as a special, indeed a very special activity, special in the way in which singing is one special activity and gardening is a battery of other special activities. For while there certainly are lots of special kinds or brands of thinking, such as computing, sonnet-composing, anagram-solving, philosophizing, and translating, still thinking is not an activity in which we are engaged only when we are *not* singing, writing testimonials, gardening, and so on. Thinking is not a rival occupation to these special occupations, in the sense that our time has to be parcelled out between them and thinking, in the way in which our time does have to be parcelled out between golf and gardening, between testimonial-writing and lecturing, between anagram-solving and chess-playing, and so on. For we have to be thinking if we are to be singing well, writing a just testimonial, or gardening efficiently. Certainly, we had better not be doing sums or anagrams in our heads while singing or lecturing; but this is because we had better be thinking how to perform our present task of singing or lecturing. We had unwittingly sold the central fort from the start, when we asked ourselves, in effect, 'Given that noise-making, of a certain sort, is what goes to make singing the proprietary occupation that it is, what is it that, analogously, makes thinking the proprietary occupation that it is?' The verbal noun 'thinking' does not, as we knew in our bones all along, denote a special or proprietary activity in the way in which 'singing' does. Thinking is not one department in a department-store, such that we can ask, What line of goods does it provide, and what lines of goods does it, *ex officio, not* provide? Its proper place is in all the departments—that is, there is no particular place which is its proper place, and there are no particular places which are not its proper place.

If we had worded our original programme by asking 'What department and what proprietary apparatus are reserved for *the using of our wits*?' we should have seen through this question straightaway. We do not, notoriously, use our wits wherever and whenever we should use them, but there is no field or department of human activity or experience of which we can say 'Here people can use their fingers, their noses, their vocal chords or their golf-clubs, but not their wits.' Or if we had worded our early question by asking 'In what special medium or with what special instruments is our use of our wits conducted?', we should have seen through this question too. We swim in water, we sing in noises, we hammer with hammers, but using our wits is not a co-ordinate special operation with its own counterpart medium, material, or implements. For one can use one's wits in swimming, singing, hammering, or in anything else whatsoever. I do not suggest that the idiom of *using one's wits* is a pure substitute for the idiom of *thinking*. There is an element of congratulation in our description of someone as having used his wits, an element which would be out of place, for example, in talking of my widower's thinking of roses as his wife's favourite flower. None the less, if we realize why it would be absurd to try to isolate out a proprietary activity of using one's wits and a reserved field for it, we realize why it actually was absurd to try to isolate out a proprietary activity of thinking and a reserved field for it.

Why do we not require our schools to give separate lessons in thinking, as they do give separate lessons in computing, translating, swimming, and cricket? The answer is obvious. It is because all the lessons that they give are lessons in thinking. Yet they are not lessons in two subjects at the same time.

Privacy

I

In spite of the misgivings of philosophers, it is still a common practice to distinguish fairly sharply between mind and matter; and one of the principal features of this distinction is that a privacy which is denied to matter is attributed to mind. There are, however, many sorts of privacy: the word 'private' is used in a number of different ways, and the sense in which the contents of our minds are supposed to be private requires to be made clear. By making it clear we may also come to discover how far this supposition can be justified.

Since the privacy of mind is contrasted with the publicity of matter, it may be helpful first to consider what is meant by saying that the material world is public. A plausible answer is that the publicity of physical objects, or events, or activities, or processes consists in their having to satisfy the following condition: that in whatever way their existence is detectable by any one person, it be also detectable by others; not necessarily by any other person that one chooses to describe, since the specification of an observer may itself restrict the range of observations that it is open to him to make, but at least by other persons in general; and not necessarily in practice but at least in principle. There may be physical objects that only one person ever in fact has the opportunity to perceive, but it must be logically possible for others to perceive them too; it must make sense to say of other persons that they perceive the very same physical objects and perceive them in the very same manner as he does. It is sufficiently obvious that this usually does make sense, so that our condition of publicity for the physical domain is at least very widely satisfied.

I am not sure, however, that it is universally satisfied. It holds for shoes and ships and sealing-wax and cabbages, but possibly not for kings. For when we come to human bodies, the events or processes which occur in them, and the activities in which they engage, it is arguable that we find exceptions to our general rule. The argument would be that one may, through organic sensation, be aware of one's body and of some of its activities in a way that it is not even logically possible for any one else to be aware of them. Thus, walking, pushing, frowning, coughing, sighing are physical activities. They can be witnessed by other people; indeed, other people may well be in a better position to testify to their occurrence than the person who is engaged in them. Even so, it may be said, he has one way of detecting these processes or activities which is not available to others. He alone can *feel* that they are going on.

To evaluate this argument we have to decide what we are to understand by saying that something is or is not detected by different people in the same way. How is the expression 'in the same way' to be interpreted? In the sense in which I am using it here, two people may be said to detect the existence of an object in the same way, if, for example, they both see it. The fact that they see it through different pairs of eyes, or from different angles, or with different degrees of clarity is left out of account. Questions arise as to whether we are still to say that the existence of an object is detected in the same way when it is seen, for example, in a mirror, or on a screen, or through a microscope, and here I do not think that there is any general method of drawing the line. We have to take special decisions: but it does not matter for our present argument which way such cases are decided. In general, also, two people may be said to detect the existence of an object in the same way if they both are touching it, though here again one may wish to draw a distinction between the case where one explores the shape of the object and that in which one only feels it with one's finger tips. And the same applies to other forms of sense-perception, including organic sensation. For example, two people may be said to detect in the same way that an object is moving, if it is attached to a rope which they are holding and both feel the strain in their arms when the rope is pulled.

But in that case, it may be argued, there is no ground for holding that one's organic awareness of the physical activities of one's own body affords one a means of detecting them which is logically denied to others. For there is no logical difficulty in supposing that some other person is also able to detect them through kinaesthetic sensation. It is conceivable, for example, that two people should be so attuned to one another that when one of them was organically aware of some bodily state or activity, the other had a sympathetic feeling of the same kind. Or, if this be thought too fanciful, one might suppose that the condition of a person's body was recorded by a machine which was so constructed that it could be read kinaesthetically. With a little ingenuity, I have no doubt that we could find other examples. They might not be practical, but their being intelligible and free from contradiction would be enough to prove the point.

But is this all that we are going to require? Surely, the case in which one person feels himself to be engaged in some physical activity and another detects it by having sympathetic sensations, or by reading a machine kinaesthetically, is considerably different from that of two persons feeling the pull of a rope. In the latter case one has no hesitation in saying that they each discover in the same way that the object which is attached to the rope is moving: but in the former case I think that the corresponding conclusion would not be generally admitted. I think that if it is to be said that one detects what is going on in someone else's body in the same way as he does, it is not sufficient in this instance that one should have similar sensations: it is necessary also that they play the same role as his do, which means that they would have to be located not in one's own body but in his.

Now it might be maintained that even this was logically possible. After all, it is known that kinaesthetic sensations can be located outside one's body: for example, many people have had the experience of feeling pressure at the end of a stick rather than in the hand which is holding it. And if one's range of feeling can go beyond one's own body, why should it not at least theoretically extend to another person's? Might one not detect, for example, that someone was frowning, not merely by feeling the corresponding sensation in one's own forehead, but by locating it in his? The difficulty is even to imagine what such an experience would be like.

An argument against its possibility would be that it is a defining property of 'my' body to be the locus of my organic sensations. This would not entail that these sensations could never be located outside my body, but only that any human body in which they were located would necessarily be mine. According to this argument, we may think that it makes sense to talk of one person's locating a sensation of frowning in another's forehead because we already think of the two bodies as separately identified; but here we fall into contradiction. For what distinguishes my body from his is just, among other things, that my sensations of frowning are located in this forehead and not in that. Of course nothing of this sort is needed for distinguishing the two bodies as physical objects; but it is needed for distinguishing them as one person's or another's. Not, indeed, that one has to observe where one's feelings are located in order to discover which body is one's own. It is not suggested that one identifies one's own body in the way that one may identify a piece of personal property. No doubt arises for me about this body's being mine. But, it is argued, the reason why no doubt arises is that it necessarily is the body in which my feelings are located. To suppose otherwise, to try to extend the possible range of feeling in the way that we have been doing, would be to undermine the ground on which we are standing; we should be presupposing the distinction between one person's body and another's and at the same time robbing it of its usual sense.

I think that this argument has some force. One obvious objection to it is that my body is not distinguished only by being the locus of my feelings. It also supplies, as it were, the viewpoint from which I survey the world, so that even if I had no organic sensations, or located them elsewhere, it would still play a special role in my experience. Another most important feature is that it responds to my will in a way that other bodies do not. The control which I exercise over it when I focus my eyes, for example, or nod my head, or raise my arm is not the same, not of the same kind, as any control that I can exercise over the corresponding movements of others. I

B

doubt indeed if it is logically possible that it should be the same. One might, through hypnosis or some other method, obtain such power over another person that he responded automatically to one's will: even so, the sense in which one could be said to be raising his arm, for example, would still be rather different from that in which one raises one's own. But what if we took more fanciful examples? Suppose, for instance, that when I decided to make a movement, I found as often as not that it was executed not by me but by someone else, and this quite independently of any decision that he made. Could it not then be said that I controlled his body in just the way that I control my own? Here again, it might be objected that this piece of science fiction is inconsistent with the distinction between persons which it presupposes. And here again there seems to be no method of deciding whether this show of inconsistency amounts to a formal contradiction or not.

Perhaps, then, the most that can be said is that it is characteristic of 'my' body that it normally is the locus of my sensations, just as it is characteristic of it that it normally responds to my will in a way that other bodies do not. These rules are part of the logical framework which gives to our talk about persons and their bodies the meaning that it has. But this framework may be sufficiently flexible to allow for the abnormal case in which one or other of these rules is broken. Thus it may not be a logical impossibility that someone should on occasion be aware of another's physical state in the way that the other is himself aware of it.

I say only that it *may* not be because, as I have already indicated, this does not seem to me to be the sort of question that has a correct answer in terms of standard usage. We have to decide what attitude to take. If we admit the possibility of such abnormal cases, then we may hold that our criterion of publicity is satisfied in principle throughout the physical domain, though in the case of human bodies and some of their activities there will be a rather disturbing difference between what is sanctioned in principle and what occurs in fact. If on the other hand we refuse to give this sanction, two courses will be open to us. Either we can maintain our criterion of publicity, and accept the consequence that there are physical processes which do not satisfy it, so that if the mental activities of human beings are private in this sense, this does not distinguish them from the physical. Or if we insist that everything physical is to be public we can adopt a weaker criterion of publicity. Thus, instead of requiring of what is public that in any way in which its existence is detectable by any one person it be detectable in the *same* way by others, we might require only that it be detectable in *some* way by others. If we took this course we should again be blunting the distinction between the mental and the physical; for we shall find that what are ordinarily classified as mental processes or activities are public in this weaker sense.

11

Returning now to the stronger criterion, I wish to suggest that one thing that is commonly meant by saying that mental happenings are private is just that they fail to satisfy it. Thus it is held not to be true of such states or processes as thinking, wishing, dreaming, intending, imagining, or feeling that in whatever way their occurrence is detectable by any one person it is detectable also by others. It is not detectable by others in a way in which it is detectable by the person to whom these states or processes are attributed. He alone can be directly aware of their existence and their character. He knows what he thinks or feels in a way that it is logically impossible that any other person should.

This view has been contested on various grounds. An initial objection is that it is not at all clear what is meant by saying that a person is directly aware of his own mental processes or states. If it is just that he usually knows what he is thinking or feeling, then, even if this is true, it does not yield the desired result; for this knowledge might be shared by others. Neither does this explain the use of the word 'directly'. It is not just that he knows what he thinks or feels, but that the knowledge somehow automatically accrues to him through the fact that these thoughts and feelings are his own. But what sense can we make of this?

Some philosophers, especially those influenced by Wittgenstein, hold that there is no sense to be made of it. They would say, not that a person normally does not know what he is thinking or feeling, nor yet that he does not gain this knowledge in the way suggested, but rather that it is a mistake to talk of knowledge in this case.

People *have* thoughts and feelings, but this is not a matter of their knowing anything. To say, as philosophers do, that they are conscious of their thoughts and feelings is permissible only if it is just a way of saying that they have them. 'It can't be said of me at all', says Wittgenstein, '(except perhaps a joke) that I *know* that I am in pain.'[1] But is this really so? What is true is that we seldom, if ever, find occasion to use such sentences as 'he knows that he is in pain' or 'I know that I am thinking about a philosophical problem' or even 'I know that I am looking at a sheet of paper'. The prefixing of the words 'I know that' or 'he knows that' makes what would otherwise be respectable, if not very interesting, sentences appear somewhat ridiculous. But the reason for this, surely, is not that the claim to knowledge is inapplicable in these cases, but rather that it is superfluous. We find it silly for someone to tell us that he knows that he is in pain, because if he is in pain we take it for granted that he knows it; and similarly with the other examples. But from the fact that the claim is superfluous it does not follow that it is unjustified. If, in the course of a discussion about knowledge, or as part of a game, one were challenged to give a list of things that one knew, I think it would be quite proper to give such replies as 'I know that I am thinking about a philosophical problem' or 'I know that I am looking at a sheet of paper' or 'I know that I am in pain'. Indeed this is about the only context in which sentences of this kind do have a natural use: as furnishing examples of what one may safely claim to know. A proof that they are legitimate examples is that the information which they convey can be made the subject of a lie. I do not think anyone would maintain that to speak of telling lies about one's thoughts or feelings was an unnatural or even an uncommon use of language. If he did, he would certainly be wrong. But to tell a lie is not just to make a false statement: it is to make a statement that one knows to be false; and this implies denying what one knows to be true.

One reason why philosophers dispute the legitimacy of such examples is that they assume that expressions of the form 'I know that . . .' must be completed by sentences which are used to make statements: and they hold that this condition is not satisfied by sentences like 'I am in pain'. Thus it is alleged that to say that I am

[1] *Philosophical Investigations*, i. 246.

in pain, as to say that I am bored or that I am amused, or to make any other pronouncement of that sort, is not to deliver a report about my feelings, but rather just to express them. It is as if I were to groan or to yawn or to laugh. In short these sentences are construed as having the force of ejaculations; and one does not say of an ejaculation that it is known to be true. In these instances, indeed, this argument has some plausibility: there does not seem to be much difference between saying that one is in pain and showing it by crying out. But even here the argument works both ways: whatever reason it gives for saying that the apparent statement has the force of an ejaculation is equally a reason for saying that the ejaculation has the force of a statement. And in other cases of this autobiographical type it hardly works at all. If a man says, for example, that he is worrying about his debts, it is surely very perverse to maintain that he is merely expressing a feeling and not making a report of it as well. Or, to return to one of my previous examples, if I say that I am thinking about a philosophical problem, I am surely not doing anything like emitting an ejaculation: I am making a statement which is in fact true and known to me to be so. Even in the case of declarations of intention, which there is some ground for refusing to treat as narrative statements, the fact that one can lie about one's intentions implies that one can know what they are. So if it is to be said that sentences like 'I intend to go to Paris tomorrow' do not report anything and consequently are not used to make statements, then the principle that 'knowing that' applies only to statements will have to be given up, together with the principle that it is only when words are used to make statements that they express what can be either true or false: for if I can know what my intentions are, it follows that a verbal formulation of these intentions can be true. This being so, it seems to me preferable to allow that such formulations are used to make statements, whatever expressive function they may perform besides.

I conclude then that one can properly be said to have knowledge of one's own thoughts or feelings or intentions; but it is not easy to give an account of the way in which this knowledge arises. One of its peculiarities is that it does not depend upon investigation; it is not, or need not be, the outcome of an inquiry. It is indeed possible to conduct a kind of inner research, to interrogate oneself about one's thoughts or feelings, and to learn something from the answer. But this is not an activity in which many people engage for much of their time, and as a rule it is not necessary to engage in it in order to know what one thinks or feels. It is possible also to be a detached spectator of one's mental states or processes, to stand aside from them and contemplate them as though they were being unfolded upon a stage. No doubt this has helped to sustain the view that one's knowledge of what one thinks and feels is obtained by introspection, a kind of inner perception analogous to the 'outer' perception of physical events. But, as critics of this view have pointed out, the analogy is misleading. Our thoughts and feelings do not normally 'pose' for us in the way that physical objects do. This is, indeed, a dispute in which both sides are at fault; the champions of introspection in assuming that our mental states and processes are constantly surveyed by us, their opponents in denying that this ever happens at all. The critics are right, however, on the main point; in the sense in which having thoughts and feelings entails being conscious of them, it does not entail observing them after the fashion either of an investigator or of a spectator. Therefore to say that we know what goes on in our minds by introspection is either false or trivial: false, if it implies that we are made aware of our mental states by passing them under review; trivial if it is taken, as it sometimes is, to mean no more than that we obtain this sort of knowledge in the special way that we do.

But what difference is there then, it may be asked, between knowing what our thoughts and feelings are and merely having them? Whatever its other defects, the model of the inner theatre does at least mark out a distinction; the spectator is separated from the scene of which he is a witness. This is indeed the feature of the model that makes it attractive. If we discard this model, as I think we must, will not the distinction disappear with it? What other account of it can we give?

The distinction is all the more difficult to preserve, as there is a tendency to make the connection between having thoughts and feelings and knowing what they are a logical one, that is, to make it logically impossible for anyone not to know what conscious thoughts and feelings he has. There is an easy transition from saying that if one is in pain one knows it to saying that if one is in pain one *must* know it. In the first case the possibility of one's being in pain and not knowing it is left theoretically open, however seldom it may in fact be realized: in the second it is logically excluded. But to take the second course is to play into the hands of those who maintain, in my opinion wrongly, that one should not talk of knowledge at all in this context. For if my knowing what my thoughts and feelings are were a logical consequence of my having them, the reference to knowledge would be otiose; the words 'I know that' in such an expression as 'I know that I am in pain' would add nothing to the sense of the phrase that followed them: and since their presence would suggest that they did add something, it would in that case be better that they should be dropped.

But if they are not to be dropped, what can they be understood to add? The answer which I propose is that knowing what one's thoughts and feelings are, as distinct from merely having them, may be taken to consist in being able to give a true report of them. The two normally go together, but they are not logically connected. Animals and young children, who have not acquired the use of language, have feelings and images of which they may be said to be conscious, but, on this view, they do not know that they have them; they may think in images but they do not know what it is that they are thinking. On the other hand it is very rare for an adult human being not to know what he is thinking or feeling. Only in exceptional cases will one be unable to give any report at all, or unable to give a correct report. It is not of course necessary that these reports should actually be made, but only that they should be forthcoming if required. Neither, on the occasions when they are made, does it matter whether they are strictly simultaneous with the occurrences to which they refer, or slightly retrospective. I shall not at this stage enter into the question whether these reports are ever infallible. For the claim to knowledge to be justified it is sufficient that they should be true. And this helps us to explain why expressions like 'I know that I am in pain' or 'I know that I am thinking about a philosophical problem' sound so odd. It is not just that we expect people to know what they are thinking or feeling. It is also that if someone *says* truly that he is in pain or says truly that he is thinking about a philosophical problem, it follows that he knows it.

This gives us the clue also to what may be meant by saying that knowledge of this kind is direct. In other cases where knowledge is claimed it is not sufficient that one be able to give a true report of what one claims to know: it is necessary also that the claim be authorized, and this is done by adducing some other statement which in some way supports the statement for which the claim is made. But in this case no such authority is needed; there is no demand for evidence; the question how one knows does not arise. It would clearly be absurd to ask anyone how he knew that he was thinking about a philosophical problem, or how he knew that he was in pain. For what could he answer except that this *was* what he was thinking about, or that this *was* what he was feeling? Our knowledge of our thoughts and feelings accrues to us automatically in the sense that having them puts us in a position and gives us the authority to report them. All that is then required is that the reports be true.

III

I have tried to show that there is a sense in which it can properly be said that a person is directly aware of his own thoughts and feelings. If this be accepted, does it follow that he alone can be directly aware of them? Are they private to him in the sense that this is at least one way in which they are detectable by him but not by anybody else?

Many philosophers would conclude that this was so, for the following reason: they would argue that being directly aware of someone's, say Mr. X's, thoughts or feelings entailed having them, that having Mr. X's thoughts or feelings entailed being Mr. X, and that it was logically impossible that anyone should be Mr. X but Mr. X himself.

I shall not dispute the last of these propositions though I think that it raises interesting and difficult problems about individuation. It does seem clear, however, that if you refer to people in a way which implies that they are different, you cannot consistently with this form of reference suppose that they might be the same. And this is all that the present argument requires. On the other hand, the second proposition seems to me less secure. I do not think it should be taken for granted that having the thoughts or feelings of Mr. X entails being Mr. X, if this is understood to imply that no two persons' thoughts or feelings can be the same. But I shall return to this question later on. I wish now to discuss the first step in the argument: the proposition that being directly aware of someone's thoughts or feelings entails actually having them.

It might be thought that this was a question which we had already settled. For in explaining what could be meant by direct awareness in this sense, I said that having certain thoughts or feelings put one in a position and gave one the authority to report them; and this would appear to make the possession of the thoughts or feelings in question a necessary condition for being directly aware of them. Nevertheless, I think it might still be argued that there is at least a logical possibility of being in a similar position with regard to thoughts and feelings that one does not have; that is, of being able to make reports about the mental states of others in the same 'immediate' way as one makes them about one's own, to report on them, in short, as if they were one's own. I believe that this is what psychologists have in mind when they talk of the possibility of co-consciousness. An example would be the relation of Eve Black to Eve White and of Jane to both of them in *The Three Faces of Eve*, a much publicized recent account of a startling case of multiple personality. The claim of Eve Black to be conscious of what went on in the mind of Eve White, and that of Jane, the third personality to emerge, to be conscious of what went on in the minds of both Eves were in fact admitted by the doctors to be valid. It is enough for our purposes, however, that they could significantly be made.

In these cases of split or multiple personality, the several persons are indeed housed in the same body, for the control of which they compete; and it may therefore be objected that they are not sufficiently separate. We may choose to speak of the two Eves as being different persons; but we should do no less justice to the facts if we spoke of there being only one person with two or more different personalities. More justice, indeed; for the only reason there is for speaking of different persons in such a case is that the personalities appear to be so different. The only use of this example, therefore, is to show what might count as one person's being directly aware of the mental state of another, when they occupied different bodies: and it is doubtful whether this occurs. It is not established that different persons, in this sense, display the type of co-consciousness that is credited to different characters in a multiple personality.

But is it not conceivable that they should? To some extent, this idea is already favoured by the evidence which supports the existence of telepathy. The accounts which are given of telepathic experiences do indeed suggest that it is more like receiving a message than anything analogous to reporting one's own feelings: their oddity consists in the fact that the message is not transmitted by any ordinary means. But suppose that someone did claim to be 'telepathically' aware of some other person's mental states and that his reports of them were found to be consistently true: and suppose that when he was asked how he did it he said that it was like asking him how he knew what his own thoughts and feelings were; so far as he was concerned the only difference was that the other person's thoughts and feelings came to him under a different label. Might we not accept this account? And might we not then decide to say that he was directly aware of thoughts and feelings which were not his own? In the same way, if someone claimed to be able to remember the experiences of another, in the same 'automatic' fashion as he remembered his own, and was found to be generally right, might we not discard another apparent source of privacy, in this weaker sense, by allowing the possibility of one's experiences being remembered by others as well as by oneself? I do not press these suggestions, but they seem to me less fanciful than the idea of the possible displacement of bodily sensations which we considered earlier on.

There is, however, one important respect in which being directly aware of another person's thoughts or feelings would differ from remembering them, and differ also from detecting his physical movements by organic sensations in the way that he did: I am assuming for the sake of argument that all these procedures are allowed to be logically possible. As we have already remarked, the fact that I may become aware of some of my physical activities through kinaesthetic or organic sensation does not put me in a better position to testify to their occurrence than are those who merely observe them 'from the outside': their acquisition of the power to detect them 'from the inside' would not raise the level of their testimony to mine, since it is on as good a level already. The case of memory is slightly different in that one's claims to remember at any rate one's more recent experiences tend to be taken as authoritative, although in special circumstances this authority may be overridden. But if someone else were to be credited with the power of 'remembering' one's experiences, his testimony on this subject might come to be regarded as equal in value, or even superior, to one's own. I suppose there would have to be an initial period in which it was checked by one's own; otherwise his claim to possess this power would never be admitted. But once it had been admitted, his reports of one's past experiences might, in a conflict of testimony, outweigh one's own, if they were found to agree better with any external evidence that went to show what these experiences had been. In many cases, such as that of remembering one's dreams, there might indeed not be any external evidence, and here it would be natural to give preference to the subject's own reports. Even so I do not think that we should be logically bound to regard them as decisive.

When it comes, on the other hand, to a person's knowledge of his present thoughts and feelings, then I do think that there are many cases in which we logically are obliged to give him the last word. Even if we allow it to be possible for others to become aware of his thoughts and feelings in the way that he does, their knowledge of them will be subordinate to his. The accuracy of their reports will be checked by his, and where there is disagreement his verdict must prevail. Thus, even if one's mental states are not private in the sense that there is any single way in which, of necessity, they are detectable by oneself alone, they may still be private in yet another sense. One may be the final authority concerning their existence and their character.

This is, indeed, a version of the doctrine of 'privileged access' which has come in for such heavy criticism in recent years. On many points I think that its critics have been justified: but I also think that they have made things too easy for themselves by their choice of examples. They are right in maintaining that when it is a question of a person's motives, or of his being in an emotional state, such as that of anger or jealousy or fear, his word is not authoritative: he may deceive himself about his motives; he may honestly believe that he is angry when his behaviour shows that he is not, or, as more commonly happens, refuse to admit that he is angry when he very plainly is. In all such cases, some outside observer may prove to be a better judge of the facts. But these examples are weighted: in so far as the terms in which we talk of a man's motives or his emotions involve a reference to his behaviour, there is clearly no reason to regard his accounts of them as privileged. On the other hand, when it comes to simple sensations, such things as Professor Ryle calls twinges or pangs, then surely there can be no better witness to their occurrence than the person who feels them? If someone else who claimed to be co-conscious with him gave a different report, we might suspect that our subject was lying about his sensations, but not that he was just mistaken: if we believed him to be honest, it is the other's claim to co-consciousness that would be discredited. This comes out even more strongly when it is a question not of feeling but of thinking. If I am lost in a day-dream, and offered a penny for my thoughts, I may choose not to avow them; but if I do honestly avow them there can surely be no question of anyone's word for them being taken against mine. It is not possible that any other person, whatever may be his parapsychological powers, should know better than I do what I am day-dreaming about. Or, to take another example which was suggested to me by Professor Ryle, to the detriment of the position which he took in the *Concept of Mind*, suppose that a child tells you that he is drawing a ship, you may feel that the drawing does not at all resemble a ship, a psychologist may discover that it is 'really' a symbol for something else, but in a straightforward sense the child knows what he is trying to draw; and if he himself says that he means it to be a ship, then no one else can be in a position to override him. Of course, he may be using the word 'ship' incorrectly, but that is a different question. The point is that whatever the word means in his usage, he is the final authority as to whether it applies, in this usage, to what he is setting out to draw.

There is, however, a problem here. If we maintain that in cases of this kind one is oneself the best possible authority as to what one thinks or intends or feels, does this not commit us to the view that one cannot be mistaken, that one's reports of these matters are, in the technical sense, incorrigible? For if one could be mistaken, it is conceivable that one's mistakes should be corrected by some other person, it is conceivable that he should be more often right about the nature of one's thoughts or feelings than one was oneself; and in that case there would seem to be no justification for insisting that one's word must be taken against his. There would be every justification, on the other hand, if one's reports were incorrigible. And indeed it is hard to see how in these special cases they could fail to be so. If verbal mistakes are excluded, it is hard to see what could be meant by saying that someone honestly believed that he was feeling a twinge, or thinking about a philosophical problem, or day-dreaming about being rich, or trying to draw a ship, and yet was really doing nothing of the sort. What would such a situation be like? Admittedly, the range of what I am calling a verbal mistake is fairly wide. It covers not only the use of the wrong word, but also mis-identification, referring to what one has in mind by a name or description which does not apply to it. I might for example honestly believe that I was thinking of Beau Brummell when I was really thinking of Beau Nash. And if this kind of mistake is not to count, the claim to infallibility is very much softened. Yet something of importance remains. Even if I refer to him wrongly, it is still true, in this example, that I am thinking of a man of such and such a sort; and about this at least, it may be said, it is impossible that I should be mistaken.

This is a question that has been much debated, and I cannot here go over it again in detail. It does seem to me, however, that there is much to be said on the other side. In particular, apart from the very special cases where the statement expresses a necessary condition for its being believed by whoever it may be, as if I were to say, for example, that I believe that I am capable of forming beliefs, I feel very reluctant to admit that the truth of any statement can simply follow from the fact that someone believes it. I am inclined to say that it must always be logically possible that the belief should be false. But then it may be argued that it is just these cases, where the statement refers to our present thoughts or feelings, that furnish the exceptions. I do not see how this argument is to be settled except by devising counter-examples. If someone wishes to maintain that these statements are not incorrigible, he must light upon a set of circumstances in which such a sentence as 'he thinks that he is thinking about a philosophical problem but he is really not' could plausibly be taken to express something true, and this not simply in the sense that the problem which he is thinking about should not be classified as *philosophical*. I think that this would be very difficult but I am not prepared to say dogmatically that it is impossible.

I am content to leave this question open because I am going to argue that my thesis does not depend upon it. The position which I wish to take is that one may be the best authority with regard to one's present thoughts and feelings, even though one's reports of them are not infallible. An obvious analogy would be that of a judge whose decisions are not subject to review by any higher court. There is a sense in which his decisions may be bad, so that he is to this extent fallible; but since his ruling settles the question at issue his authority is supreme. In one very important way, however, this analogy does not suit our purpose. For the point about the judge is that he is not issuing reports: when he delivers a verdict he is not making a statement which can be either true or false. Whereas, in the cases we are now considering, it is part of my thesis that when people make pronouncements about their thoughts and feelings, they are expressing statements, which they know to be true.

Surprisingly, I think a closer parallel may be found in the observation of physical events. The notion of an eyewitness is not precise. It leaves open the question how good a view one must have of the scene which one can be said to witness, whether one sees it with the naked eye or with the help of some instrument, what sort of instrument this may be. For instance, I think it would commonly be said that a person was an eyewitness of a scene that he had viewed through a telescope or seen reflected in a mirror, but not of one that he viewed only on a cinema or television screen; but it is to some extent an arbitrary matter where one draws the line. In any case it must surely be admitted that not even the best-placed eyewitnesses are infallible. One proof of this is that their reports may disagree. All the same, they are collectively the best authorities with regard to the events which come within their view. Suppose, for example, that we were able to find a group of clairvoyants who claimed to know what was happening at a great distance from them. Suppose that their reports were always in agreement and that when checked against the testimony of observers who were present at the scenes which they described, they were consistently found to be right. We might very well come, in certain circumstances, to prefer the evidence of these clairvoyants to that of some individual eye-witness. But if a reasonable number of eyewitnesses agreed in their reports, then I think we should be bound to take their word against that of the clairvoyants, however reliable the clairvoyants had so far proved to be. The only possible exception would be the case in which the eyewitnesses' reports contradicted some well-established natural law; and this is only an apparent exception since the law itself would have been established on the basis of first-hand testimony. The reason why I think we should be bound to give the eyewitnesses preference is that it is only through its agreement with their evidence that the testimony of the clairvoyants could come to merit any credence at all. If they triumph over one set of eye-witnesses it is only because they are supported by another. In short, it enters into the logic of statements about perceptible physical events that the eyewitnesses have the final say in deciding whether they are true or false.

If this is correct, it provides us with a satisfactory model for the logic of the statements that a person may make about his present thoughts or feelings. He may not be infallible, but still his word is sovereign. If he is not infallible, others may be right when he is wrong. Even so their testimony is subordinate to his in the same way and for the same reason as the testimony of the clairvoyants is subordinate to that of the eyewitnesses. If his reports are corrigible it must be that he himself is ready to correct them, not after an interval of time in which a lapse of memory would rob him of his authority, but as it were in the same breath. We might allow that others were right against him if they pressed upon him a correction which he was immediately willing to accept. This is not sufficient, he might be wrongly overborne by them, but something of this sort is necessary. The logic of these statements that a person makes about himself is such that if others were to contradict him we should not be entitled to say that they were right so long as he honestly maintained his stand against them.

IV

To allow that a person's access to his own thoughts and feelings is, in this sense, privileged is not to maintain that it is exclusive. He may be the final authority on the subject of what he thinks or feels, but that does not imply that the opinions of others on this subject have no standing at all. The question how we are justified in ascribing certain thoughts and feelings to others on the basis of their physical demeanour, and of what they say and do, presents a stubborn philosophical problem. I am not sure that it has yet been satisfactorily answered, but I do not think that this obliges us to say that we can never have any good reason for the beliefs that we hold concerning other people's states of mind, any more than the lack of a satisfactory theory of perception would oblige us to say that we had no good reason for the beliefs that we hold concerning physical objects. In particular instances, we can justify such beliefs by adducing our evidence. And this is not conditional upon our being able to give a general proof that evidence of this type is reliable.

A feature which lends plausibility to the sceptical position concerning our knowledge of other minds is, once again, the construing of privileged access as the privilege of entering a private theatre. A person's thoughts and feelings are held to be private to him, in the sense of being his private property. They are objects which manifest themselves directly to him, and at best only indirectly to others. The question is then raised how these others can have any right to their belief in the existence of objects with which *ex hypothesi* they could never be acquainted.

But from the fact that a person is, in the sense and to the degree that we have explained, the best witness regarding what he thinks or feels, it does not follow that he is acquainted with any private objects, or indeed with any objects at all. For this is not a case in which we are committed to an existential inference. We can maintain that someone thinks or feels something without being bound to draw the conclusion that there *is* something which he thinks or feels. And if we do draw this conclusion, if we decide that it is convenient to speak of thoughts and feelings as objects, we are not bound to hold that they are private property. The privilege that I enjoy with respect to knowledge of my thoughts and feelings does depend upon my having them; but not necessarily upon my being the only one to have them. It is not incompatible with their being shared by somebody else.

But is it conceivable that anyone else should share them? This is a question that we are free to answer as we please. We do often talk as if they could be shared. We talk of a feeling spreading from one person to another, of people having memories or beliefs in common, of their having the same sensation, of their entertaining the same wishes or hopes; we use such expressions as 'the same thought struck them both'. But, some philosopher will protest, what we really mean in such cases is that they were struck by similar thoughts, by thoughts of the same kind, that when one person has a feeling another comes to have a feeling like it. We cannot mean that these thoughts and feelings are numerically the same; in other words, that there is in these cases only one thought or feeling which any number of different people can literally share. But why can we not mean this? What should prevent us? All that our philosopher is doing is to lay down a criterion of identity. He insists that if we treat thoughts and feelings as objects that can be counted, we are to count 'the same thought' in two different people's minds as two and not as one. This is a perfectly feasible suggestion, but, at least so far as thoughts are concerned, I cannot find any strong reason why we should adopt it; or indeed, why we should not.

We might have a motive for resisting it if the ruling that thoughts and feelings could be literally shared were a means to the solution of the other minds problem. But the most it could do in this way would be to weaken the hold upon us of the image of the private theatre. It would not help to vindicate our claims to know what was going on in other people's minds. For the fact, if it be made a fact, that if you are thinking what I am thinking, there exists a thought which we have in common, does not enable me to infer that you actually are thinking this at all. And if I do know what your thoughts are, and find that they coincide with mine, it can hardly matter to me whether or not I am entitled to say that they are literally the same. It is to be remarked also that if we do make thoughts public, in this special sense of making them common, they would still not be common in the way that physical objects are. For in the case of physical objects it is not just a matter of our being entitled to say that an object which is perceived by one person is literally the same as that which is perceived by another; the important point is that if they are perceptible, then it is a necessary condition of their existence that they be perceptible, at least in theory, by more than one person. If I think that I am perceiving a physical object and become convinced that others, who would be in a position to perceive it if it existed, do not do so, then I have reason to doubt whether it exists. But this does not apply to thoughts. In certain circumstances I may expect others to have the same thoughts as I do: but the existence of a thought which I am thinking in no way depends upon another's sharing it.

In so far as feelings are spatially located, there is a special reason for denying that they can be shared. For the fact that they are spatially located may make us inclined to regard them as particular existents: and we are reluctant to allow that a particular can exist discontinuously in time, or that it can be in different places at once. But if feelings are to be treated as objects, they will be objects of a peculiar kind, and we are free to apply special criteria of identity to them. As I have argued elsewhere,[1] it might even suit us to go further and make them public in a fuller sense. If it were an empirical fact that people in a given neighbourhood habitually felt the same, or, if you prefer it, similar, feelings on the same occasions, we might come to think of such a feeling as an object, analogous to a physical sound, which pervaded the region and existed independently of any given person's feeling it, perhaps even independently of its being felt at all. What we now describe as a person's locating this feeling in some part of his body would then be regarded as his feeling it from a special point of view. Further, the fact that someone had the experience of feeling it would not be a sufficient proof that the feeling existed, nor therefore that he really did feel it. If others, who would be expected to share the feeling, did not do so, this would be an indication that the feeling did not exist, and consequently that the man who claimed to feel it really did not but only thought he did. In these circumstances,

[1] *Vide* 'Can there be a Private Language?', *Aristotelian Society: Supplementary Proceedings* 1954.

a return to our present way of speech would be a move in the direction of phenomenalism.

I think that the reverse process would also be possible. Instead of socializing what we now tend to regard as private property, we could as it were enclose the common land; we could deny any object the power of being accessible to more persons than one. This would be in line with the phenomenalist view that physical objects can be constructed out of private sense-data, but it would not commit us to it. All that would be needed would be to restrict our rules of identity so that it became impossible for the same thing to be perceived by different people. What we should then obtain would be a set of private 'worlds', where the things which appeared in one world coexisted in a large measure with those that appeared in another. One could refer to the things in another person's world, but not by the same names as he did, unless it were understood that these names were systematically ambiguous: the same would apply of course to references to the persons themselves. It is clear that such a language would be intolerably inconvenient, but I do not think that the idea of it is logically vicious.

The moral which I draw from these speculations is that, so far as the problem of solipsism is concerned, it does not matter whether the objects with which we suppose ourselves to be acquainted are private, in the sense of being 'owned' by only one person, or public, in the sense of being available to many. If we surround ourselves with private sense-data we are obviously landed with the problem of showing how they can supply us with a reason for attributing experiences to others or for assuming the existence of a common world. But equally, though less obviously, a similar problem arises if we claim to be directly aware of physical objects. Admittedly, if we really do perceive the physical objects that we think we do, it will follow that they are capable, at least in theory, of being perceived by others. But this means that unless we have reason to believe that other people could perceive them, we are not justified in believing that we perceive them ourselves, since to say that we really do perceive them is to imply that they exist and so, in this case, to imply that they are public. Thus the problem of perception depends upon the problem of other minds. But the problem of other minds depends in its turn upon the problem of perception. For unless we knew that what appeared to be other human bodies really were so, the question of their being inhabited by other conscious persons would not arise.

V

In the course of this discussion I have distinguished four different criteria of privacy. One, which I only fleetingly considered, would make things private to a given person if their existence could be detected by him but not conceivably by anybody else. I maintain that nothing, whether it be mental or physical, is private in this sense. A weaker criterion of the same type would make things private to a given person if there is at least one way in which he can detect their existence but others cannot: it is not implied in this case that others cannot detect it in any way at all. If the possibility of co-consciousness is excluded, all mental states and processes at the conscious level are private in this sense: but so also are many bodily states and processes, unless we admit the possibility of our locating our kinaesthetic sensations in bodies other than our own. And if we take the doubtful step of distinguishing thoughts and feelings, as objects, from the processes of thinking and feeling them, we cannot say that the privacy of these mental activities extends, in this sense, to their accusatives, unless we also hold that thoughts and feelings cannot be literally shared.

Thirdly, a person might be said to have private access to those things concerning which his authority could not be overridden. This would not extend to anything physical, but neither would it cover a great deal that is ordinarily classified as mental. Perhaps we might say that only the thoughts and feelings to which it did apply were *strictly* mental. If we allow that one's present thoughts and feelings can be shared, one may not be the only final authority with regard to their existence, since others may have them too, though this will remain a point on which one cannot be overridden: one will in any case be the only final authority with regard to the fact that one is having them. Finally, the attribution of privacy may be made to turn on the question whether something is public or private property, in the sense that it is or is not capable of being shared.

This is the criterion to which philosophers have perhaps paid most attention, without as a rule distinguishing it at all clearly from the others. It is not applied unambiguously, since physical objects are held to be sharable on the ground that different people can *perceive* the same physical object, while feelings are held to be unsharable on the different ground that two people cannot *have* the same feeling. Even if these rules of identity be accepted, this criterion does not in general distinguish between the mental and the physical, since if it is true that you cannot have my feelings, it is equally true that you cannot sleep my sleep, or smile my smile or speak with my voice. How ambiguously this criterion works is shown by the fact that it also makes these things public, since my sleeping, my voice, and my smile are all perceptible by others. I have included it not for its merits but because it is so often used.

A word remains to be said about the logical relations of these criteria. If anything were private according to the first criterion, in the order in which I have just listed them, it would be private according to the other three; but in no case does the converse hold. The fourth criterion may be thought to be a muddled version of the second but it operates differently. To say of something that its existence is detectable by a given person in at least one way in which it is not detectable by others neither implies nor excludes the possibility of its being something that he can be said to share. I maintain also that the third criterion is logically independent of the second and fourth. Plainly from the fact that something is exclusively mine, it does not follow, as was shown by the example of a smile, that I have privileged access to it; and I have also tried to show that from the fact that I do have privileged access to my present thoughts and feelings, in the sense that my testimony concerning them cannot be overridden, it does not follow that they are exclusively mine. Again it is obvious that having a private method of detecting the existence of something is not sufficient to make one a final authority concerning it: neither, in my view, is it necessary. For I have argued that this authority is not destroyed even by the admission of co-consciousness. Why indeed such a privilege should exist in the cases where it does is a question to which I have not found an answer. We may just have to take it as a fact for which no further reason can be given.

STUART HAMPSHIRE

Spinoza and the Idea of Freedom

I believe that everyone who has ever written about Spinoza, and who has tried to interpret his thought as a whole, either has been, or ought to have been, uneasily aware of some partiality in his interpretation, when he turns once again from his own words to the original. Certainly this is my own position. When the study of Spinoza is reviewed historically, one sees that each commentator, unconsciously faithful to his own age and to his own philosophical culture, has seized upon some one element in Spinoza's thought; he then proceeds to develop the whole of the philosophy from this single centre. Spinoza as the critic of Cartesianism: Spinoza as the free-thinker and destroyer of Judaeo-Christian theology: Spinoza as the pure deductive metaphysician: Spinoza as the near-mystic, who imagines a level of intuitive understanding beyond discursive reason: lastly, Spinoza as the scientific determinist, who anticipates the more crude materialists, and the more crude secular moralists, of the nineteenth century: as the precursor of George Henry Lewes. All these masks have been fitted on him and each of them does to some extent fit. But they remain masks, and not the living face. They do not show the moving tensions and unresolved conflicts in Spinoza's *Ethics*. They remain interpretations that have been imposed from outside. They smooth over and cover up the opposing strains within the original thought. His writing has a hard, finished, unyielding surface. One can return to it again and again without ever being sure that one has penetrated to the centre of his intentions.

He could only state; he could not loosely explain, or betray his intentions in an approximation. Yet I have the persisting feeling— I cannot yet properly call it a belief—that in the philosophy of mind he is nearer to the truth at certain points than any other philosopher ever has been. I do not therefore propose historical accuracy and historical justice as motives for returning once again to the original *Ethics* at one of its most difficult points. Rather I believe that there is something very relevant to moral and political philosophy at this time to be learnt from an entirely literal, unprejudiced, and uncondescending attention to Spinoza's idea of freedom. Perhaps his conception of freedom is after all a valid one; and perhaps we are now in a better position than our ancestors to find the true significance of it.

The two most obvious facts about Spinoza are the two most important facts in understanding his intentions: first, that his definitive philosophical work was justly called *Ethics*: second, that the only evaluative distinction finally recognized in his philosophy, other than the distinctions between true and false, and between adequate and inadequate, ideas, is the distinction between freedom and servitude. These are the terms, positive and negative, in which a man, and a man's life, his actions and passions, are to be finally judged. These are the terms in which a wise man reviews and criticizes his own conduct, his own emotions and attitudes, and it is by reference to this contrast that he will, if he is wise, make his own decisions. A man is wise in proportion as his thought at all times proceeds by active reasoning from premises that are well known to him as self-evident truths. These self-evident truths are necessarily available to him, as instruments for his enlightenment, among the many confused and inadequate ideas that he must also have. They are necessarily available to every thinking being, as the reflections in his thought of the universal and unchanging features of the natural order of extended things. His inadequate ideas reflect only his particular and temporary standpoint as one extended thing among others. If once he concentrates his attention on these timeless truths, independent of his own standpoint and perceptions, and argues carefully from them, he cannot help coming to the conclusion that human conduct has to be judged, and his own decisions made, by reference to this single standard, the standard of freedom of mind as opposed to servitude of mind; and he will unavoidably agree that the distinction between freedom and its opposite is the distinction between active reasoning, internally determined, and the mind's passive reception of ideas impressed upon it from without.

'He cannot help coming to the conclusion', 'He will unavoidably agree that it *must* be interpreted'—here already there are the signs of necessity. As soon as we start to argue strictly, these and other signs of necessity will always enter in. As will be seen later, these marks of necessity, rightly understood and in the appropriate context, are the marks of freedom and activity of mind. The mind is active and free when, and only when, the argument is strict, when the conclusion of a passage of thought is internally determined by the thinking process itself. A man whose attention has been drawn to self-evident, primary truths, the terms of which he understands, will unavoidably follow a continuous train of thought and will unavoidably affirm the necessary conclusions. If he fully understands, he has no choice. If he has a choice, and if he can doubt and hesitate until he settles the matter by a decision, his conclusion will be determined, at least in part, by something that is external to the thinking process itself.

Some of these primary truths are concerned with the notion of cause or of explanation, in the widest sense of these words. In the widest sense of the word 'cause', anything that is an appropriate answer to the question 'Why?' gives a cause, irrespective of the category to which the thing to be explained belongs. The question 'Why?' may, for example, be asked with reference to a belief, a human action, a human attitude or sentiment, the existence of a physical object, or the properties of numbers and geometrical figures. Anything that counts as an answer to the question 'Why?' is an explanation, whether true or false, of the belief, action, attitude, sentiment, physical object, or mathematical entity. In the vocabulary that Spinoza inherited, the word 'cause' can be substituted for the word 'explanation', without prejudging any questions about the type of explanation appropriate to these different cases. The distinguishing of different types, or categories, of causes, which is the distinguishing of different types or categories of explanation, has always been the proper work of philosophy, and of that reflexive knowledge that is peculiar to philosophy. Spinoza draws these distinctions between types of explanation in the *Ethics*, adapting an inherited scholastic vocabulary for his own purpose.

Let us assume the standpoint of an individual thinker, a finite mode, with his necessarily limited knowledge. Reflecting on the range of his knowledge, he will find at least one clear distinction: the distinction between an understanding of causes that is complete and self-justifying, and an understanding of causes that is not complete and self-justifying. There are ideas in reference to which the question 'Why is it so?' receives a complete answer, in the sense that, in looking for the explanation, we arrive at self-evident truths, and definitions, in a finite number of steps. There are other ideas in reference to which the question 'Why is it so?' leads us back along an infinite series of ideas, with no final and sufficient explanation to be found within the series, however long we continue. So much is common to Leibniz and Spinoza. They diverge when they specify the limits of application of the two orders of explanation, the complete and the incomplete For Spinoza the fundamental difference between the two orders of causes is the difference between the series of eternal things and the series of things that come into existence and pass away at a certain time. There is no further difference between the two orders of explanation which is not entailed by this primary difference. There is no ultimate contingency in the existence of things in the common order of nature, no contingency imputable to a creator's free choice among logically possible alternatives. The difference is only between that which is eternal and that which is finite in its existence. The existence of things that are not eternal, and that occupy a determinate position in the time-order, can only be incompletely explained. There must always be an infinite regress of causes required to explain why this particular thing exists at this particular time. The existence of this thing was contingent upon the prior existence of some other thing and so on *ad infinitum*. No limit can be set on the universe of individual things that come into existence and pass away. But there are objects conceived as eternal things, about which it does not make sense to ask when they came into existence and when they will perish: numbers, for example, or the whole of extended Nature, which can be referred to as a thing, as *Res extensa*. About such things an explanation can be given of why their properties must be ordered as they are, an explanation that will terminate in self-evident, primary propositions defining the nature of the objects referred to.

This distinction between the two orders of explanation, the two kinds of answer to 'Why is it so?', the temporal and the non-temporal order, corresponds to Leibniz's distinction between truths of reason and truths of fact, and also to familiar post-Kantian distinctions between analytic and synthetic propositions. But it is a different distinction, not the same distinction with a different label. Every philosopher has to draw some similar line between the two types of knowledge. As the chosen ground of distinction differs, the line will fall in a different place and will suggest different groupings and exclusions. Spinoza expresses the distinction, not only as a distinction between different types of object, eternal things and finite things, but also as a distinction between the ways in which any given subject-matter can be studied. Whether we are inquiring into human emotions, including our own emotions, or into the nature and movements of physical objects, we can always, if we choose, look for the eternally valid laws that explain the variety of human emotions and the movements of physical objects. We can always regard the particular case of an emotion or of a physical movement, occurring at exactly this time and soon to disappear, as an instance, or illustration, of a constant, unchanging pattern. Such a pattern has its own ultimate explanation in the permanent structure of things. We can always regard the thing to be explained *sub specie aeternitatis*, without attention to the date on which it occurred, or to the standpoint from which it was observed, and not *sub specie durationis*, which would involve explaining its place in the time-order that leads up to this particular occasion. If we are interested only in ourselves and in our own environment, and therefore in the occurrence of the emotion, or of the physical movement, at this particular time, and if we wish to trace the causes in their historical sequence up to this moment, we will of course need to invoke the eternally valid laws in looking for the historical explanation of this particular case. But the interest is then an historical interest, and this is an interest that can never be finally satisfied. Some uncertainty will always attach to any historical explanation that we attempt. Some of the infinitely numerous factors, which should ideally have been mentioned, have always eluded us. We fall into error, and an error that has serious consequences in our practical activities, if we do not always bear in mind the intrinsic difference between the two types of explanation, the two orders of causes, the intellectual order and the common order of nature. We must always be aware of the incompleteness and necessary uncertainty of any historical explanation of things in the common order of nature. Intellectually, the error is to take some cause picked out from the temporal sequence of events and to concentrate our attention upon it as *the* cause, and then to suppose that we can know that, if only this had been different, which it might have been, the effect would never have followed. Then it will seem to us contingent that things happened as they did. But the appearance of contingency is due to the necessary limitation of our knowledge, to our incapacity to follow to its conclusion every path of investigation, where the paths are infinitely many. When we isolate some one cause as the sole object of interest, and think of it as something that really might have been different, we are simply failing to realize the infinite complexity of the connections between things in the temporal order. Practically and morally, the corresponding error will be to love or to hate with blind concentration the particular thing which, through weakness of mind, has become isolated in our thought from the infinitely complex network in the common order of nature. Instead of being detached and sceptical in reflecting on the infinite complexity of the causes, we shall be uncritically certain that we have identified the original good or evil within our own environment. We shall therefore for a time tend to act as if our welfare depended solely on the destruction or preservation of this particular thing. Our conduct will for a time correspondingly exhibit the same blind and helpless partiality, the same imaginative obsession with one thing, suggested to us by our environment, as the true cause of our present pleasure or suffering.

Most men spend their lives in an alternation between one object and another as the temporary object of desire or aversion, absorbed in their own partial view of their own environment, and unable to see this environment, and their own passive reactions to it, as formed by a concatenation of causes that extends infinitely in every direction. They have therefore no consistent plan, no stable and central direction of their interests. This alternation of desires, this fluctuation of the mind, is the state of fantasy, obsession, and un-enlightenment. The mind is then to a greater or less degree disintegrated, in the sense that the succession of its states is not determined by the subject's own activity of thought. Their states of mind are only to be explained as more or less unconnected responses of their imagination to the stimulus of the environment, which evokes desires and aversions that have no adequate foundation in the subject's own directed reasoning. This condition of unfreedom, of slavery to the passions, is the equivalent in Spinoza of the heteronomy of the will in Kant. But it is not an enslavement of the will, but rather of the understanding. The remedy is the correction of the understanding and an appeal to its natural powers. The remedy is available to everyone who is able to reflect upon, and who never forgets, the two levels of explanation, the two orders of causes, and therefore the two kinds of knowledge which each man necessarily possesses. As long as a man is reflectively aware, whenever he thinks, of the nature of his own thought, as either actively directed towards eternal and demonstrable truths, or else as absorbed in uncriticized fantasies traceable to his own sensations and memories, he is not misled either in that which he claims to know with certainty, or in that which he considers desirable or undesirable, as good or bad. He will reflectively examine the reasons for his own desires and aversions, and he will distinguish those that are to be explained as the effects of events on his imagination, from those that are explained by an active consideration, independent of his own situation, of the tendency of an object to serve the purposes common to all thinking beings as such. Because he knows when he truly knows and when he only incompletely knows, he always knows when he has an entirely sufficient reason for his actions and attitudes, and when he has not. As he is by nature an active thinking being, he will prefer the type of explanation of things that is complete and intellectually satisfying when it is presented to him. As a body naturally tends to maintain itself, and restore itself, against the effects of the environment, so correspondingly a mind tends to assert its power of thought, and to prefer rational argument, whenever it is presented, to the passive association of ideas in the common order of nature. But we need to be awakened to the recognition and the use of the powers that our minds possess. This is part of the work of a philosopher, which includes, as in the example of Spinoza's own writing, exhortation, a call to reflection, alongside purely intellectual analysis.

Perhaps this picture of the free man as self-directing, as an integrated mind with a continuous controlling reason, is so far a clear one. But the notion of freedom itself is still unclarified: what is the precise connection between a man's knowledge of the distinction between different levels of knowledge and his freedom in action? The connection is to be found in Spinoza's theory of individuals. Like every other identifiable particular thing in the natural order, a man tries in his characteristic activity to preserve himself and his own distinct nature as an individual, and to increase his own power and activity in relation to his environment. This trying (*conatus*), or inner force of self-preservation, is that which makes any individual an individual. Regarded as a physical organism, his overriding interest is to preserve his own stability as a distinct organism in relation to the physical environment. Regarded as a thinking being, his overriding interest is to preserve the coherence and continuity of his own thought against the flow of unconnected ideas which are his perceptions, sensations, and imaginations. The conatus of the individual, conceived as a physical organism, is the body's tendency to repair itself and to maintain itself in relation to the environment. The conatus of the individual, conceived as a thinking being, is the *vis animi*, which is the essential and natural tendency of the mind to assert active thinking and knowledge against the passive association of ideas in imagination. The more the sequence of a man's own ideas can be explained without reference to causes outside his own thinking, the more active and self-determining he is, regarded as a thinking being. The more active and self-determining he is, to that degree also he can be more properly regarded as a distinct thing, having an individuality that sets him apart from his particular environment. The more self-determining and active he is, and the more free, in this sense of 'free', the more he can be regarded as a real individual, real as an individual thinking being.

Because a thing's reality as a distinct individual depends on its activity and freedom, Spinoza must take the word 'free', rather than the word 'good', as the fundamental term of evaluation. He is a scholastic and an Aristotelian in taking it for granted that praise and evaluation of a thing are necessarily an assessment of the degree to which it realizes its nature or essence in its activity. The nearer a thing approaches perfection in the activity proper to it, the more praiseworthy it is. He takes the virtue, objectively regarded, of any thing to be the same as the perfect realization of its nature. But, unlike Aristotle, he identifies the essential nature of any individual thing with its individuality, with that which makes it a distinct individual: and this is its power of self-maintenance in relation to other things. Its virtue is its power as an individual. A particular thing's nature or essence is its nature or essence as a distinct individual rather than as a specimen of a kind. Peter or Paul are therefore not to be judged as being more or less good men, that is, as realizing more or less completely the potentialities of their species. They are to be judged as more or less complete individuals, that is, as more or less distinguishable as active agents from the temporary influences of their environment in the common order of nature. A man's natural tendency or conatus is not to make himself a good or perfect specimen of his kind, to realize in his activity some general ideal of humanity, but rather to preserve himself, this individual, as an active being, who is, as far as possible, independent in his activity. He has achieved virtue, and succeeded in that which he necessarily desires, when, and only when, he is comparatively free and self-determining in his activity. He would be a perfect being, if he were perfectly self-determining, active, and free. His happiness, and enjoyment of action, does not depend on a choice of ends of action that he, as an individual, has to make and that he is free to make: the choice of whether to pursue the ideal of excellence that is proper to his species. In the last analysis, and speaking philosophically, there is no such choice of an ideal or end. Philosophically speaking, the choice is of the right means to an end that is already determined for him by his nature and appetites as an individual thinking and physical thing. The real choice is between the first step of reflection, preliminary to the use of his intellectual powers, and an undirected passive response to experience. His desires, as they emerge into consciousness, are determined by the thought of the causes of his pleasure and suffering. If the thought is confused, and is largely fantasy, he will pursue, *sub specie boni*, temporary ends, which, by the laws of his nature, must lead to frustration, instability, and suffering. Therefore he needs to be stirred to take this first step of reflection. His happiness consists in his sense of his activities as having their originating cause within him, and in his enjoyment of his own activity as unimpeded activity. He is frustrated, and therefore suffers, when his activity is not self-directed, but is rather the immediate effect of causes external to himself. The suffering is the loss of his sense of his own power and vitality as a distinct and active being.

The notion of an individual nature or essence may be found altogether obscure. We can, I think, still attach a sense to the notion of the essential characteristics of a species, and to the judgement of individuals as more or less perfect specimens of their kinds. But can we intelligibly speak of an individual or particular thing becoming more or less of an individual? Spinoza provides a criterion by which the approach in perfection of an individual *qua* individual is to be judged: the criterion is the degree to which the individual is active and self-determining. Any thing that is identifiable as a particular thing can be judged by this single criterion, irrespective of the kind to which it is allotted within conventional classifications. One may review the scale of the increasing activity and self-determination of particular things, and therefore of their increasing individuality, from physical objects of various orders of complexity, to living organisms, to human beings. Human beings, at the top of the scale, can be completely self-determining when their activity is continuous thought, with each idea following its predecessor, in the intellectual sense of 'follow' as well as in the temporal sense. At such moments—and the moments cannot be indefinitely prolonged —men rise above their normal human condition as finite modes.

In the ordinary vocabulary we conventionally classify things into kinds according to their typical human uses. Spinoza demands that, as moralists and philosophers, we should see through these anthropocentric classifications to the true individuality of particular things. When we group them into kinds, we should follow this single principle in differentiating the kinds: their characteristic power and form of self-maintenance as individuals. From the standpoint of the true natural philosopher, the natural order should be seen as a system of individuals within individuals, of increasing power and

complexity, each type of individual differentiated by its characteristic activity in self-maintenance. The more fully we study and
understand particular things, not as specimens of the conventionally
recognized kinds, but as types of structure each acting and maintaining their identity according to the laws of the type, the more we
shall understand Nature as a whole. This is the form in which natural
knowledge, objectively valid for the whole of Nature, is properly to
be expressed. Psychology as a science can be no exception.

There is one case in which each man is well qualified to achieve
such a true understanding of an individual: himself. Starting from
this secure example, he can work outwards towards a true and
objective understanding of Nature as a whole. He will become dis-
satisfied with the conventional classifications of things by their
ordinary human uses, and he will find a more objective and truly
scientific principle of classification in their various modes of self-
maintenance. Spinoza's objective study of the emotions, the outline
of a psychopathology, illustrates these principles. There are systematic connections, laws of unconscious memory, to be found behind
the conventional classifications of the passions. Systematic knowledge of these laws is the necessary first step to useful self-knowledge.

It is now possible to state the connection between a constant
awareness of the distinction between adequate and inadequate
knowledge and the notion of freedom. We need to apply the doctrine
of the individual as essentially active to a thinking being who is a
person. For every belief that I have, and for every claim to knowledge that I make, there is an explanation of why I have this belief
and why I claim to have this knowledge. Every passion that can be
attributed to me is a pleasure or a pain combined with an idea of the
cause of this pleasure or pain. There must therefore be an explanation of my having this idea about the cause of my pleasure or suffering. Suppose then that I am at all times asking myself the question
—Is the sequence of ideas that has terminated in this idea a self-
contained sequence that, by itself, completely explains my idea of
the cause? In other words, was the conclusion reached by a rational
process? Or must I mention ideas that are associated in my experience, but that are without intrinsic connection, in explaining my
conclusion? Under these conditions of self-conscious reflection, I
never affirm a proposition, or commit myself to a belief, without

qualifying it as adequately or inadequately founded. If this condition were fulfilled, I could not be a victim of those passions that consist in the association of my pleasure or suffering with the idea of a particular transient thing, or person, in the common order of nature as its adequate cause. And when I say that I *could* not be a victim of the passion, the impossibility here is a logical impossibility. The unexamined links of association, which are necessary to the belief that is part of the passion, depend for their existence on my not being reflectively aware of them. As soon as I am self-consciously aware of them, I must then know that it is only through the fantasies engendered by my particular history that my present pleasure or suffering has become associated in my mind with the idea of these particular things or persons, which I now in consequence hate or love. If I actively inquire into the true causes of my pleasure or suffering, the passive association of ideas is broken, and the attention focused on the particular thing, or person, as the adequate cause is dissolved. An emotion necessarily involves a thought of the cause or occasion of the pleasure or unpleasure, and it is in this sense directed towards an object. Spinoza's theory of the emotions represents them as states of pleasure or unpleasure, and of desire and aversion, combined with a thought of the causes, simple or complex, of the pleasure or unpleasure. To change the accompanying thought is therefore to change the emotion, and therefore to change the desire or the aversion that determines conduct. Suppose that I am angry with someone and am angry about something that he has done. To be angry is to be displeased and to be disposed to injure someone, together with the thought that he has been the cause of injury to me. When I consider my true interests as an active thinking being, and also examine a train of unconscious associations that leads to the idea of him as the original cause of my displeasure, and recognize the inadequacy of the idea, the passion of anger disappears. When I realize the contributing causes of my displeasure in my own unconscious memories and consequent dispositions, the idea of an adequate external cause disappears, and there is nothing left to be angry with. When on reflection I realize that no one external thing can be isolated as the cause of my displeasure, I not only realize my error in imagining a simple external cause of my state: I open the way to the activity of intellectual inquiry, regarding this particular case wholly as an instance of general laws. I thereby substitute the active enjoyment of my own powers of thought for the suffering associated with my imagination of an adequate external cause of my displeasure.

To interpret Spinoza as expecting emancipation solely from an intellectual understanding of causes is not entirely correct. It is equally incorrect to represent him as defining freedom simply as knowledge of the causes that determine my emotions and actions. Reason is the expression of my primary desire of self-assertion as a thinking being, of the urge to extend my own activity and freedom as far as I can. I am to the highest degree free when I am engaged in an intellectual inquiry, and when the subject of this inquiry is the order of my thought, as an instance of something that may be understood *sub specie aeternitatis*, and not as it is affected by particular causes in the common order of nature. My happiness then consists, first, in immunity from hatred of particular things, and from the other negative and depressive passions, as an immunity that an adequate understanding of causes necessarily brings: secondly, it consists in the positive enjoyment of my own freedom *as* freedom, as the active exercise of the power of thought. These two necessary conditions of happiness, which may be distinguished in other philosophies, are inseparable, even if distinguishable, in Spinoza's thought. He is often represented as implausibly asserting that knowledge of the causes of suffering by itself brings liberation from suffering. This is a double over-simplification. First, the liberation consists in the substitution of a free activity and of self-assertion, which is as such enjoyable, for a passive reaction, which is as such depressing and frustrating. Secondly, in the definition of any of the passions the pleasure or suffering, and the thought of its cause, are indissolubly connected. If the confused thought, or imagination, of an external cause is replaced by thought in an intellectual order, an active emotion replaces a passion.

We may now ask whether, and with what qualifications, this idea of human freedom is still defensible, and whether it suggests the true grounds of our present interest in the freedom of the individual as the main end of policy, both in private and political affairs. Let it be remembered that a man is most free, according to Spinoza, and also feels himself to be most free, when he cannot help drawing a certain conclusion, and cannot help embarking on a certain course of action in view of the evidently compelling reasons in favour of it. He has a compelling reason for following a certain course of action when he knows with certainty that it will promote his power and freedom as an active thinking being, and therefore that it will promote his enjoyment of his own existence. Then he cannot hesitate. The issue is decided for him without any need for the exercise of his will in decision, exactly as the issue is decided for him when the arguments in support of a theoretical conclusion are conclusive arguments. The only difference between theoretical conclusions and practical decisions is that the latter are always governed by the agent's desire for his own good, rationally or irrationally interpreted. When a man finds himself divided in mind between conflicting and inconclusive arguments, and between conflicting inclinations, he is, and feels himself to be, so much less a free man in his affirmations and in his actions. In such a case that which has determined his final decision, whatever it is, must be, at least in part, external to his own thought. In such cases some explanation could always in principle be given, a cause found in the common order of nature, for his deciding as he did. But it would not be a complete explanation of the right kind, namely, something that was present to his mind as a universally sufficient ground. He was moved to affirmation or action by something that was outside the rational sequence of thought. He was not entirely active and self-determining, but, at least in part, unknowing and passive in his motivation, since that which moved him to action was below the level of conscious thought. He was not altogether free in his decision, and he knows and feels that he was not, because he did not himself recognize its necessity. When some part of the explanation of my believing something, or of my doing something, is to be found in a cause unrecognized by my reason, and in something external to my thought, I had not sufficient grounds for my belief or action. If I have a full awareness of the adequate explanation of my affirming or acting, I necessarily have sufficient grounds for my affirmation or action. The knowledge of the necessity of affirming something, or of doing something, by itself converts an external cause into an inner ground of affirmation or action. If I know clearly why I believe something or why I am doing something, I must have my own sufficient reasons for affirming or doing. If I cannot completely explain why I reach the conclusion, and if I allow that there are other possibilities open to me, my conclusion, whatever it is, will have been motivated by something other than my own reasoning.

It should now be evident that the too simple question 'Was Spinoza a determinist?' admits of no clear answer. The doctrine of the two orders of causes, the intellectual and the temporal orders, by itself makes the question indeterminate—almost meaningless. But there is a question that always lies behind any mention of 'determinism' and that certainly is worth asking: 'Did Spinoza provide clear and acceptable grounds for familiar moral distinctions? Or is his idea of human freedom incompatible with the acceptance of any familiar moral distinctions?' We cannot answer without considering the concept of morality itself: what kind of classifications of men and of their activities are to be counted as moral classifications, as resting on moral distinctions? There is no philosophically neutral answer to this question. Following Kant, one may distinguish between the moral and natural qualities of men on the basis of some doctrine of the will, which is taken to define the domain of the moral. And there is certainly no place for any such distinction as this in Spinoza's thought. Or one may so restrict the notion of morality that nothing counts as a moral judgement, or as a moral choice, unless the free choice of some specific end, or specific standard, of human activity is prescribed, an end or standard that all men, as men, unconditionally ought to aim to achieve or to conform to. If, following Spinoza, the freedom of the individual, as an individual, is taken as the supreme evaluative term, and not the goodness of a man, as a man, one cannot properly speak of a specific end, or specific standard, of human performance which each man ought to achieve or to conform to. Within the terms of his meta-physical theory, there is no sense in saying that men ought to be free, that they ought to be self-determining, integrated in mind and constant in their desires, and actively rational, in an unconditional sense of 'ought'. The unconditional injunction to them to pursue a certain end implies that they have a choice among various possibilities, and that they may make the wrong choice, unless they are enlightened by the moralist. Philosophically speaking and in the last analysis, they have no such choice of the ultimate ends of action.

They are all, the virtuous and the vicious, the enlightened and the unenlightened, in any case trying to survive as active individuals and are trying to assert their power and freedom as individuals. The only question that arises, either in their own decisions or in judgement upon them, is—'How completely are they succeeding in asserting themselves as self-determining individuals? How can they become more successful than they are in maintaining and extending their own freedom and activity?' Of the ideally free man one can say that he will necessarily have certain virtues—for instance, the virtues of liberality and benevolence. In this sense there is indeed a standard or norm of conduct: that we can specify the dispositions that are inseparable from freedom of mind, and therefore we can specify the essential public and private virtues. Spinoza clearly explains in the Preface to Part IV of the *Ethics*: although the words 'good' and 'bad' indicate nothing positive in the things to which they are applied, we do indeed need to retain them in use, because (I quote) 'we want to form for ourselves an idea of man upon which we may look as a model of human nature'. This is part of the technique of self-improvement, a preparation for the life of reason. And he explains again in Part V that reflection upon maxims of virtue and wise conduct is a useful starting-point for the life of reason. But it is, strictly speaking, a misstatement, a philosophical error of the kind that occurs only in speaking to the unenlightened, to represent the virtues of the free, rational man as duties imposed upon us, or as appropriate matter for unconditional moral imperatives. There is no law, and therefore there are no duties, other than the natural law of self-preservation, which states that we try to extend our power and liberty as far as we can. How far we can, and by what methods of intellectual discipline, is the proper subject of any book that has the title 'Ethics'. Its conclusions are properly called the dictates of reason. Most of the duties recognized in conventional morality are in fact irrational foreshadowings of behaviour that would be the natural and unconstrained behaviour of a free man. He has his own adequate reasons for being a peaceful, friendly, just, and co-operative member of society. He may need to appeal to the myth of the moral law to persuade the mass of his fellow citizens to co-operate in civil society. Some of the conventional virtues of civil society, those associated with renunciation, unworldliness, and repression, are not virtues but defects. They are signs of weakness and of failure in the individual's realization of his own vitality as an individual. They have been taken for virtues, when myths of a transcendent God and of another world have been taken seriously as metaphysical truths. Preoccupation with death, and with human weakness, and with the passage of time, rather than with the enjoyment of present activity, are the emotional counterparts of these false philosophies. In a well-known and significant paragraph (Scholium to Prop. X in Part V), Spinoza says that the attitude of the severe moralist, which issues in denunciations of the vices and vanities of man, and of the common conditions of human life, is always the mark of a diseased mind. Pathos and virtue are opposed to each other, because, for Spinoza, virtue is energy—in a rather more precise sense than Blake intended.

There is therefore a sense in which Spinoza is representing the study of ethics, in the then dominant Christian and Jewish tradition, as one immense error, as the pursuit of a harmful illusion. The illusion is that various goals or ends of human effort, towards which our actions might be directed, are open to us for decision and for appraisal, and that the discussion and comparison of the various ends of action is the proper subject-matter of ethics. The ultimate ends of action are not open for decision or discussion. They are fixed by the laws of our nature as mind-body organisms struggling to preserve ourselves against our environment. That which we generally take, in our ignorance of these natural laws, to be our own free decision between alternative ends is to be explained as the complicated working of these laws in our own individual psychology. They are laws governing increases and decreases of vitality in the mind-body organism, and, derivatively, of unconscious appetites and conscious desires. I am only self-directing and independent when I am actively studying the laws of nature themselves, free from any concentration of interest exclusively on myself and on my relation to other particular things. Unless I continually reflect in this detached, philosophical manner, my particular judgement of ends of action, of good and bad, will correspond only to my particular desires and needs, due to the complications of my particular environment, and to the fantasies that have arisen from this history. I am deceived, if I do not discover the element of fantasy, and of unconscious memories, in my original judgements of value. Moral argument, that which replaces the traditional free discussion of ends of action, should be an attempt to bring to light, and to recognize, our own motives and their sources, and thereby to make our pursuit of our own safety, and the enjoyment of our own activity, fully self-conscious and therefore fully rational.

I think it is at least possible that Spinoza is right in his opinion that traditional ethics is the pursuit of an illusion, and that gradually, in the course of years, he may be shown to be right. But for him of course this conclusion was not opinion, but knowledge. Nor did he think that it required, or could receive, confirmation from further observation and scientific inquiry. I am assuming a view of his philosophy, and of philosophy itself, which was not his, and which many living British philosophers would certainly not accept: the view that a philosophy such as his, which began with a claim to final truth demonstrable by *a priori* argument, is to be judged now as a speculative anticipation of truths that may gradually be supported by scientific inquiry, and by accumulating human experience. The confirmation, if it comes, will not be like the confirmation of an empirical hypothesis. It will not be direct confirmation, which leaves one with no reasonable alternative other than to accept the hypothesis as true. Rather the confirmation would be that some notions closely resembling Spinoza's key notions become widely accepted as peculiarly appropriate in studying and in evaluating human behaviour. New psychological knowledge might fit better into this framework than into any other, and psychologists themselves, and those who must now be directly or indirectly influenced by them, might come to employ concepts closely akin to Spinoza's. Certainly anyone who altogether rejects Spinoza's naturalistic standpoint, and anyone who has some religious and transcendental ground for his moral beliefs, would remain unpersuaded: and, given his premisses, justifiably so. But those of us who have no such transcendental grounds may at least pause and consider the possibility that much of our habitual moralizing about the ends of action is altogether mistaken. Certainly we should not deceive ourselves by dismissing Spinoza as the kind of determinist who allows no possibility of deliberate self-improvement, as if this were the dividing line between him and the traditional moralists. It is not. An unprejudiced reading of the introduction to the *De Intellectus Emendatione*, and of Part V of the *Ethics*, will show that it is not. The dividing line is his theory of individuals maintaining themselves as individuals and of the mind and body as the two aspects of a single organism; and this line can be traced back to his nominalistic logic and to his philosophy of nature.

I have elsewhere suggested that there is an illuminating, and more than superficial, resemblance between Spinoza's and Freud's conception of personality. The more closely one considers this resemblance, the more clearly it appears to be traceable to common philosophical beliefs, which lie far below the surface of a shared terminology. That simple, misleading question 'Was Spinoza, was Freud, a determinist?' has to be put on one side, and for the same reason, in both cases: that determinism, as a label, is associated with a particular model of the type of explanation to be aimed at in individual psychology and in the assessment of character: and this is a type which was certainly not theirs and which they had no interest either in accepting or rejecting. A determinist, as this label is commonly understood, has the single idea that any human behaviour is to be explained by well-confirmed natural laws which, taken together with a statement of initial conditions, exhibit the behaviour, whatever it may be, as always in principle predictable. This is not the kind of understanding, and of self-understanding, that is proposed by Spinoza and Freud.

Let me briefly list their points of agreement. First: there is the 'economic' conception of the mind: that any individual is a psychophysical organism with a quantity of undifferentiated energy that appears in consciousness as desire and, below the level of consciousness, as appetite. This is the instinctual energy that must find its outlet, however deformed and deflected it may be by its interactions with the environment. Desires and appetites are projected upon objects, as objects of love or of hate, in accordance, first, with the primary economic needs of the organism, as objects promoting or depressing its vitality, and, secondly, upon objects that are derivatively associated, through the complex mechanisms of memory, with increase or depression of vitality. Following this conception of a person's undifferentiated energy of self-assertion, Spinoza's account of passive emotions, and of the laws of transference that govern them, is very close to Freud's mechanisms of projection, transference, displacement, and identification, in forming the objects of love and aggression. Second: that the way towards freedom and self-direction is through the recognition of the unreality of the causes with which an individual associates pleasures and sufferings. A man's discrimination between good objects and bad objects will be explained to him as imaginative projection upon reality of unconsciously remembered incidents in his personal history. Third: the purpose of such an explanation is to give him an overriding interest in the objective order of things, an interest independent of his own fantasies and of the passive association of ideas. The recall to reason is a recall from fantasy, and from the attachment to past experience through unconscious memories, towards an active and present enjoyment of his energies. He therefore becomes free to direct his mind naturally to its proper objects, instead of endlessly and helplessly repeating patterns of pursuit and aversion that originally established themselves below the level of his consciousness. Fourth: in his original state of uncriticized passive emotions, based upon fantasy, and the projection of his conflicts on to external objects, a man necessarily follows contrary and violently conflicting inclinations, and not a stable and consistent policy. Taken as a whole, his behaviour, in realizing his own desires, is therefore self-defeating. He is in this sense a divided and disintegrated personality. Freedom consists in the integration of all his desires and aversions into a coherent policy, the policy of developing his own powers of understanding, and of enjoying his active energies.

The point of philosophical interest here is the conception of mental causation which in turn determines the conception of freedom as the proper subject of ethics. For both Spinoza and Freud, the starting-point was the individual who, although part of the common order of nature, has to assert his individuality, his activity as an individual, against the common order of nature: in later, un-Spinozistic language, to assert the self, as agent, against the not-self, the external reality which resists him. His only means of achieving this distinctness as an individual, this freedom in relation to the common order of nature, is the power of the mind freely to follow in its thought an intellectual order. Then the flow of his reasonable thought and his reasonable action is predictable with greater certainty than when his thoughts and actions were determined by causes external to his own thinking. Spinoza and Freud alike argued that it is the common condition of men that their conduct and their judgements of value, their desires and aversions, are in each individual determined by unconscious memories. This is the nature of the passions—that their objects can be explained only from knowledge of unconsciously remembered satisfactions and frustrations in the individual's history, and not from the properties of the objects themselves. The future activity of a reasonable man is predictable on the basis of his present activity, while the future of the man who is a slave to his passions is to be inferred only from fantasies that he formed in the remote past. When a man's thought follows the objective order of things in nature, he is, and knows that he is, for a time an autonomous individual, asserting his own power and independence of mind. I repeat 'for a time'. For neither Spinoza nor Freud were optimists. Freedom is at the best only intermittent and partial, and the general condition of men, as parts of nature, is one of fantasy and of passion determined by unconscious memory and therefore by conflict and frustration. But Freud's was certainly the deeper pessimism. Attending to the evidence of fact, he found no reason to believe that the mere force of intellect and of reflection could by itself open the way to self-knowledge, and therefore to freedom of mind. And one traditional form of philosophical writing, which still survives in Spinoza, is disappearing from our literature: the exhortation addressed to reason, the call to reflection on the right way of life, which used to be the preface, as in the *De Intellectus Emendatione*, to intellectual analysis.

Spinoza's philosophy can be construed as a metaphysical justification of individualism in ethics and politics. In so interpreting him, we only follow his design of his own work, which has never, I think, been treated with sufficient seriousness, largely because the attention of political philosophers has been concentrated on the more crude and inapplicable metaphysics of Hobbes. Whatever may be our judgement on the metaphysical premises from which it was deduced, Spinoza's theory of the passions is indeed a justification for taking the freedom of the individual as the supreme goal of political action. The now prevailing liberal conceptions of freedom, based on an empiricist philosophy, leave a mystery: why is the individual's act of choice, free from outside interference and threats of force, the supremely valuable activity of a man? Mill himself drew his answer from his utilitarian philosophy. The freedom of the individual was not for him a supreme and absolute end, but rather a means to the general progress of mankind. The individual's freedom of choice is a means to diversity and experiment, and diversity and experiment are means to the discovery of the most desirable forms of life. There is nothing in this philosophy that requires that the freedom of any individual is as such to be respected before all other things. Perhaps a revived doctrine of natural rights could give a sense to the absolute, as opposed to the conditional, value of the freedom of the individual. But no sense is given to the notion of natural rights within the empiricist philosophies of this time. If every man is by the law of his nature as an individual trying to assert his own power and freedom, in Spinoza's sense, in his thought and action, there is indeed a natural basis for the insistence on freedom as the supreme value in politics as in personal morality. The pursuit of any incompatible end will only lead to conflict and violence.

I return to my starting-point. It is, I think, at least possible that Spinoza has presented the outline of a defensible conception of individual freedom as the ultimate value in politics. In the *Tractatus Theologico-Politicus*, particularly in Chapter 20, he undertakes to show both that a civilized social order, based on freedom of thought and toleration, is a necessary condition of the use of reason, and therefore of the individual's fulfilment and enjoyment of his active powers: also, and more important now, to show that violence and social conflict are the projections into the external world of conflicts of passion within the individual. The first demonstration is in its conclusion, though not in its method, a commonplace. The second is not. We continue to speculate without conviction about freedom and social co-operation in the traditional terms of political philosophy, without any serious attention to the psychopathology of the individual, and as if all the discoveries in clinical psychology in the last fifty years had never been made. And this is, I think, why political philosophy seems now dying or dead, and lacks all conviction, except as an interpretation of the past. It has lost contact with the revolutionary and relevant moral science of its time. It is contrary to reason, and contrary also to John Stuart Mill's own principles in philosophy, that we should still cling to Mill's definition of freedom, when the philosophy of mind upon which he based it is discredited. We thereby preserve the letter, and lose the spirit, of empiricism, and of the liberal beliefs that were derived from it.

P. F. STRAWSON

Freedom and Resentment

Some philosophers say they do not know what the thesis of determinism is. Others say, or imply, that they do know what it is. Of these, some—the pessimists perhaps—hold that if the thesis is true, then the concepts of moral obligation and responsibility really have no application, and the practices of punishing and blaming, of expressing moral condemnation and approval, are really unjustified. Others—the optimists perhaps—hold that these concepts and practices in no way lose their *raison d'être* if the thesis of determinism is true. Some hold even that the justification of these concepts and practices requires the truth of the thesis. There is another opinion which is less frequently voiced: the opinion, it might be said, of the genuine moral sceptic. This is that the notions of moral guilt, of blame, of moral responsibility are inherently confused and that we can see this to be so if we consider the consequences either of the truth of determinism or of its falsity. The holders of this opinion agree with the pessimists that these notions lack application if determinism is true, and add simply that they also lack it if determinism is false. If I am asked which of these parties I belong to, I must say it is the first of all, the party of those who do not know what the thesis of determinism is. But this does not stop me from having some sympathy with the others, and a wish to reconcile them. Should not ignorance, rationally, inhibit such sympathies? Well, of course, though darkling, one has some inkling—some notion of what sort of thing is being talked about. This lecture is intended as a move towards reconciliation; so is likely to seem wrongheaded to everyone.

But can there be any possibility of reconciliation between such clearly opposed positions as those of pessimists and optimists about determinism? Well, there might be a formal withdrawal on one side in return for a substantial concession on the other. Thus, suppose the optimist's position were put like this: (1) the facts as we know them do not show determinism to be false; (2) the facts as we know them supply an adequate basis for the concepts and practices which the pessimist feels to be imperilled by the possibility of determinism's truth. Now it might be that the optimist is right in this, but is apt to give an inadequate account of the facts as we know them, and of how they constitute an adequate basis for the problematic concepts and practices; that the reasons he gives for the adequacy of the basis are themselves inadequate and leave out something vital. It might be that the pessimist is rightly anxious to get this vital thing back and, in the grip of his anxiety, feels he has to go beyond the facts as we know them; feels that the vital thing can be secure only if, beyond the facts as we know them, there is the further fact that determinism is false. Might *he* not be brought to make a formal withdrawal in return for a vital concession?

2. Let me enlarge very briefly on this, by way of preliminary only. Some optimists about determinism point to the efficacy of the practices of punishment, and of moral condemnation and approval, in regulating behaviour in socially desirable ways.[1] In the fact of their efficacy, they suggest, is an adequate basis for these practices; and this fact certainly does not show determinism to be false. To this the pessimists reply, all in a rush, that *just* punishment and *moral* condemnation imply moral guilt and guilt implies moral responsibility and moral responsibility implies freedom and freedom implies the falsity of determinism. And to this the optimists are wont to reply in turn that it is true that these practices require freedom in a sense, and the existence of freedom in this sense is one of the facts as we know them. But what 'freedom' means here is nothing but the absence of certain conditions the presence of which would make moral condemnation or punishment inappropriate.

[1] Cf. P. H. Nowell-Smith, 'Freewill and Moral Responsibility', *Mind*, 1948.

They have in mind conditions like compulsion by another, or innate incapacity, or insanity, or other less extreme forms of psychological disorder, or the existence of circumstances in which the making of any other choice would be morally inadmissible or would be too much to expect of any man. To this list they are constrained to add other factors which, without exactly being limitations of freedom, may also make moral condemnation or punishment inappropriate or mitigate their force: as some forms of ignorance, mistake, or accident. And the general reason why moral condemnation or punishment are inappropriate when these factors or conditions are present is held to be that the practices in question will be generally efficacious means of regulating behaviour in desirable ways only in cases where these factors are *not* present. Now the pessimist admits that the facts as we know them include the existence of freedom, the occurrence of cases of free action, in the negative sense which the optimist concedes; and admits, or rather insists, that the existence of freedom in this sense is compatible with the truth of determinism. Then what does the pessimist find missing? When he tries to answer this question, his language is apt to alternate between the very familiar and the very unfamiliar.[1] Thus he may say, familiarly enough, that the man who is the subject of justified punishment, blame or moral condemnation must really *deserve* it; and then add, perhaps, that, in the case at least where he is blamed for a positive act rather than an omission, the condition of his really deserving blame is something that goes beyond the negative freedoms that the optimist concedes. It is, say, a genuinely free identification of the will with the act. And this is the condition that is incompatible with the truth of determinism.

The conventional, but conciliatory, optimist need not give up yet. He may say: Well, people often decide to do things, really intend to do what they do, know just what they're doing in doing it; the reasons they think they have for doing what they do, often really are their reasons and not their rationalizations. These facts, too, are included in the facts as we know them. If this is what you mean by freedom—by the identification of the will with the act—then freedom may again be conceded. But again the concession is compatible

---

[1] As Nowell-Smith pointed out in a later article: 'Determinists and Libertarians', *Mind*, 1954.

with the truth of the determinist thesis. For it would not follow from that thesis that nobody decides to do anything; that nobody ever does anything intentionally; that it is false that people sometimes know perfectly well what they are doing. I tried to define freedom negatively. You want to give it a more positive look. But it comes to the same thing. Nobody denies freedom in this sense, or these senses, and nobody claims that the existence of freedom in these senses shows determinism to be false.

But it is here that the lacuna in the optimistic story can be made to show. For the pessimist may be supposed to ask: But *why* does freedom in this sense justify blame, etc.? You turn towards me first the negative, and then the positive, faces of a freedom which nobody challenges. But the only reason you have given for the practices of moral condemnation and punishment in cases where this freedom is present is the efficacy of these practices in regulating behaviour in socially desirable ways. But this is not a sufficient basis, it is not even the right *sort* of basis, for these practices as we understand them.

Now my optimist, being the sort of man he is, is not likely to invoke an intuition of fittingness at this point. So he really has no more to say. And my pessimist, being the sort of man he is, has only one more thing to say; and that is that the admissibility of these practices, as we understand them, demands another kind of freedom, the kind that in turn demands the falsity of the thesis of determinism. But might we not induce the pessimist to give up saying this by giving the optimist something more to say?

3. I have mentioned punishing and moral condemnation and approval; and it is in connection with these practices or attitudes that the issue between optimists and pessimists—or, if one is a pessimist, the issue between determinists and libertarians—is felt to be particularly important. But it is not of these practices and attitudes that I propose, at first, to speak. These practices or attitudes permit, where they do not imply, a certain detachment from the actions or agents which are their objects. I want to speak, at least at first, of something else: of the non-detached attitudes and reactions of people directly involved in transactions with each other; of the attitudes and reactions of offended parties and beneficiaries;

of such things as gratitude, resentment, forgiveness, love, and hurt feelings. Perhaps something like the issue between optimists and pessimists arises in this neighbouring field too; and since this field is less crowded with disputants, the issue might here be easier to settle; and if it is settled here, then it might become easier to settle it in the disputant-crowded field.

What I have to say consists largely of commonplaces. So my language, like that of commonplaces generally, will be quite unscientific and imprecise. The central commonplace that I want to insist on is the very great importance that we attach to the attitudes and intentions towards us of other human beings, and the great extent to which our personal feelings and reactions depend upon, or involve, our beliefs about these attitudes and intentions. I can give no simple description of the field of phenomena at the centre of which stands this commonplace truth; for the field is too complex. Much imaginative literature is devoted to exploring its complexities; and we have a large vocabulary for the purpose. There are simplifying styles of handling it in a general way. Thus we may, like La Rochefoucauld, put self-love or self-esteem or vanity at the centre of the picture and point out how it may be caressed by the esteem, or wounded by the indifference or contempt, of others. We might speak, in another jargon, of the need for love, and the loss of security which results from its withdrawal; or, in another, of human self-respect and its connection with the recognition of the individual's dignity. These simplifications are of use to me only if they help to emphasize how much we actually mind, how much it matters to us, whether the actions of other people—and particularly of *some* other people—reflect attitudes towards us of goodwill, affection, or esteem on the one hand or contempt, indifference, or malevolence on the other. If someone treads on my hand accidentally, while trying to help me, the pain may be no less acute than if he treads on it in contemptuous disregard of my existence or with a malevolent wish to injure me. But I shall generally feel in the second case a kind and degree of resentment that I shall not feel in the first. If someone's actions help me to some benefit I desire, then I am benefited in any case; but if he intended them so to benefit me because of his general goodwill towards me, I shall reasonably feel a gratitude which I should not feel at all if the benefit was an incidental consequence, unintended or even regretted by him, of some plan of action with a different aim.

These examples are of actions which confer benefits or inflict injuries over and above any conferred or inflicted by the mere manifestation of attitude and intention themselves. We should consider also in how much of our behaviour the benefit or injury resides mainly or entirely in the manifestation of attitude itself. So it is with good manners, and much of what we call kindness, on the one hand; with deliberate rudeness, studied indifference, or insult on the other.

Besides resentment and gratitude, I mentioned just now forgiveness. This is a rather unfashionable subject in moral philosophy at present; but to be forgiven is something we sometimes ask, and forgiving is something we sometimes say we do. To ask to be forgiven is in part to acknowledge that the attitude displayed in our actions was such as might properly be resented and in part to repudiate that attitude for the future (or at least for the immediate future); and to forgive is to accept the repudiation and to forswear the resentment.

We should think of the many different kinds of relationship which we can have with other people—as sharers of a common interest; as members of the same family; as colleagues; as friends; as lovers; as chance parties to an enormous range of transactions and encounters. Then we should think, in each of these connections in turn, and in others, of the kind of importance we attach to the attitudes and intentions towards us of those who stand in these relationships to us, and of the kinds of *reactive* attitudes and feelings to which we ourselves are prone. In general, we demand some degree of goodwill or regard on the part of those who stand in these relationships to us, though the forms we require it to take vary widely in different connections. The range and intensity of our *reactive* attitudes towards goodwill, its absence or its opposite vary no less widely. I have mentioned, specifically, resentment and gratitude; and they are a usefully opposed pair. But, of course, there is a whole continuum of reactive attitude and feeling stretching on both sides of these and—the most comfortable area—in between them.

The object of these commonplaces is to try to keep before our minds something it is easy to forget when we are engaged in philosophy, especially in our cool, contemporary style, viz. what it is actually like to be involved in ordinary inter-personal relationships, ranging from the most intimate to the most casual.

4. It is one thing to ask about the general causes of these reactive attitudes I have alluded to; it is another to ask about the variations to which they are subject, the particular conditions in which they do or do not seem natural or reasonable or appropriate; and it is a third thing to ask what it would be like, what it *is* like, not to suffer them. I am not much concerned with the first question; but I am with the second; and perhaps even more with the third.

Let us consider, then, occasions for resentment: situations in which one person is offended or injured by the action of another and in which—in the absence of special considerations—the offended person might naturally or normally be expected to feel resentment. Then let us consider what sorts of special considerations might be expected to modify or mollify this feeling or remove it altogether. It needs no saying now how multifarious these considerations are. But, for my purpose, I think they can be roughly divided into two kinds. To the first group belong all those which might give occasion for the employment of such expressions as 'He didn't mean to', 'He hadn't realized', 'He didn't know'; and also all those which might give occasion for the use of the phrase 'He couldn't help it', when this is supported by such phrases as 'He was pushed', 'He had to do it', 'It was the only way', 'They left him no alternative', etc. Obviously these various pleas, and the kinds of situations in which they would be appropriate, differ from each other in striking and important ways. But for my present purpose they have something still more important in common. None of them invites us to suspend towards the agent, either at the time of his action or in general, our ordinary reactive attitudes. They do not invite us to view the *agent* as one in respect of whom these attitudes are in any way inappropriate. They invite us to view the *injury* as one in respect of which a particular one of these attitudes is inappropriate. They do not invite us to see the *agent* as other than a fully responsible agent. They invite us to see the *injury* as one for which he was not fully, or at all, responsible. They do not suggest that the agent is in any way an inappropriate object of that kind of demand for goodwill or regard which is reflected in our ordinary reactive attitudes. They suggest instead that the fact of injury was not in this case incompatible with that demand's being fulfilled, that the fact of injury was quite consistent with the agent's attitude and intentions being just what we demand they should be.[1] The agent was just ignorant of the injury he was causing, or had lost his balance through being pushed or had reluctantly to cause the injury for reasons which acceptably override his reluctance. The offering of such pleas by the agent and their acceptance by the sufferer is something in no way opposed to, or outside the context of, ordinary inter-personal relationships and the manifestation of ordinary reactive attitudes. Since things go wrong and situations are complicated, it is an essential and integral element in the transactions which are the life of these relationships.

The second group of considerations is very different. I shall take them in two subgroups of which the first is far less important than the second. In connection with the first subgroup we may think of such statements as 'He wasn't himself', 'He has been under very great strain recently', 'He was acting under post-hypnotic suggestion'; in connection with the second, we may think of 'He's only a child', 'He's a hopeless schizophrenic', 'His mind has been systematically perverted', 'That's purely compulsive behaviour on his part'. Such pleas as these do, as pleas of my first general group do not, invite us to suspend our ordinary reactive attitudes towards the agent, either at the time of his action or all the time. They do not invite us to see the agent's action in a way consistent with the full retention of ordinary inter-personal attitudes and merely inconsistent with one particular attitude. They invite us to view the agent himself in a different light from the light in which we should normally view one who has acted as he has acted. I shall not linger over the first subgroup of cases. Though they perhaps raise, in the short term, questions akin to those raised, in the long term, by the second subgroup, we may dismiss them without considering those questions by taking that admirably suggestive phrase, 'He wasn't himself', with the seriousness that—for all its being logically comic—it deserves. We shall not feel resentment against the man he is for the action done by the man he is not; or at least we shall feel less.

[1] Perhaps not in every case *just* what we demand they should be, but in any case *not* just what we demand they should not be. For my present purpose these differences do not matter.

We normally have to deal with him under normal stresses; so we shall not feel towards him, when he acts as he does under abnormal stresses, as we should have felt towards him had he acted as he did under normal stresses.

The second and more important subgroup of cases allows that the circumstances were normal, but presents the agent as psychologically abnormal—or as morally undeveloped. The agent was himself; but he is warped or deranged, neurotic or just a child. When we see someone in such a light as this, all our reactive attitudes tend to be profoundly modified. I must deal here in crude dichotomies and ignore the ever-interesting and ever-illuminating varieties of case. What I want to contrast is the attitude (or range of attitudes) of involvement or participation in a human relationship, on the one hand, and what might be called the objective attitude (or range of attitudes) to another human being, on the other. Even in the same situation, I must add, they are not altogether *exclusive* of each other; but they are, profoundly, *opposed* to each other. To adopt the objective attitude to another human being is to see him, perhaps, as an object of social policy; as a subject for what, in a wide range of sense, might be called treatment; as something certainly to be taken account, perhaps precautionary account, of; to be managed or handled or cured or trained; perhaps simply to be avoided, though *this* gerundive is not peculiar to cases of objectivity of attitude. The objective attitude may be emotionally toned in many ways, but not in all ways: it may include repulsion or fear, it may include pity or even love, though not all kinds of love. But it cannot include the range of reactive feelings and attitudes which belong to involvement or participation with others in inter-personal human relationships; it cannot include resentment, gratitude, forgiveness, anger, or the sort of love which two adults can sometimes be said to feel reciprocally, for each other. If your attitude towards someone is wholly objective, then though you may fight him, you cannot quarrel with him, and though you may talk to him, even negotiate with him, you cannot reason with him. You can at most pretend to quarrel, or to reason, with him.

Seeing someone, then, as warped or deranged or compulsive in behaviour or peculiarly unfortunate in his formative circumstances —seeing someone so tends, at least to some extent, to set him apart from normal participant reactive attitudes on the part of one who so sees him, tends to promote, at least in the civilized, objective attitudes. But there is something curious to add to this. The objective attitude is not only something we naturally tend to fall into in cases like these, where participant attitudes are partially or wholly inhibited by abnormalities or by immaturity. It is also something which is available as a resource in other cases too. We look with an objective eye on the compulsive behaviour of the neurotic or the tiresome behaviour of a very young child, thinking in terms of treatment or training. But we *can* sometimes look with something like the same eye on the behaviour of the normal and the mature. We *have* this resource and can sometimes use it: as a refuge, say, from the strains of involvement; or as an aid to policy; or simply out of intellectual curiosity. Being human, we cannot, in the normal case, do this for long, or altogether. If the strains of involvement, say, continue to be too great, then we have to do something else— like severing a relationship. But what is above all interesting is the tension there is, in us, between the participant attitude and the objective attitude. One is tempted to say: between our humanity and our intelligence. But to say this would be to distort both notions.

What I have called the participant reactive attitudes are essentially natural human reactions to the good or ill will or indifference of others towards us, as displayed in *their* attitudes and actions. The question we have to ask is: What effect would, or should, the acceptance of the truth of a general thesis of determinism have upon these reactive attitudes? More specifically, would, or should, the acceptance of the truth of the thesis lead to the decay or the repudiation of all such attitudes? Would, or should, it mean the end of gratitude, resentment, and forgiveness; of all reciprocated adult loves; of all the essentially *personal* antagonisms?

But how can I answer, or even pose, this question without knowing *exactly* what the thesis of determinism is? Well, there is one thing we do know: that if there is a coherent thesis of determinism, then there must be a sense of 'determined' such that, if that thesis is true, then all behaviour whatever is determined in that sense. Remembering this, we can consider at least what possibilities lie formally open; and then perhaps we shall see that the question can be answered *without* knowing exactly what the thesis of determinism is. We can consider what possibilities lie open because we have already before us an account of the ways in which particular reactive attitudes, or reactive attitudes in general, may be, and, sometimes, we judge, should be, inhibited. Thus I considered earlier a group of considerations which tend to inhibit, and, we judge, should inhibit, resentment, in particular cases of an agent causing an injury, without inhibiting reactive attitudes in general towards that agent. Obviously this group of considerations cannot strictly bear upon our question; for that question concerns reactive attitudes in general. But resentment has a particular interest; so it is worth adding that it has never been claimed as a consequence of the truth of determinism that one or another of *these* considerations was operative in every case of an injury being caused by an agent; that it would follow from the truth of determinism that anyone who caused an injury *either* was quite simply ignorant of causing it *or* had acceptably overriding reasons for acquiescing reluctantly in causing it *or* . . ., etc. The prevalence of this happy state of affairs would not be a consequence of the reign of universal determinism, but of the reign of universal goodwill. We cannot, then, find here the possibility of an affirmative answer to our question, even for the particular case of resentment.

Next, I remarked that the participant attitude, and the personal reactive attitudes in general, tend to give place, and it is judged by the civilized should give place, to objective attitudes, just in so far as the agent is seen as excluded from ordinary adult human relationships by deep-rooted psychological abnormality—or simply by being a child. But it cannot be a consequence of any thesis which is not itself self-contradictory that abnormality is the universal condition.

Now this dismissal might seem altogether too facile; and so, in a sense, it is. But whatever is too quickly dismissed in this dismissal is allowed for in the only possible form of affirmative answer that remains. We can sometimes, and in part, I have remarked, look on the normal (those we rate as 'normal') in the objective way in which we have learned to look on certain classified cases of abnormality. And our question reduces to this: could, or should, the acceptance of the determinist thesis lead us always to look on everyone exclusively in this way? For this is the only condition worth considering under which the acceptance of determinism could lead to the decay or repudiation of participant reactive attitudes.

It does not seem to be self-contradictory to suppose that this might happen. So I suppose we must say that it is not absolutely inconceivable that it should happen. But I am strongly inclined to think that it is, for us as we are, practically inconceivable. The human commitment to participation in ordinary inter-personal relationships is, I think, too thoroughgoing and deeply rooted for us to take seriously the thought that a general theoretical conviction might so change our world that, in it, there were no longer any such things as inter-personal relationships as we normally understand them; and being involved in inter-personal relationships as we normally understand them precisely is being exposed to the range of reactive attitudes and feelings that is in question.

This, then, is a part of the reply to our question. A sustained objectivity of inter-personal attitude, and the human isolation which that would entail, does not seem to be something of which human beings would be capable, even if some general truth were a theoretical ground for it. But this is not all. There is a further point, implicit in the foregoing, which must be made explicit. Exceptionally, I have said, we can have direct dealings with human beings without any degree of personal involvement, treating them simply as creatures to be handled in our own interest, or our side's, or society's—or even theirs. In the extreme case of the mentally deranged, it is easy to see the connection between the possibility of a wholly objective attitude and the impossibility of what we understand by ordinary interpersonal relationships. Given this latter impossibility, no other civilized attitude is available than that of viewing the deranged person simply as something to be understood and controlled in the most desirable fashion. To view him as outside the reach of personal relationships is already, for the civilized, to view him in this way. For reasons of policy or self-protection we may have occasion, perhaps temporary, to adopt a fundamentally similar attitude to a 'normal' human being; to concentrate, that is, on understanding 'how he works', with a view to determining our policy accordingly, or to finding in that very understanding a relief from the strains of involvement. Now it is certainly true that in the case of the abnormal, though not in the case of the normal, our adoption of the objective attitude is a consequence of our viewing the agent as *incapacitated* in some or all respects for ordinary inter-personal relationships. He is thus incapacitated, perhaps, by the fact that his picture of reality is pure fantasy, that he does not, in a sense, live in the real world at all; or by the fact that his behaviour is, in part, an unrealistic acting out of unconscious purposes; or by the fact that he is an idiot, or a moral idiot. But there is something else which, *because* this is true, is equally certainly *not* true. And that is that there is a sense of 'determined' such that (1) if determinism is true, all behaviour is determined in this sense, and (2) determinism might be true, i.e. it is not inconsistent with the facts as we know them to suppose that all behaviour might be determined in this sense, and (3) our adoption of the objective attitude towards the abnormal is the result of a prior embracing of the belief that the behaviour, or the relevant stretch of behaviour, of the human being in question *is* determined in this sense. Neither in the case of the normal, then, nor in the case of the abnormal is it true that, when we adopt an objective attitude, we do so *because* we hold such a belief. So my answer has two parts. The first is that we cannot, as we are, seriously envisage ourselves adopting a thoroughgoing objectivity of attitude to others as a result of theoretical conviction of the truth of determinism; and the second is that when we do in fact adopt such an attitude in a particular case, our doing so is not the consequence of a theoretical conviction which might be expressed as 'Determinism in this case', but is a consequence of our abandoning, for different reasons in different cases, the ordinary inter-personal attitudes.

It might be said that all this leaves the real question unanswered, and that we cannot hope to answer it without knowing exactly what the thesis of determinism is. For the real question is not a question about what we actually do, or why we do it. It is not even a question about what we would *in fact* do if a certain theoretical conviction gained general acceptance. It is a question about what it would be *rational* to do if determinism were true, a question about the rational justification of ordinary inter-personal attitudes in general. To this I shall reply, first, that such a question could seem real only to one who had utterly failed to grasp the purport of the preceding answer, the fact of our natural human commitment to ordinary inter-personal attitudes. This commitment is part of the general framework of human life, not something that can come up for review as particular cases can come up for review within this general framework. And I shall reply, second, that if we could imagine what we cannot have, viz. a choice in this matter, then we could choose rationally only in the light of an assessment of the gains and losses to human life, its enrichment or impoverishment; and the truth or falsity of a general thesis of determinism would not bear on the rationality of *this* choice.[1]

5. The point of this discussion of the reactive attitudes in their relation—or lack of it—to the thesis of determinism was to bring us, if possible, nearer to a position of compromise in a more usual area of debate. We are not now to discuss reactive attitudes which are essentially those of offended parties or beneficiaries. We are to discuss reactive attitudes which are essentially not those, or only incidentally are those, of offended parties or beneficiaries, but are nevertheless, I shall claim, kindred attitudes to those I have discussed. I put resentment in the centre of the previous discussion. I shall put moral indignation—or, more weakly, moral disapprobation—in the centre of this one.

The reactive attitudes I have so far discussed are essentially reactions to the quality of others' wills towards us, as manifested in their behaviour: to their good or ill will or indifference or lack of concern. Thus resentment, or what I have called resentment, is a reaction to injury or indifference. The reactive attitudes I have now to discuss might be described as the sympathetic or vicarious or impersonal or disinterested or generalized analogues of the reactive attitudes I have already discussed. They are reactions to the qualities of others' wills, not towards ourselves, but towards others. Because of this impersonal or vicarious character, we give them

---

[1] The question, then, of the connection between rationality and the adoption of the objective attitude to others is misposed when it is made to seem dependent on the issue of determinism. But there is another question which should be raised, if only to distinguish it from the misposed question. Quite apart from the issue of determinism, might it not be said that we should be nearer to being purely rational creatures in proportion as our relation to others was in fact dominated by the objective attitude? I think this might be said; only it would have to be added, once more, that if such a choice were possible, it would not necessarily be rational to choose to be more purely rational than we are.

different names. Thus one who experiences the vicarious analogue of resentment is said to be indignant or disapproving, or morally indignant or disapproving. What we have here is, as it were, resentment on behalf of another, where one's own interest and dignity are not involved; and it is this impersonal or vicarious character of the attitude, added to its others, which entitle it to the qualification 'moral'. Both my description of, and my name for, these attitudes are, in one important respect, a little misleading. It is not that these attitudes are essentially vicarious—one can feel indignation on one's own account—but that they are essentially capable of being vicarious. But I shall retain the name for the sake of its suggestiveness; and I hope that what is misleading about it will be corrected in what follows.

The personal reactive attitudes rest on, and reflect, an expectation of, and demand for, the manifestation of a certain degree of goodwill or regard on the part of other human beings towards ourselves; or at least on the expectation of, and demand for, an absence of the manifestation of active ill will or indifferent disregard. (What will, in particular cases, *count* as manifestations of good or ill will or disregard will vary in accordance with the particular relationship in which we stand to another human being.) The generalized or vicarious analogues of the personal reactive attitudes rest on, and reflect, exactly the same expectation or demand in a generalized form; they rest on, or reflect, that is, the demand for the manifestation of a reasonable degree of goodwill or regard, on the part of others, not simply towards oneself, but towards all those on whose behalf moral indignation may be felt, i.e., as we now think, towards all men. The generalized and non-generalized forms of demand, and the vicarious and personal reactive attitudes which rest upon, and reflect, them are connected not merely logically. They are connected humanly; and not merely with each other. They are connected also with yet another set of attitudes which I must mention now in order to complete the picture. I have considered from two points of view the demands we make on others and our reactions to their possibly injurious actions. These were the points of view of one whose interest was directly involved (who suffers, say, the injury) and of others whose interest was not directly involved (who do not themselves suffer the injury). Thus I have spoken of personal reactive attitudes in the first connection and of their vicarious analogues in the second. But the picture is not complete unless we consider also the correlates of these attitudes on the part of those on whom the demands are made, on the part of the agents. Just as there are personal and vicarious reactive attitudes associated with demands on others for oneself and demands on others for others, so there are self-reactive attitudes associated with demands on oneself for others. And here we have to mention such phenomena as feeling bound or obliged (the 'sense of obligation'); feeling compunction; feeling guilty or remorseful or at least responsible; and the more complicated phenomenon of shame.

All these three types of attitude are humanly connected. One who manifested the personal reactive attitudes in a high degree but showed no inclination at all to their vicarious analogues would appear as an abnormal case of moral egocentricity, as a kind of moral solipsist. Let him be supposed fully to acknowledge the claims to regard that others had on him, to be susceptible of the whole range of self-reactive attitudes. He would then see himself as unique both as one (*the* one) who had a general claim on human regard and as one (*the* one) on whom human beings in general had such a claim. This would be a kind of moral solipsism. But it is barely more than a conceptual possibility; if it is that. In general, though within varying limits, we demand of others for others, as well as of ourselves for others, something of the regard which we demand of others for ourselves. Can we imagine, besides that of the moral solipsist, any other case of one or two of these three types of attitude being fully developed, but quite unaccompanied by any trace, however slight, of the remaining two or one? If we can, then we imagine something far below or far above the level of our common humanity—a moral idiot or a saint. For all these types of attitude alike have common roots in our human nature and our membership of human communities.

Now, as of the personal reactive attitudes, so of their vicarious analogues, we must ask in what ways, and by what considerations, they tend to be inhibited. Both types of attitude involve, or express, a certain sort of demand for inter-personal regard. The fact of injury constitutes a prima facie appearance of this demand's being flouted or unfulfilled. We saw, in the case of resentment, how one class of considerations may show this appearance to be mere appearance, and hence inhibit resentment, *without* inhibiting, or displacing, the sort of demand of which resentment can be an expression, without in any way tending to make us suspend our ordinary interpersonal attitudes to the agent. Considerations of this class operate in just the same way, for just the same reasons, in connection with moral disapprobation or indignation; they inhibit indignation without in any way inhibiting the sort of demand on the agent of which indignation can be an expression, the range of attitudes towards him to which it belongs. But in this connection we may express the facts with a new emphasis. We may say, stressing the moral, the generalized aspect of the demand: considerations of this group have no tendency to make us see the agent as other than a morally responsible agent; they simply make us see the injury as one for which he was not morally responsible. The offering and acceptance of such exculpatory pleas as are here in question in no way detracts in our eyes from the agent's status as a term of moral relationships. On the contrary, since things go wrong and situations are complicated, it is an essential part of the life of such relationships.

But suppose we see the agent in a different light: as one whose picture of the world is an insane delusion; or as one whose behaviour, or a part of whose behaviour, is unintelligible to us, perhaps even to him, in terms of conscious purposes, and intelligible only in terms of unconscious purposes; or even, perhaps, as one wholly impervious to the self-reactive attitudes I spoke of, wholly lacking, as we say, in moral sense. Seeing an agent in such a light as this tends, I said, to inhibit resentment in a wholly different way. It tends to inhibit resentment because it tends to inhibit ordinary interpersonal attitudes in general, and the kind of demand and expectation which those attitudes involve; and tends to promote instead the purely objective view of the agent as one posing problems simply of intellectual understanding, management, treatment, and control. Again the parallel holds for those generalized or moral attitudes towards the agent which we are now concerned with. The same abnormal light which shows the agent to us as one in respect of whom the personal attitudes, the personal demand, are to be suspended, shows him to us also as one in respect of whom the impersonal attitudes, the generalized demand, are to be suspended. Only, abstracting now from direct personal interest, we may express the facts with a new emphasis. We may say: to the extent to which the agent is seen in this light, he is not seen as one on whom demands and expectations lie in that particular way in which we think of them as lying when we speak of moral obligation; he is not, to that extent, seen as a morally responsible agent, as a term of moral relationships, as a member of the moral community.

I remarked also that the suspension of ordinary inter-personal attitudes and the cultivation of a purely objective view is sometimes possible even when we have no such reasons for it as I have just mentioned. Is this possible also in the case of the moral reactive attitudes? I think so; and perhaps it is easier. But the motives for a total suspension of moral reactive attitudes are fewer, and perhaps weaker: fewer, because only where there is antecedent personal involvement can there be the motive of seeking refuge from the strains of such involvement; perhaps weaker, because the tension between objectivity of view and the moral reactive attitudes is perhaps less than the tension between objectivity of view and the personal reactive attitudes, so that we can in the case of the moral reactive attitudes more easily secure the speculative or political gains of objectivity of view by a kind of setting on one side, rather than a total suspension, of those attitudes.

These last remarks are uncertain; but also, for the present purpose, unimportant. What concerns us now is to inquire, as previously in connection with the personal reactive attitudes, what relevance any general thesis of determinism might have to their vicarious analogues. The answers once more are parallel; though I shall take them in a slightly different order. First, we must note, as before, that when the suspension of such an attitude or such attitudes occurs in a particular case, it is *never* the consequence of the belief that the piece of behaviour in question was determined in a sense such that all behaviour *might be*, and, if determinism is true, all behaviour *is*, determined in that sense. For it is not a consequence of any general thesis of determinism which might be true that nobody knows what he's doing or that everybody's behaviour is unintelligible in terms of conscious purposes or that everybody lives in a world of delusion or that nobody has a moral sense, i.e. is susceptible of self-reactive attitudes, etc. In fact no such sense of

'determined' as would be required for a general thesis of determinism is ever relevant to our actual suspensions of moral reactive
attitudes. Second, suppose it granted, as I have already argued, that
we cannot take seriously the thought that theoretical conviction of
such a general thesis would lead to the total decay of the personal
reactive attitudes. Can we then take seriously the thought that such
a conviction—a conviction, after all, that many have held or said
they held—would nevertheless lead to the total decay or repudiation
of the vicarious analogues of these attitudes? I think that the change
in our social world which would leave us exposed to the personal
reactive attitudes but not at all to their vicarious analogues, the
generalization of abnormal egocentricity which this would entail,
is perhaps even harder for us to envisage as a real possibility than
the decay of both kinds of attitude together. Though there are some
necessary and some contingent differences between the ways and
cases in which these two kinds of attitudes operate or are inhibited
in their operation, yet, as general human capacities or pronenesses,
they stand or lapse together. Finally, to the further question whether
it would not be *rational*, given a general theoretical conviction of
the truth of determinism, so to change our world that in it all these
attitudes were wholly suspended, I must answer, as before, that
one who presses this question has wholly failed to grasp the import
of the preceding answer, the nature of the human commitment that
is here involved: it is *useless* to ask whether it would not be rational
for us to do what it is not in our nature to (be able to) do. To this
I must add, as before, that if there were, say, for a moment open to
us the possibility of such a god-like choice, the rationality of making
or refusing it would be determined by quite other considerations
than the truth or falsity of the general theoretical doctrine in
question. The latter would be simply irrelevant; and this becomes
ironically clear when we remember that for those convinced that
the truth of determinism nevertheless really would make the one
choice rational, there has always been the insuperable difficulty of
explaining in intelligible terms how its falsity would make the
opposite choice rational.

I am aware that in presenting the argument as I have done,
neglecting the ever-interesting varieties of case, I have presented
nothing more than a schema, using sometimes a crude opposition

of phrase where we have a great intricacy of phenomena. In particular the simple opposition of objective attitudes on the one hand and the various contrasted attitudes which I have opposed to them must seem as grossly crude as it is central. Let me pause to mitigate this crudity a little, and also to strengthen one of my central contentions, by mentioning some things which straddle these contrasted kinds of attitude. Thus parents and others concerned with the care and upbringing of young children cannot have to their charges either kind of attitude in a pure or unqualified form. They are dealing with creatures who are potentially and increasingly capable both of holding, and being objects of, the full range of human and moral attitudes, but are not yet truly capable of either. The treatment of such creatures must therefore represent a kind of compromise, constantly shifting in one direction, between objectivity of attitude and developed human attitudes. Rehearsals insensibly modulate towards true performances. The punishment of a child is both like and unlike the punishment of an adult. Suppose we try to relate this progressive emergence of the child as a responsible being, as an object of non-objective attitudes, to that sense of 'determined' in which, if determinism is a possibly true thesis, all behaviour *may* be determined, and in which, if it is a true thesis, all behaviour *is* determined. What bearing *could* such a sense of 'determined' have upon the progressive modification of attitudes towards the child? Would it not be grotesque to think of the development of the child as a progressive or patchy emergence from an area in which its behaviour is in this sense determined into an area in which it isn't? Whatever sense of 'determined' is required for stating the thesis of determinism, it can scarcely be such as to allow of compromise, border-line-style answers to the question, 'Is this bit of behaviour determined or isn't it?' But in this matter of young children, it is essentially a border-line, penumbral area that we move in. Again, consider—a very different matter—the strain in the attitude of a psycho-analyst to his patient. *His* objectivity of attitude, *his* suspension of ordinary moral reactive attitudes, is profoundly modified by the fact that the aim of the enterprise is to make such suspension unnecessary or less necessary. Here we may and do naturally speak of restoring the agent's freedom. But here the restoring of freedom means bringing it about that the agent's behaviour shall be intelligible in terms of conscious purposes rather than in terms only of unconscious purposes. *This* is the object of the enterprise; and it is in so far as *this* object is attained that the suspension, or half-suspension, of ordinary moral attitudes is deemed no longer necessary or appropriate. And in this we see once again the *irrelevance* of that concept of 'being determined' which must be the central concept of determinism. For we cannot both agree that this object is attainable and that its attainment has this consequence and yet hold (1) that neurotic behaviour is determined in a sense in which, it may be, all behaviour is determined, and (2) that it is because neurotic behaviour is determined in this sense that objective attitudes are deemed appropriate to neurotic behaviour. Not, at least, without accusing ourselves of incoherence in our attitude to psycho-analytic treatment.

6. And now we can try to fill in the lacuna which the pessimist finds in the optimist's account of the concept of moral responsibility, and of the bases of moral condemnation and punishment; and to fill it in from the facts as we know them. For, as I have already remarked, when the pessimist himself seeks to fill it in, he rushes beyond the facts as we know them and proclaims that it cannot be filled in at all unless determinism is false.

Yet a partial sense of the facts as we know them is certainly present to the pessimist's mind. When his opponent, the optimist, undertakes to show that the truth of determinism would not shake the foundations of the concept of moral responsibility and of the practices of moral condemnation and punishment, he typically refers, in a more or less elaborated way, to the efficacy of these practices in regulating behaviour in socially desirable ways. These practices are represented solely as instruments of policy, as methods of individual treatment and social control. The pessimist recoils from this picture; and in his recoil there is, typically, an element of emotional shock. He is apt to say, among much else, that the humanity of the offender himself is offended by *this* picture of his condemnation and punishment.

The reasons for this recoil—the explanation of the sense of an emotional, as well as a conceptual, shock—we have already before us. The picture painted by the optimists is painted in a style

D

appropriate to a situation envisaged as wholly dominated by objectivity of attitude. The only operative notions invoked in this picture
are such as those of policy, treatment, control. But a thoroughgoing
objectivity of attitude, excluding as it does the moral reactive attitudes, excludes at the same time essential elements in the concepts
of *moral* condemnation and *moral* responsibility. This is the reason
for the conceptual shock. The deeper emotional shock is a reaction,
not simply to an inadequate conceptual analysis, but to the suggestion of a change in our world. I have remarked that it is possible to
cultivate an exclusive objectivity of attitude in some cases, and for
some reasons, where the object of the attitude is not set aside from
developed inter-personal and moral attitudes by immaturity or
abnormality. And the suggestion which seems to be contained in
the optimist's account is that such an attitude should be universally
adopted to all offenders. This is shocking enough in the pessimist's
eyes. But, sharpened by shock, his eyes see further. It would be
hard to make *this* division in our natures. If to all offenders, then to
all mankind. Moreover, to whom could this recommendation be, in
any real sense, addressed? Only to the powerful, the authorities.
So abysses seem to open.[1]

But we will confine our attention to the case of the offenders.
The concepts we are concerned with are those of responsibility and
guilt, qualified as 'moral', on the one hand—together with that of
membership of a moral community; of demand, indignation, disapprobation and condemnation, qualified as 'moral', on the other
hand—together with that of punishment. Indignation, disapprobation, like resentment, tend to inhibit or at least to limit our goodwill
towards the object of these attitudes, tend to promote an at least
partial and temporary withdrawal of goodwill; they do so in proportion as they are strong; and their strength is in general propor-
tioned to what is felt to be the magnitude of the injury and to the
degree to which the agent's will is identified with, or indifferent to,
it. (These, of course, are not contingent connections.) But these
attitudes of disapprobation and indignation are precisely the correlates of the moral demand in the case where the demand is felt to
be disregarded. The making of the demand *is* the proneness to such

[1] Peered into by Mr. J. D. Mabbott, in his article 'Freewill and Punishment', published
in *Contemporary British Philosophy*, 3rd ser., 1956.

attitudes. The holding of them does not, as the holding of objective attitudes does, involve as a part of itself viewing their object other than as a member of the moral community. The partial withdrawal of goodwill which *these* attitudes entail, the modification *they* entail of the general demand that another should, if possible, be spared suffering, is, rather, the consequence of *continuing* to view him as a member of the moral community; only as one who has offended against its demands. So the preparedness to acquiesce in that infliction of suffering on the offender which is an essential part of punishment is all of a piece with this whole range of attitudes of which I have been speaking. It is not only moral reactive attitudes towards the offender which are in question here. We must mention also the self-reactive attitudes of offenders themselves. Just as the other-reactive attitudes are associated with a readiness to acquiesce in the infliction of suffering on an offender, within the 'institution' of punishment, so the self-reactive attitudes are associated with a readiness on the part of the offender to acquiesce in such infliction *without* developing the reactions (e.g. of resentment) which he would normally develop to the infliction of injury upon him; i.e. with a readiness, as we say, to accept punishment[1] as 'his due' or as 'just'.

I am not in the least suggesting that these readinesses to acquiesce, either on the part of the offender himself or on the part of others, are always or commonly accompanied or preceded by indignant boilings or remorseful pangs; only that we have here a continuum of attitudes and feelings to which these readinesses to acquiesce themselves belong. Nor am I in the least suggesting that it belongs to this continuum of attitudes that we should be ready to acquiesce in the infliction of injury on offenders in a fashion which we saw to be quite indiscriminate or in accordance with procedures which we knew to be wholly useless. On the contrary, savage or civilized, we have some belief in the utility of practices of condemnation and punishment. But the social utility of these practices, on which the optimist lays such exclusive stress, is not what is now in question. What is in question is the pessimist's justified sense that to speak in terms of social utility alone is to leave out something vital in our conception of these practices. The vital thing can be restored by attending to that complicated web of attitudes and feelings which

[1] Of course not *any* punishment for *anything* deemed an offence.

form an essential part of the moral life as we know it, and which are quite opposed to objectivity of attitude. Only by attending to this range of attitudes can we recover from the facts as we know them a sense of what we mean, i.e. of *all* we mean, when, speaking the language of morals, we speak of desert, responsibility, guilt, condemnation, and justice. But we *do* recover it from the facts as we know them. We do not have to go beyond them. Because the optimist neglects or misconstrues these attitudes, the pessimist rightly claims to find a lacuna in his account. We can fill the lacuna for him. But in return we must demand of the pessimist a surrender of his metaphysics.

Optimist and pessimist misconstrue the facts in very different styles. But in a profound sense there is something in common to their misunderstandings. Both seek, in different ways, to over-intellectualize the facts. Inside the general structure or web of human attitudes and feelings of which I have been speaking, there is endless room for modification, redirection, criticism, and justification. But questions of justification are internal to the structure or relate to modifications internal to it. The existence of the general framework of attitudes itself is something we are given with the fact of human society. As a whole, it neither calls for, nor permits, an external 'rational' justification. Pessimist and optimist alike show themselves, in different ways, unable to accept this.[1] The optimist's style of over-intellectualizing the facts is that of a characteristically incomplete empiricism, a one-eyed utilitarianism. He seeks to find an adequate basis for certain social practices in calculated consequences, and loses sight (perhaps wishes to lose sight) of the human attitudes of which these practices are, in part, the expression. The pessimist does not lose sight of these attitudes, but is unable to accept the fact that it is just these attitudes themselves which fill the gap in the optimist's account. Because of this, he thinks the gap can be filled only if some general metaphysical proposition is repeatedly verified, verified in all cases where it is appropriate to attribute moral responsibility. This proposition he finds it as

---

[1] Compare the question of the justification of induction. The human commitment to inductive belief-formation is original, natural, non-rational (not *ir*rational), in no way something we choose or could give up. Yet rational criticism and reflection can refine standards and their application, supply 'rules for judging of cause and effect'. Ever since the facts were made clear by Hume, people have been resisting acceptance of them.

difficult to state coherently and with intelligible relevance as its determinist contradictory. Even when a formula has been found ('contra-causal freedom' or something of the kind) there still seems to remain a gap between its applicability in particular cases and its supposed moral consequences. Sometimes he plugs this gap with an intuition of fittingness—a pitiful intellectualist trinket for a philosopher to wear as a charm against the recognition of his own humanity.

Even the moral sceptic is not immune from his own form of the wish to over-intellectualize such notions as those of moral responsibility, guilt, and blame. He sees that the optimist's account is inadequate and the pessimist's libertarian alternative inane; and finds no resource except to declare that the notions in question are inherently confused, that 'blame is metaphysical'. But the metaphysics was in the eye of the metaphysician. It is a pity that talk of the moral sentiments has fallen out of favour. The phrase would be quite a good name for that network of human attitudes in acknowledging the character and place of which we find, I suggest, the only possibility of reconciling these disputants to each other and the facts.

There are, at present, factors which add, in a slightly paradoxical way, to the difficulty of making this acknowledgement. These human attitudes themselves, in their development and in the variety of their manifestations, have to an increasing extent become objects of study in the social and psychological sciences; and this growth of human self-consciousness, which we might expect to reduce the difficulty of acceptance, in fact increases it in several ways. One factor of comparatively minor importance is an increased historical and anthropological awareness of the great variety of forms which these human attitudes may take at different times and in different cultures. This makes one rightly chary of claiming as essential features of the concept of morality in general, forms of these attitudes which may have a local and temporary prominence. No doubt to some extent my own descriptions of human attitudes have reflected local and temporary features of our own culture. But an awareness of variety of forms should not prevent us from acknowledging also that in the absence of *any* forms of these attitudes it is doubtful whether we should have anything that *we* could find intelligible as a system of human relationships, as human society. A quite different factor of greater importance is that psychological studies have made us rightly mistrustful of many particular manifestations of the attitudes I have spoken of. They are a prime realm of self-deception, of the ambiguous and the shady, of guilt-transference, unconscious sadism and the rest. But it is an exaggerated horror, itself suspect, which would make us unable to acknowledge the facts because of the seamy side of the facts. Finally, perhaps the most important factor of all is the prestige of these theoretical studies themselves. That prestige is great, and is apt to make us forget that in philosophy, though it also is a theoretical study, we have to take account of the facts in *all* their bearings; we are not to suppose that we are required, or permitted, as philosophers, to regard ourselves, as human beings, as detached from the attitudes which, as scientists, we study with detachment. This is in no way to deny the possibility and desirability of redirection and modification of our human attitudes in the light of these studies. But we may reasonably think it unlikely that our progressively greater understanding of certain aspects of ourselves will lead to the total disappearance of those aspects. Perhaps it is not inconceivable that it should; and perhaps, then, the dreams of some philosophers will be realized.

If we sufficiently, that is *radically*, modify the view of the optimist, his view is the right one. It is far from wrong to emphasize the efficacy of all those practices which express or manifest our moral attitudes, in regulating behaviour in ways considered desirable; or to add that when certain of our beliefs about the efficacy of some of these practices turn out to be false, then we may have good reason for dropping or modifying those practices. What *is* wrong is to forget that these practices, and their reception, the reactions to them, really *are* expressions of our moral attitudes and not merely devices we calculatingly employ for regulative purposes. Our practices do not merely exploit our natures, they express them. Indeed the very understanding of the kind of efficacy these expressions of our attitudes have turns on our remembering this. When we do remember this, and modify the optimist's position accordingly, we simultaneously correct its conceptual deficiencies and ward off the dangers it seems to entail, without recourse to the obscure and panicky metaphysics of libertarianism.

DAVID PEARS

Predicting and Deciding

Other people's decisions can be predicted inductively. But can anyone treat his own decisions in this way? It has been claimed[1] that the answer to this question would be a step towards the solution of the problem of free will. But my aim is at something closer. I ask the question because it opens a way to a problem about the nature of deliberation. How is one person's deliberation related to another person's prediction of its result?

If someone tries to make an inductive prediction of the result of his own deliberation, it looks as if he is trying to see the matter as another person would see it. But can he really take a spectator's seat? Certainly he can, when what he predicts is that, even if, after deliberation, he decided on an action, and never changed his mind, he still would not perform it. But that is not the point. The point that some philosophers[2] want to make is that, when he thinks that his action will depend on his decision, he cannot predict it inductively, because he cannot predict his own decision inductively. They maintain that, in such cases, what he will do must remain an open question for him until he has made his decision. It would follow that an inductive prediction, made by him, of his own decision could never come true, since his prior certainty would exclude the

[1] By Professor Hampshire in his book *Thought and Action*, chaps. ii and iii.

[2] e.g. Professor Hampshire loc cit.: Professor Hart and Professor Hampshire in their article 'Decision, Intention and Certainty' in *Mind*, 1958: and D. M. Mackay in his article 'On the Logical Indeterminacy of a Free Choice' in *Mind*, 1960.

possibility of his subsequent decision. It is admitted that the decision would be possible if he forgot, or ceased to believe, his inductive prediction after he had made it; and that, when he seems to be making an inductive prediction of his own future decision, he may really be making a present decision, expressed in a misleading way. But, it is contended, a prediction of a decision which is genuinely inductive, and made, remembered, and still believed by the agent, is strictly self-frustrating. He may take a spectator's seat in such cases, but, so long as he stays in it, he cannot play the whole of his predicted part as agent.

There are two things which make it difficult to assess this answer to my question. First, deciding and acting may be almost simultaneous, and, even when they are not, deciding need not be a definite event. It is no accident that the present tense of the verb 'to decide' leads a very marginal life outside subordinate clauses. Secondly, it is not always clear when the agent's prediction of his own decision is properly called 'inductive'.

In order to circumvent the first difficulty, I shall begin by considering cases in which the agent would naturally and easily make his decision at a definite moment which precedes the moment of action. What I shall say about these cases can be generalized, without much modification, to cover similar cases where, although the decision does not occur at a definite moment, there would be a time before the action at which he could say that he had decided. Later, I shall say something about the very different situation where he finds it hard to make up his mind before the moment of action. In that kind of situation the best way to secure examples where a decision, or something like a decision, might naturally be expected before the moment of action is to assume that there is some special consideration which makes this necessary. For instance, there might be other decisions which he could not postpone, and which depended on his decision in this matter: or other people might require him to make up his mind, perhaps for a similar reason. But, as I said, I shall begin with simpler cases.

In order to circumvent the second difficulty, I shall confine the initial scope of my inquiry even further. My first cases will all be ones in which the agent's prediction of his own decision will be obviously inductive. I shall leave the more dubious cases, where we should hesitate to call it 'inductive', until later. That will make it possible to isolate one problem, the compatibility or incompatibility of deciding with inductively predicting the decision, and to deal with it first.

One way of securing cases where the agent's prediction of his own decision is obviously inductive is to assume that he does not know all the relevant details of the situation in which he will make his decision. Then there might be special circumstances which made it possible for him to predict it inductively in spite of this gap in his knowledge. In a matter of taste, for example, he might predict that in a certain shop he would decide to buy what a friend of his, with similar tastes, had just bought, even if he did not yet know what the shop offered. Or, to take a more calculative example, he might predict that in a game of chess, confronted by the same simple position as a friend of similar skill, he would decide to make the same move, even if he did not yet know what the position was. In both these examples his prediction would be obviously inductive. Moreover, so long as he remained unaware what his friend's purchase or move specifically were, there is no doubt that, confronted by the situation—shop-counter or chess-board—he could make each of the predicted decisions. For there is not even an appearance of incompatibility between predicting one's own decision under one description and making it under another description, provided that one does not know that the two descriptions are uniquely satisfied by the same decision. But suppose that the agent, before he makes his decision, does find out what article his friend bought, or what move he made, so that he can predict his decision under the description under which it will be made. Then, when he is confronted by the situation, can he still make his decision without giving up his prediction of it? This is the controversial question.

When I ask it, I am, of course, assuming that the agent really does begin by making an inductive prediction, and does not begin by deciding to do whatever his friend does. I am also assuming that he maintains his prediction, neither forgetting it later, nor abandoning it, nor modifying it in any way. However, within these limitations, the question can be generalized a little. The agent might begin by predicting that he would decide to do what his friend advised, or what his friend predicted, on the evidence of his (the agent's) past decisions, that he would decide to do. The only restriction on the descriptions in the agent's original prediction is that they must be descriptions from which, given additional information available *before* the decision is made, it would be possible to deduce the description under which it will be made. So the description in his prediction must not be 'what my friend will imitate', if the friend will imitate whatever he does. Of course, if the agent is going to make his decision under a rationalizing description, the matter becomes more complex. But I shall ignore that complexity, and confine myself to cases where he makes his decision under a description which connects it with the desires from which it issues.

What is the answer to the controversial question? Consider first the more calculative case where the agent asks himself what move he will make when he is handed the chess-board, and predicts that it will be the same move as his friend's, and then discovers what that move was. Here, provided that the position is simple, a high degree of certainty is often justifiable.[1] For this kind of practical problem is not merely like a theoretical one: it actually contains a theoretical one. Now, whether the agent's problem is only theoretical—what move would lead to the swiftest certain check-mate—, or practical —what move to make—, there are things which remain to be done after he has predicted the result inductively, and which cannot be done before he sees the board. The question is what ought we to call these things. Had he not made a certain prediction of the result, we should say that he solved the theoretical problem, and, if there were also a practical one, that he deliberated and decided. But, since he has made the prediction, we cannot say that he solves the theoretical problem, because solving is discovering the solution by working it out. Nor can we even say that he is checking the solution. For, given his initial inductive certainty, he will be working it out from the position in order to see *how* it fits, rather than *that* it fits. Still, this is something that is related to solving. It is what is left when initial uncertainty is subtracted from solving.

If his problem is practical, what he does will be slightly more complex. For he will start not from the position alone, but from the position and his desire for the swiftest certain check-mate, and he will work forward from these two to the project. However, as

---

[1] But the degree of justifiable certainty is limited, see p. 128.

before, he will be seeing how the project fits rather than that it fits. But this time that will not be all that he is doing. Something that is not purely intellectual will be happening simultaneously. His desire will be directed on to the project. And there is a great difference between knowing that this will happen and actually feeling it happen. Can we call this deliberating and deciding? Perhaps not. But, if we do not, it is important to see that this time more that is the same is left when the initial uncertainty is taken away. For, though he may not be making the decision, nevertheless, when he sees how the project fits his desire and the position, and when he feels the direction of his desire, he is making the decision his own. No such essential part is played by desire when the problem is theoretical, since, though he may not want to solve a theoretical problem, the solution does not depend on his desires. So, if, in my example, he makes the solution of the theoretical problem his own, the sense in which he makes it his own will not be so strong as the sense in which he makes the decision his own when the problem is practical. Hence the subtraction of initial uncertainty from normal deciding leaves more that is the same. What about deliberating? There too, I think, the same considerations apply. Only, we should add that, since deliberation is a sort of working out, if we refuse to allow that an agent can deliberate with prior certainty, this refusal ought to be even more qualified.

The other example, where a choice between available articles is a matter of taste, is different in several ways. Desires that may vary from person to person play a larger part, and calculation plays a smaller part. Consequently, it would often be artificial to try to extract a theoretical problem from the practical one: exposure to the articles is almost inevitably followed by the process which has a claim to be called deliberating; and prior certainty is more rarely attainable. Still there are cases of this kind where a high degree of prior certainty is attained, and, if we ask whether the agent deliberates and decides in such cases, the answer will be much the same as before; except that, since competing desires play a larger part here, a negative answer would need to be qualified even further.

It has been suggested[1] that the idea, that there is anything like a

---

[1] By J. W. Roxbee Cox in his article 'Can I know beforehand what I am going to decide?' in the *Philosophical Review*, 1963.

contradiction concealed in the phrase 'deciding to do *A* with prior inductive certainty that one would decide to do *A*', is an illusion; an illusion which comes from thinking that the agent decides to do *A* in order to achieve certainty that he will in fact do *A*. For, if we think this, we shall naturally regard his inductive certainty that he will decide to do *A* and his actually deciding to do *A* as two competing, and therefore, perhaps, incompatible ways of achieving certainty that he will in fact do *A*. But, it is contended, people decide in order to achieve certainty about what to do, and not in order to achieve certainty about what they will do. And to those who realize this, it is suggested, the phrase will no longer even appear to be contradictory.

If this is correct, my treatment of the two examples is too cautious and qualified. But I do not think that it is correct: not just because people do sometimes decide to do *A* with the primary purpose of achieving certainty that they will in fact do *A*, and then building on it; but for the more important reason that, whatever the primary purpose of a decision may be, after it has been made, the agent will be certain what he will in fact do, and so the apparent contradiction cannot be removed in this way. In any case another apparent contradiction confronts us when we consider certainty about what to do. For in my two examples, if the agent assumes that his friend made the right choice, he will be inductively certain about what to do: and it is equally plausible to maintain that there is another contradiction concealed in the phrase 'deliberating and deciding with prior inductive certainty about what to do'. But, as I have been arguing, even in my two examples there is room for important elements of deliberating and deciding. However, it is true that in unusual cases, like these, the agent, before he is confronted with the actual situation, will not have the feeling that normally accompanies certainty about what to do. He cannot have it until he makes the decision his own by seeing how it fits the situation and his desires, and by feeling the direction of his desires. These are the elements of deliberating and deciding that come later.

I hope that a fairly general truth is beginning to emerge. To put it negatively, if an action depends on a decision, it is an exaggeration to say that the two things which yield certainty about it, deciding and predicting the decision inductively, are independent and uncombinable. To say that they are independent is exaggerated, because the description under which the decision is predicted must be one from which, given additional information available before the decision is made, it would be possible to deduce the description under which it will be made (unless the description under which it will be made is a rationalization). To say that they are uncombinable is exaggerated, because one of them, unmodified, can be combined with a modified form of the other. Even if the agent maintains the so-called spectator's viewpoint, he will not be prevented from playing his part as agent: he will only play it rather differently (unless, of course, he has a desire to falsify the prediction as such: but I am assuming that he has not).

It might be admitted that the two things that yield certainty about an action that depends on a decision can be combined, after some modification of one of them, in unusual cases where the agent predicts his decision under the description under which it will be made before he discovers the relevant features of the situation of choice. For, when he discovers them, he does something very like deliberating and deciding, and, even if he does not make his prediction come absolutely true, at least he catches up with it. But in the more usual cases, where he already knows the relevant features of the situation of choice, it is not so easy to see how his prediction can outstrip his deliberating and deciding and yet come almost true. However, this often seems to happen. How can it happen? This time there is an additional difficulty. For how can his prediction keep its inductive character, in spite of the fact that it goes through his own desires and knowledge of the situation of choice? How can it avoid becoming a decision made in advance?

I think that it is clear that we cannot go very far towards answering this question without examining the deeper operations of induction, and unearthing contingent facts which are taken for granted in everyday life and built into the structure of our concepts. However, I shall begin, as before, by taking cases in which the agent's prediction is obviously inductive, and I shall assume that naturally, and without the pressure of any special consideration, he would make, or at least would have made his decision before the moment of action. Now where the deliberation is largely calculative it will be difficult to find such cases. For the more calculative the deliberation, the more unlikely it will be that the agent's prediction will outstrip his decision and still keep its inductive character. For instance, if his desire to check-mate swiftly is firm, and, if he sees the position, and, after calculating, appears to predict with complete certainty that he will decide to make a particular move, there are strong reasons for saying that he has already decided, but is expressing his decision misleadingly. For it is irrelevant that he has not yet made the move or touched the piece, and any behavioural confirmation of the hypothesis that he had not yet made the decision would be exceedingly likely to undermine the hypothesis that he was certain that he would make it. So I shall choose examples where the deliberation is very far from being purely calculative, and involves the weighing of desires that may change.[1] In such cases there will be more than an analogy between predicting one's decision before it is made and predicting one's emotion before it is felt.

In this category there seem to be two types of case where the agent's inductive prediction outstrips his decision. First, there is the radical type of case where he predicts that the general pattern of his desires will change, and that after it has changed he will make a particular decision. For instance, he predicts that it will change after physical or psychological treatment, conversion, or some other cardinal experience. Secondly, there is the less radical, and far more frequent type of case, where he predicts only that, in some particular matter, his present desire[2] or favour will change, and that he will make a different decision in the end. Everyone would agree that this happens in matters of taste and in cases where pleasure is the avowed aim. But it also happens in other kinds of delicately balanced predicament. If we were interested only in the nature of desire, the difference between the two types of case, the more and the less radical, could be presented as simply a difference of degree. For even a desire about a particular matter contributes something to the general pattern, and a change in it might be part of a larger upheaval. But, since we are also interested in the agent's

[1] Even the desire to win a game of chess may come and go. But usually its constancy is taken for granted in deliberation about one's next move.

[2] I use the word 'desire' in an inclusive way. Contrast the exclusive use of the verb 'to want' in 'deciding to do what one does not want to do'.

ability to predict the change inductively, the difference is, perhaps, more than one of degree. For he can often predict from his own past record that his desire in a particular matter will change, but the prediction of a change in the general pattern would need to be based on a striking external cause.

What the two types of case have in common is that the agent predicts a change in his desires. He considers the possible projects, favours one of them most, and then predicts that he will decide on a different one. In the radical type of case the prediction, which is based on an external cause, is obviously inductive, and it will sometimes yield a high degree of prior certainty. If it does, will the agent be able to make the prediction come true by deliberating and deciding? I think that he will, but not quite in the way that he could in my first two examples. For in those examples, when he made the predictions, he did not know the situations: but in this case, when he made the prediction, he already knew the situation and saw how the project would fit it and the pattern of his desires, if that pattern changed. What happens later is that it does change, and the direction of his desires, which he then feels, is new. In general, in the triangle formed by situation, desire, and project, either the first point is not known by the agent when he makes his prediction, or the second point is not fixed.

The usual objection to this answer is that the agent decides, or ought to decide, before the change comes about. But ought he? Surely the idea that beneath such changes there is an unchanging source of decisions is a moralizing fiction. How can he make a decision in advance? Perhaps it will be suggested that he can decide in advance to do whatever he feels like doing later. But, when a decision is expressed in that way, there is an implied contrast between one's own later feelings and other considerations, and the decision, which issues from the present pattern of desires, is a decision to exclude those other considerations. Our case, however, is quite different. In it the implied contrast is lacking, and so that way of expressing a decision in advance would be deprived of its usual point. Moreover, the decision could only issue from a higher desire, which could not compete with the others, the desire to be true to oneself.

In the less radical cases, where the agent claims that in a

particular matter his desire will change, it might be doubted whether the claim is really inductive. As before, he knows what the possible projects are, favours one most at the moment, but predicts that in the end he will decide on a different one. But this time there is no suggestion that the general pattern of his desires will change, and the prediction is based on the outcome of his own previous deliberations in similar situations. So his reasoning is very closely connected with the usual operation of the pattern of his desires. However, it can still be called inductive. If he had waited for his desires to point in their final direction, his reasoning would not have been inductive. But he does not wait. His prediction outstrips his decision, and so, though it is closely connected with the usual operation of the pattern of his desires, the connection is not the kind of connection that would deprive his reasoning of its inductive character.

Can he, in this kind of case, make his prediction come true by deliberating and deciding? The answer seems to be that, even if he is quite certain of his prediction, he can, in much the same way that he could when the change was more radical. However, in this kind of case he would seldom in fact feel very certain about his prediction. So I ought also to ask my question about cases where his prediction is more tentative.

Tentative predictions introduce complications which are off my route. So I shall deal with their effect briefly and schematically. When the agent predicts confidently that he will decide to do A, let us suppose that he would assign the probability $1/x$ to the proposition that he will decide to do A. When he predicts it tentatively, the probability that he would assign to it would be smaller, say $1/(x+w)$. Now nobody would claim that it is absolutely certain that, if he decided to do A, he would do it, even if the moment of action were very close. For, even if nothing else changed in the interval, his desire might change. Of course, there are cases where any change would be enormously improbable, particularly if the interval were short. Let us say that in such cases the agent's decision to do A would give the proposition that he will do A the probability $1/z$. I pointed out earlier that often deciding and acting will be almost simultaneous. When this is so, $1/z$ will be almost indistinguishable from 1.

There is another complication which ought to be mentioned at this point. There is something else, which is very like a decision, but less firm. It may be that decisions are, by definition, firm. If so, the other thing ought to be called 'a tentative intention'. The noun 'intention', and the verb 'to intend', even when they are not qualified, often have this suggestion of tentativeness. Now suppose that an agent predicts inductively that he will form a tentative intention to do A.[1] Then the formation of this intention would give the proposition that he will do A a probability less than $1/z$, say $1/(z+y)$. These two assessments of probability can be made by anybody, but I am assuming that they are made by the agent.

Now, if we hear him predict that he will decide to do A, or that he will form the tentative intention of doing A, we may inquire what probability he would assign to the proposition that he will in fact do A. So far, I have only taken cases where the prediction is confident and what is predicted is a decision, and in such cases he would assign the high probability $1/xz$. But there are also three other theoretically possible types of case. He can confidently predict the formation of a tentative intention, and then the probability that he would assign would be $1/x(z+y)$: or tentatively predict a decision, and assign the probability $1/z(x+w)$: or tentatively predict the formation of a tentative intention, and assign the probability $1/(x+w)(z+y)$.

This fourfold schema generalizes the problem, and my original question can now be put in its most general form: can the agent make a decision or form an intention which, in his estimation, gives the proposition that he will perform the action a probability scarcely greater than the probability which he had already implicitly

[1] We might ask when, according to him, this tentative intention would be formed. In the cases so far examined it was natural to expect that he would have decided before the moment of action arrived. But suppose that he is going to find it difficult to make up his mind. Then why should he predict that there will be some moment before the moment of action at which he will have formed a tentative intention? Would it be a final tentative intention? As the moment approached closer to the moment of action it would become increasingly absurd for him to predict that the intention that he would then form would be only tentative. So how could he ever predict that he would form a tentative intention, unless he were using this phrase only as a synonym for the gradual emergence of a preference?

I think that the answer to this question is that, though he might be using the phrase in this way, he need not be. For there might be some special consideration which would force him to crystallize his desires, however inadequately, before the moment of action arrived. Cf. p. 98.

assigned to it when he inductively predicted the decision or the formation of the intention? I have been arguing for a qualified affirmative answer in some cases where the prediction is confident and what is predicted is a decision. Exactly the same arguments apply when the prediction is confident and what is predicted is the formation of a tentative intention. But in the other two types of case, where the prediction is tentative, the situation is quite different. For here, when the predicted decision is actually made, or the predicted tentative intention is actually formed, it will give the proposition that the agent will perform the action a probability substantially greater than the probability which he had already implicitly assigned to it when he made the inductive prediction. Consequently, in these cases, the agent's prior certainty is not great enough to modify the nature of his deliberation and decision, or the formation of his tentative intention. This explains why people find nothing puzzling in the very frequent cases where an agent predicts with less than complete certainty that in a particular matter his desire will change, and that he will make a different decision or form a different intention in the end.

The existence of these cases, which is hardly in dispute, is enough to dispel two very common prejudices. The first is the idea that an agent cannot really make an inductive prediction of his own future decision, since, if he did, that could only be because, between the moment of prediction and the moment of decision, there was going to be such a change in him that the decision would not be, in the full sense, his own. The second is the idea that, if he considers the possible projects and favours one most, he cannot help deciding on it. The first is connected with the moralizing fiction that I mentioned just now.[1] Against the second it is enough to point out that, even when the result of deliberation is a very strong preference for a particular project, the preference need not amount to a decision. Everyone would agree that it need not in cases where the agent thinks that the circumstances may change, or that the matter may be taken out of his hands. What is less obvious is the thesis for which I have been arguing, that, even if there are no considerations of this sort in his mind, his preference still will

---

[1] It is the other horn of the dilemma: 'Either there is an unchanging source of decisions, or they will not really belong to the same person.'

not amount to a decision if he has inductive reasons for thinking that it will change.

I asked my original question in the hope that the answer to it might throw some light on the way in which one person's deliberation is related to another person's prediction of its outcome. My idea was that, if we could see how the two things fit together in cases where it is the agent who predicts his own decision inductively, that might help us to see how they fit together in other cases. In all cases alike the difficult thing is to see how inductive and immediate knowledge are related. Now two distinct questions are possible here. First there is a question about deliberation. I pointed out earlier that, if what is predicted inductively is the agent's decision, then, provided that it is not made under a rationalizing description, its description in the prediction must be one from which, given additional information available before the decision is made, it would be possible to deduce the description under which it will be made. Obviously this also applies to an inductive prediction that the agent will favour a particular project most. But then what is the relationship between the agent's immediate knowledge, based on deliberation, of his own selective favour and perhaps decision, and the prediction that he would favour that project most and perhaps decide on it, which was based on inductive reasoning? That is the first question, which is about the process of deliberation. The second question concerns what follows deliberation. What is the relationship between an inductive assessment of the probability that the agent will carry out a particular project, given that he has just decided to do so, and his own immediate knowledge that he will carry it out?

I shall answer these two questions briefly and dogmatically. My answer to the first is that, if the dispositional theory of desire allowed that a desire might be manifested in the inner life of the agent as well as in his behaviour, it would explain the relationship between the two kinds of knowledge and reasoning. My answer to the second is that the concepts of intention and decision are founded on very general contingent connections, and that, when their substructure is analysed, the relationship between the two kinds of knowledge becomes intelligible. It would take more than my remaining time to defend these two answers adequately. So I shall merely sketch a defence, which, I think, might become powerful if it were elaborated.

I take the second question first. I have argued that the agent can predict inductively that his desires will change, and that he will decide on a different project from the one that he favours most at the moment. But then it looks as if, in the straightforward cases where he simply decides to do what he favours most at the moment, he must be making the inductive assumption that they will not change. Otherwise how could he be so certain that he will do it? Now there are various things which might make him uncertain. There is, for instance, the possibility that he might be prevented. But, of course, I am not concerned with that kind of possibility, but only with the possibility that his desires might change. And even that is too wide, since a change in his desires might be produced by a change in the situation, and the possibility which really exposes my difficulty is the possibility that his desires alone might change. My point is that it looks as if he must be making the inductive assumption that at least this will not happen, and naturally this assumption would sometimes be mistaken.

It will be objected that, if he takes no account of things outside himself, his certainty that he will perform the action is immediate. If this means that normally he will not use the kind of inductive argument that I have been describing, it is true. But that might show only that he assumes that his desires will not change. Admittedly, if others build on his decision, or if he himself does, a new desire will be brought in, the desire not to disappoint them,[1] or the desire not to upset his own further plans, and each of these will help to keep his favour constant. But perhaps the introduction of these new desires would only complicate his assumption without altering its inductive character.

Decisions should not be idolized. They are not very different from desires, and their effect on the future and the foreknowledge which accompanies them are not magical. There is often only a very slight difference between favouring a particular project most and deciding on it. It may be only that one dismisses the matter,

---

[1] There is a difference between keeping up with a statement of intention and keeping a statement of intention close to what one would have done even if one had not made it, and there is room for two distinct virtues here.

perhaps merely because there is no more time to consider it. And, if we are impressed by the connection between a decision and the future, at least we ought not to be superstitious about it. The announcement of a decision may be a sort of certificate, but the decision itself is not one. There really does not seem to be any reason to reject the view that even in the straightforward case, where an agent claims to know that he will perform a particular action, his claim, although it is immediate, is founded on a piece of inductive self-knowledge. Of course he may not be exceptional, and what he claims to know about himself may be merely that his constancy is average. But it could be something more interesting than this, since people vary, and it could be mistaken.

There are two theories which deny, or seem to deny this contention, or at least part of it. According to one, when the agent says 'I will do *A*', this either is a command, and not a statement, or at least it is more like a command than a statement. The other allows that it is a statement, but implies that its eventual truth or falsity,[1] in so far as it depends on things inside the agent, is always ascertainable by him at the moment of utterance. An examination of these two theories might assist the defence of my contention.

Is 'I will do *A*' like a command? Or rather, let us open the bidding at the top, and ask whether it actually is a command. This question has recently been answered in the affirmative.[2] It is said that an expression of intention, like 'I will do *A*', may be regarded as a kind of command addressed to oneself, and that the utterance 'I intend to do *A*', when it is a genuine report of a state of mind, is tantamount to the statement 'I have said in my heart "Let me do *A*"'. The kind of command that is meant must be self-exhortation, which, according to this theory, in the latter case, is said by the agent to have been done by himself in the past, and, in the former case, is actually being done by him audibly at the moment. But how can the theory allow for the fact that he might be insincere in what he says? When he says what he has done, he may, of course, be lying. But that is not possible in the other case, in which he does not make

---

[1] See p. 115 for an explanation of this phrase.

[2] By A. Kenny, in his book *Action, Emotion and Will*, pp. 216-27. However, his thesis, that an intention is a species of command, may be only an emphatic way of saying that the two things are similar to one another. It ought to mean that intentions possess the generic properties of commands and certain specific properties of their own.

a statement at all. Nor does the possibility of a lie completely cover the possibilities of insincerity when he reports his past self-exhortation. For his past self-exhortation may itself have been 'insincere'.

The solution proposed[1] is that an insincere expression of intention is a piece of overheard self-exhortation which the speaker does not mean: just as an ordinary 'insincere' command is an exhortation to another person which he does not mean; whereas an insincere statement is one which he does not believe. Similarly, the past self-exhortation, even when he reports it truthfully later, may not have been meant by him at the time.

There are many obscurities in this theory, but the points that I shall make against it are simple. To exhort oneself to do something is a way of getting oneself to decide to do it, or else a way of keeping oneself up to the mark after one has decided to do it: to form an intention to do something is neither of these things. If someone exhorts himself to do A in order to get himself to decide to do it, he has not yet fully formed the intention to do it. Consequently, in this case, though it is true that, if he does not really mean his self-exhortation, and if he knows that he is overheard by another person, then that would be a devious kind of insincerity, nevertheless he would not be deceiving the other about his intention to do A, but only about his intention to get himself to decide to do A. If, on the other hand, he exhorts himself in order to keep himself up to the mark after deciding to do A, this piece of self-exhortation comes too late to express the intention to do A at the moment when it is formed. Consequently, in this case, though it is true that, if he believed that the self-exhortation was necessary, and if he did not mean it and knew that it was overheard, then that too would be a devious kind of insincerity, nevertheless he would be deceiving the other not about the present formation of an intention to do A, but, rather, about the efficacy[2] of that intention, which had been formed in the past: for he would be implying that it needed reinforcing, and yet he would only be pretending to reinforce it. Therefore, when 'I will do A' expresses an intention that is formed at the moment of utterance, it cannot be right to regard it as a piece of self-exhortation. It follows that the other half of the theory, which analyses the

---

[1] A. Kenny, loc. cit.   [2] Efficacy of intention is defined on p. 117.

formation of an intention in the past in a similar way, cannot be right either.

Moreover, even if the thing about which the speaker might deceive his audience when he says 'I will do *A*' or 'I intend to do *A*' had been the thing about which he might deceive them when he produces what the theory regards as the equivalent of these utterances, it is also important that the method of deception suggested by the theory is too devious. For conveying information is not the primary purpose of self-exhortation, whereas it is the primary purpose of the two utterances.

So it looks as if we ought not to expect more than an analogy between intentions and commands. The most important point of analogy that has been suggested concerns their direction of fit. It has been said that, when an action does not fit what the agent said that he would do, it is the action that is mistaken and not what he said:[1] and this direction of fit is characteristic of commands, whereas the opposite direction of fit is characteristic of statements. Let us signalize this by calling commands and intentions 'dominant partners', and statements 'subordinate partners'. Then another point of similarity that has been suggested is that intentions, like commands, produce the subordinate partners that fit them.[2] But already it is not clear exactly what the dominant partner here is supposed to be. Commands can be heard or seen, but in the case of intentions many of the candidates for the position of dominant partner are not perceptible. Is the dominant partner the announcement that one will perform the action, or the decision to perform it, or the knowledge that one will perform it, or, perhaps, the intention itself? A third point of analogy that has been suggested[3] is that, if someone says that he will do something, the contradictory rejoinder would not be that he will not, because he never does such things, but, rather, that he will not, because you are going to stop him: just as, it is said, the contradictory of a command is not the prediction that for some reason the thing will not be done, but, rather, another command, not to do it.

In these suggestions too there are many obscurities. My discussion

[1] By E. Anscombe in her book *Intention*, pp. 55-7. A. Kenny agrees with this—loc. cit., p. 216.
[2] By E. Anscombe, loc. cit., p. 87.   [3] By E. Anscombe, loc. cit., p. 55.

of them will be aimed at establishing only one thing: that, whatever the exact analogy between intentions and commands, it ceases at the point where my problem begins, since it contributes nothing to an account of the agent's knowledge that he will in fact do A:[1] indeed, if it is exaggerated, it actually blocks any account of this knowledge.

First, it is true that an action which does not conform to an unchanged intention is often a mistake. But it does not follow that the agent did not make another mistake when he said what he would do. He did. Admittedly, if what he said turned out to be mistaken because he changed his mind later, there would not also be a mistake in his action. But it does not follow that the two kinds of mistake are incompatible; nor, of course, if it did, could it follow from this that there never could be a mistake in what he said. The idea that the two kinds of mistake are incompatible comes from assuming that there can be only one direction of fit here. But why? What fits what? Certainly the action (subordinate) fits the intention (dominant). But also, if the agent says that he will perform the action, his statement (subordinate) fits the action (dominant).

Of course, those who deny that the agent can make a mistake when he says 'I will do A' do not think that he is using the future tense to make a future perfect report of his present state of mind. Their idea is that there is a logical connection between sincere utterances of this kind and subsequent performances. This connection is, up to a certain point, flexible: for failure to perform the action does not prove insincerity if a suitable explanation is forthcoming. But their contention is—and it is this contention that I am now challenging—that, whether or not an explanation is forthcoming, the fact that the action is not performed cannot show that the agent was mistaken in what he said earlier.

Admittedly, in such a situation we are at least reluctant to call

[1] E. Anscombe herself makes this point, loc. cit., p. 55. 'But, returning to the order and the description by the agent of his own intentional action, is there not a point at which the parallelism ceases: namely, just where we begin to speak of knowledge? For we say that the agent's description is a piece of knowledge, but an order is not a piece of knowledge. So though the parallelism is interesting and illuminates the periphery of the problem, it fails at the centre and leaves that in the darkness that we have found ourselves in.'

The point on which I disagree with her is this: it seems to me that she exaggerates the analogy between intentions and commands, and that the exaggeration blocks any account of the agent's knowledge.

what he said 'false', or even 'not true'. For these predicates, used by themselves, home on to a different target, the agent's implication[1] that he intended to perform the action. There seems to be a very reasonable feeling that the front-line target for truth and falsity is the thing that the agent has the best chance of getting right. So I prefer to say that his statement, that he will perform the action, may come out true, or may possess eventual truth. But, whatever semantic phrases are used, the pejorative one may imply that a mistake has been made. Why should a mistake have to be signalized by the word 'False', or by the phrase 'Not true'?

To say 'I will do *A*' is, on any view, to hold up a rather complex target. If someone retorts 'You will not in fact do *A* (although you intend to)', that will hit the target. If he retorts 'You do not intend to do *A*', that too will hit the target. How should we characterize these two impacts? The simplest answer to this question is that the target is a conjunction, and that each retort is the contradictory of one of its members. If that answer were right, the contradictory rejoinder would be the disjunction of the two retorts, and the complete denial would be the conjunction of them. However, there are reasons for regarding this simple answer as too crude. I shall not explore those reasons, or try to refine on the answer. But, if what I have been saying is right, any refinement of it must allow the first retort to be characterized as the imputation of some kind of mistake in what was said. This does not require that the first retort should be the contradictory rejoinder.[2]

But at least, it will be said, intentions, like commands, produce actions. But what exactly produces an action? Certainly not the agent's statement, nor even his knowledge that he will perform it. And, in order to see what a small fraction of truth there is in the idea that the decision produces the action, it is only necessary to reflect how much its efficacy would be reduced if one remembered

---

[1] It is difficult to determine the logical character of this implication, and in what follows I make no attempt to do so.

[2] The idea that the contradictory rejoinder is 'You will not because I am going to stop you' seems to be produced by the requirement that a contradictory rejoinder must be the same kind of utterance as its target, and in the same person (i.e. in this example the first person singular). But if this exceedingly stiff requirement has to be met as well as the usual requirement for contradictories, how can there be such a thing as the contradictory rejoinder to 'I will do *A*'?

it without remembering the reasons for it. The efficacy of an intention would be similarly reduced if one remembered only that one had formed it, and not why. If, on the other hand, the thesis, that decisions or intentions produce actions, means that desires produce actions through decisions or intentions, there is much more truth in it, but, correspondingly, less room for the analogy with commands.

So, though the analogy between intentions and commands may well be worth exploring further, it clearly does not account for the agent's knowledge that he will in fact do A. Indeed, if the analogy is exaggerated and if the similarity between 'I will do A' and 'It will rain' is underestimated, any account of this knowledge will be blocked.

The second theory which I said that I would examine is simply the denial of a corollary of my contention. My contention is that, when an agent says that he will do A, his knowledge that he will in fact do A is based partly on the inductive assumption that his desires will not change. It would follow that the eventual truth or falsity of his statement, in so far as it depends on things inside him, is not always ascertainable by him at the moment of utterance. But the second theory, although it concedes that he makes a statement, maintains that its eventual truth or falsity, in so far as it depends on things inside him, is always ascertainable by him at the moment of utterance.

This theory is connected with a particular kind of analysis of sincerity, and it is that analysis that I am going to challenge. The analysis exaggerates the rigidity of the connection between sincere statements of the form 'I will do A' and subsequent performances. Everyone agrees that there must be some flexibility in this connection, since, even if such a statement were sincere, external things might prevent it from coming out true. But exactly how flexible is the connection? The theory implies that its flexibility ceases at the point where we begin to consider things inside the agent. It maintains that, if anything of that kind prevented it from coming out true, that could only be because he had spoken insincerely. For insincerity is avoidable distortion of the truth, and, according to the theory, the eventual truth or falsity of his statement, in so far as it depended on things inside him, was ascertainable by him at the moment of utterance.

But how could this always be so? Sometimes his statement that he will perform the action will be a downright lie. But it may be insincere because his reasons for suspecting that he will not are strong enough to make it an exaggeration. Now, if we confine our attention to his inner life, there are two reasons why he may suspect that he will not perform it. It may be that he does not favour the project enough, or it may be that he does, but has reasons for predicting a change in his favour (if so, his present favour, as I pointed out earlier, would not amount to a decision). If the fact is that he will not do it simply because his present favour is deficient, it is very largely correct to say, as the theory does, that he is aware of the eventual falsehood of his statement at the moment of utterance. If the fact is that he will not do it because his favour will change in a way which he is in a position to predict, it is still often correct to say this, or at least to say that he might suspect that it would not come out true. But if the fact is that he will not do it because his favour will change in a way which he is not in a position to predict, it is never correct to say anything of this kind.

The theory that the eventual truth-value of his statement, in so far as it depends on things inside him, is always ascertainable by him at the moment of utterance is another moralizing prejudice. The idea is that, though his favour at one moment may not be a sufficient basis for a decision because it may change later, nevertheless his psyche is a crystal in which any such change may be seen in the future. But how can it be seen? How could such foresight fail to have an inductive basis, explicit or buried? How, then, could the future always be clear to him?

It is understandable that some recent analyses of sincerity should credit the agent with more foreknowledge than he always possesses at the moment when he says 'I will do *A*'. Let us call an intention which will not fail to be fulfilled because of anything inside the agent 'an efficacious intention'.[1] Then what recent treatments of this problem have stressed is that there must be a logical connection between sincere announcement and efficacy. But, if the connection is not rigid, the analysis should be cast in the following form: if

---

[1] An efficacious intention need not be fulfilled, since something outside the agent might prevent its fulfilment. There could be an external impediment, or there could be a change in the circumstances which produced a change of mind.

the intention is not efficacious, the agent was necessarily insincere unless . . . and here a list of escape-clauses is given. But what sort of escape-clauses should be put on this list? If a photographic film does not react to light, it was necessarily insensitive when it was bought, unless it suffered some specifiable change in the interval. But this is a treacherous analogy. For when the agent's favour is strong[1] but his intention is not efficacious, he can be fairly charged with insincerity, but only if he foresaw the later change in himself. It is so easy to forget that this difference between him and a material object, which appears to, but does not really possess a dispositional property, must produce a difference between the two analyses. If this is forgotten, we shall think that we are testing his sincerity when we are not.

This trap is avoided if the analysis of sincerity allows for possible lack of foreknowledge. But, if it does this, it will lose another point of similarity with the analysis of the defect in the film. For in that case the escape-clauses would all mention things that might have happened between the moment of purchase and the moment of use. But that part of the analysis of sincerity which allows for the agent's possible lack of foreknowledge of later changes in himself will not necessarily confine itself to developments in his history between the moment of utterance and the moment for action. For instance, we might know from his earlier history that he must know that his present favour is likely to change. This sort of possibility is forgotten by those who put too much trust in the analogy between the two analyses.

The sincerity of the agent's statement cannot be connected with the efficacy of his intention in the way proposed by some recent analyses. But perhaps there is something else which can be, namely, the strength of his favour at the moment of utterance. Can we produce an analysis of strength of favour which will be closely analogous to the analysis of the sensitivity of the film? Perhaps we may say that, if an intention is not efficacious, then the favour was not strong at the moment of utterance, unless . . . and here will follow a list of escape-clauses, all of which will mention possible developments in the history of the agent between the moment of

---

[1] Strength of favour is not the same as efficacy of intention. The latter is defined above: the former is explained, but not defined, on pp. 118-120.

utterance and the moment for action. For instance, he might definitely change his mind, or suffer from aboulia. If this schema for the analysis is correct, the strength of an agent's favour is very nearly a necessary but far from a sufficient condition of his sincerity when he says 'I will do A'. It is very nearly a necessary condition, because his statement is at least exceedingly unlikely to be sincere if his favour is weak:[1] it is far from a sufficient condition, since, even if his favour is strong, he may expect it to change.

But what would happen if his favour seemed to be strong and his intention turned out to be inefficacious, and yet none of the escape-clauses applied? Either we would say that his favour was not really strong, or we should have to admit that the explanation eluded us, and that the list of escape-clauses was not complete. The choice between these two alternatives would be difficult. For, if we believe that it is almost inconceivable that he should make a mistake about the present strength of his favour,[2] his sincerity when he reports its strength[3] and its actual strength will be judged together. Shall we argue that, since he seems to be sincere when he says that his favour is strong, it must be strong, or that, since it does not seem possible that it is strong, he cannot be sincere? He himself will nearly always be in a position to distinguish between these two possibilities. But we are like astronomers trying to plot the positions of two stars from the gravitational effects of the binary system. If, impressed by the agent's apparent sincerity and influenced by our general knowledge of his preferences, we chose the first alternative, we would be admitting that our first attempt at a list of escape-clauses yielded a generalization which was not analytic, but contingent and false. However, we could still maintain that there was an unspecific analytic statement connecting strength of favour, judged by criteria independent of the sequel, with the sequel: i.e. we could still say that it was analytic that there must be some further factor, as yet undiscovered, which would explain why the action was not performed. But then we should have to try to discover what that factor was. Certainly we would

---

[1] But there is the odd case in which his favour is now weak, but he thinks that it will become stronger.

[2] But this belief needs considerable qualification. Much depends on the way in which he assesses the present strength of his favour. See pp. 123-125.

[3] This is not the same thing as his sincerity when he says 'I will do A'.

not accept the situation with equanimity.[1] Even more certainly the concept of favour, in its present form, could not survive a general dissociation from action. But from none of this does it follow, nor is it true that, when the agent says 'I will do *A*', he cannot be sincere if his intention is inefficacious.

My use of the concept of favour is, admittedly, a distortion, because favour is not sufficiently basic or generic,[2] and an over-simplification, because the different species in the genus are built up in various complicated ways. But it is sometimes legitimate to ignore the finished surface of our conceptual system, and I hope that, though I have not isolated the basic generic concept that I mean, I have at least indicated it. It ought to be possible to take it as a foundation, and, using such things as intensity, belief, and agency, to reconstruct our present system in a way that would show in detail how inductive and immediate knowledge fit together. For instance, deprive an agent of any confidence that he will continue to favour a project, and what is left of his decision to carry it out is only his present favour.

There remains to be considered the other transition where it is difficult to see how inductive and immediate knowledge fit together, the transition from desire through deliberation to selective favour, and, perhaps, decision. Here the question is what is the relationship between the agent's immediate knowledge, based on deliberation, of his own selective favour, and perhaps decision, and the prediction that he would favour that particular project most and perhaps decide on it, which was based on inductive reasoning. Now we have seen what happens when he tries to combine both things. His prediction in some cases alters to a certain extent the nature of what

[1] There is an element of rather transparent bluff in the phrase 'unspecific analytic statement'. It suggests that in a particular case, when the agent did not perform the action and none of the escape-clauses applied, we could use the analytic statement as a premiss and argue that his favour could not have been strong. But how could we ever verify that there was no further factor operating? Struck by this doubt, we might reverse the argument and, convinced on other grounds that his favour was strong, infer that there must be some further factor operating, which ought therefore to be added to our list.

Even when such a crisis has not yet occurred, it might occur at any time. Before it occurs, it is possible to treat the list of escape-clauses as if it were complete, and to base the concept of strength of favour on two working criteria which may not continue to be satisfied together. Saying that their joint satisfaction must continue would be like saying that there must be a point at which two lines meet, although it is not geometrically necessary.

[2] What is?

he predicted. But when they are not combined, the fit ought to be exact, provided that the prediction goes through the pattern of his desires, and there is no rationalization. How does this exact fit come about? At first sight it looks as if nothing could be simpler. The agent just does the things that were predicted of him, and, though he is unaware of the prediction, he knows that he is doing them. The prediction was based on knowledge of his desires, and his decision, if there is one, is based on the same desires, of which he will usually be aware. But it is not so easy to see how the decision is based on the desires, or how the same desires can be known in two different ways.

How is the decision based on the desires? What is acting for a reason? It could hardly fail to be true that the agent's reason for his decision or action is a cause in some sense of that versatile word. The difficulty begins when we try to fix the sense in which it is true. On the one hand, Wittgensteinian discussions of this problem fail to do justice to the force of the word 'because' in 'I did it because . . .';[1] and, on the other hand, those who do justice to its force usually understate the differences between reasons for decisions or actions and other kinds of causes. The problem is notoriously difficult, and it is easier to say how it will not be solved than to say how it will be. For instance, the idea that a solution might be extracted from the analogy between intentions and commands cannot be right, if only because issuing and obeying commands are both instances of the very thing that requires to be explained.

I shall approach the problem by first trying to answer the other question: How can the same desires be known in two different ways? Now the way which is open to agent and spectator alike strongly suggests a dispositional analysis of desire. It is, however, well known that this analysis sometimes errs by over-simplification and omission. It over-simplifies by assimilating ascriptions of reasons for actions to ascriptions of traits of character. What it omits is the way of knowledge that is open only to the agent.

It is not difficult to begin to correct the over-simplification. The first step is to distinguish between a desire to do a particular thing

---

[1] This is argued by Professor Davidson in his article 'Actions, Reasons and Causes' in the *Journal of Philosophy*, 1963.

and a general desire. Now a desire to do a particular thing may be blocked either by another such desire, or by an impediment that is not a desire at all. But, even if it is blocked, its existence must make some difference to the world. Perhaps it will show itself at some other point in the person's behaviour. At least, the prevailing desire should be implemented with some reluctance, or the impediment should produce some frustration. Alternatively, or perhaps in addition, we may require that he should have, and show by his behaviour that he has, a general desire that gives some support to the rejected project. If so, it does not matter that often there will be no name of a trait of character associated with the general desire. All that is needed for this version of the dispositional analysis is that the kind of thing that is desired should be identifiable, and that the agent's desire for it should be manifested in his behaviour. If the strength of his desire and its manifestation in his behaviour were below the average, as they might be, the relevant trait of character, even if it had a name, would not be ascribed to him. The dispositional analysis of desire is not so closely tied to the dispositional analysis of traits of character or even of moods.

But, however much we elaborate this version of the dispositional analysis of desire, it does not allow for the way of knowledge that is open only to the agent. In order to correct this omission, we must add the kind of thing that I mentioned in my account of deliberation: we must say that a desire is a tendency not only to behavioural manifestations but also to inward favourable reactions. It is quite absurd to neglect the pervasive influence of desires on thoughts and fantasies.

The concept of a reaction does not cover the whole of this wide field. For a favourable reaction to an idea is not the only kind of inward effect of a desire. Desires do not merely add colour to our thoughts and fantasies: they also exert an influence on their structure, and even on their existence. The word 'reaction' suggests a definite situation, in which something is presented for assessment. That is why it is appropriate when the agent is deliberating, and in practical matters it applies both to the outward and to the inward effects of desires. But, for that very reason, it fails to cover the whole field of the inward influence of desire.

However, the fact that human beings have inward favourable

reactions supplies most of one part of the explanation of the way of knowing desires which is open only to the agent. The other part of the explanation is supplied by a fact which much of this lecture has been devoted to emphasizing, the fact that in most, but not all people these reactions are on the whole, but not always consistent with each other and with behaviour. Of course, a reaction of this kind does not have to occur every time that anyone acts, or even decides to act. Nor, when it does occur does the agent need to remember earlier reactions in the same set, as he would, if he were carefully testing a thing for a dispositional property. These reactions point beyond themselves: that is to say his inductive assumption, that they are on the whole constant, is confirmed.

These things might have been otherwise. Human beings might not have been capable of thought. Or they might not have been susceptible to any kind of pleasure or pain. In either case they would have had no inward reactions of favour. Or, although they had both these capacities, they might have been incapable of action. In that case the concept of favour would have developed differently: it might perhaps have produced the concept of wishing, but not the concept of intending or the other concepts in that family. But, given all three things, there is the possibility that there should be, on the whole, consistency between the inward favourable reactions of one person, consistency in his behaviour, and consistency between his inward favourable reactions and his behaviour. This possibility is realized for most people, and it explains our concept of favour and the way of knowing desires which is open to the agent.

This brief sketch of the way in which the two kinds of knowledge fit together at this point leaves many problems unsolved. For instance, there is the fundamental question how the agent knows what the object of his present favourable reaction is. There is also the question, how he knows that his reaction to a particular project is more favourable than his reaction to its rivals. So far, I have discussed only the possibility that he might be mistaken when he predicts that he will continue to favour most the project that he favours most at the moment. But can he be mistaken when he says that he favours it most at the moment? Or, to make things even easier for him, can he be mistaken when he says that he favours it to some extent at the moment? Here, at least, he seems to be infallible.

E

But suppose that he is asked why he favours it, and that he answers that he just does favour it under the description already given, or else gives further descriptions under which he says that he favours it. Can his present reaction to the features picked out by his descriptions be favourable even if none of them are connected with the general pattern of his desires? To put this question in the form which is required by the extended version of the dispositional analysis, can his present reaction to the features that he gives be favourable even if none of them are believed by him to be, or to be connected with, a kind of thing desire for which has made, or will make, some difference either to his inward life or to his behaviour? If not, could he think that his reaction was favourable when it was not?

These are marginal questions. They suggest things that are on the brink of conceptual impossibility. If we give them a negative answer, our position might be that it is psychologically impossible for him to be mistaken when he reports that his present reaction is favourable, and that, if *per impossibile* he were mistaken, we could rely on another psychological impossibility, the impossibility of a totally aberrant reaction, and correct him. Can we credit him with the same infallibility when he says which of two projects he favours most at the moment? If we do, the position will be different. For if *per impossibile* he did make a mistake when he said that at the moment he favoured a particular project most, we should not always be able to correct him, since, however well we may know a person, we never possess a system of reliable general statements assigning precise and unvarying relative strengths to his desires.

But is it really psychologically impossible for a person to be mistaken when he says which of two projects he favours most at the moment? Perhaps it is, even when the predicament is very delicately balanced. But this infallibility would be secured only by restricting his report to the present moment. When what he reports is less restricted in time he can certainly make a mistake. Moreover, there is another connected way of assessing present favour which is certainly liable to error, even when it is restricted in time. Let us apply the word 'par' to the degree of favour which is just sufficient to produce the following result: if he were now given the opportunity to perform the action, provided that there were no impediments except other desires, he would do so. Then if he reports that his present favour is at least par, he may well be mistaken.

It would take too long to complete this sketch of the way in which the two kinds of knowledge fit together at this point, but I would like to defend it against one criticism. The suggestion that desire is partly an inward reaction of favour might be criticized for assimilating a desire, to that extent, to a sensation, and for implying that the agent has to recognize it in the same way that he has to recognize a sensation as one that accompanies a bodily need. But there is no such assimilation. For he does not start from the reaction, and ask himself what its object is: the direction of fit is the opposite one, so that, by the time that he has the reaction, it is already distinguished from others by its object, and his problem is to assess its strength. Of course, this does not dispose of the fundamental question, how he knows that the thing which seems to be the object of his reaction really is its object. My present point is only that the question which he asks himself is not whether it is the object of his reaction, but, rather, how strong his reaction to it is.

Finally, there is the question how the agent's decision is related to his desires. I have implied that this question is likely to get the same answer as the question how his action is related to his desires, and that the answer would provide an analysis of the concept of acting for a reason. In the discussion that follows I shall concentrate on this concept. What I shall say about it can be generalized, without much modification, to cover the concept of deciding for a reason. I have already suggested that the answer could hardly fail to be that the relationship between desire and action is, in some sense, causal. But in what sense? Is some general statement implied by the statement that a person did something because he believed it to be, or to be connected with something that he desired?

It has been pointed out that the statement, that A caused B, does not imply that A, under the description 'A' was a sufficient condition of B, under the description 'B'; and so does not imply the straightforward generalization that whenever A occurs, B ensues: it only implies that A and B fall under some descriptions, perhaps as yet unknown, which would yield a true generalization of that form.[1]

---

[1] By Professor Davidson, loc. cit.

Now those who say that a reason for an action is a kind of cause usually mean at least that the agent's desires and beliefs about the situation caused his action. It is then natural for them to assume that, if they are going to give the word 'cause' anything like its usual meaning, they must say that the statement that he did something for a particular reason implies a generalization of the following form: Whenever the state of desire and belief, as described in the singular statement, recurs, the action, as described in the singular statement, ensues. But this assumption is said to be mistaken.¹ The singular statement only implies that there is some true generalization satisfied by the particular case. It might even be a neurological generalization.

It is true and important that an ordinary singular causal statement does not imply its own straightforward generalization. If we knew that the only true generalization which was satisfied by the particular case contained terms which were totally unknown to the person who made the singular statement, we would not deny either that his singular statement was true or that it was causal. So, if what he says is that a person did something for a particular reason, and if the case satisfies only one true generalization, and that one is neurological, his singular statement may well be both true and causal. We could not even object that the agent must have made his decision under a rationalizing description. For that would mean that his action had not really issued from the stated desire.²

However, it is also important that, when someone wants to know another person's reasons for his action and cannot ask him, he is not necessarily reduced to guessing them, and that the evidence for such ascriptions is not neurological but psychological. How does the spectator use this evidence? There are two distinct steps in his ascription. First, he argues from his knowledge of the agent and his situation to the present state of his desires and beliefs. Then he

---

¹ By Professor Davidson, loc. cit.
² But I suppose that we might regard the desire as epiphenomenal. The assessment of epiphenomenalism turns on the answer to a question which will not be discussed: if a desire is always accompanied by a neurological state, how can we determine which of the two is causally efficacious? In any case, there must be some kind of general connection between the desire and the neurological state. Otherwise, the singular statement would be a pure guess (not because the speaker would be unaware of the general connection, but because it would not exist).

argues that the present state of his desires and beliefs sufficiently explains the action. He might generalize each of these steps. He would generalize the first step by maintaining that, whenever this agent is in a similar situation, that state of desires and beliefs will recur in him. He would generalize the second step by maintaining that, whenever the state of desires and beliefs recurs in him, he will perform a similar action unless there is some specifiable factor to explain why he will not.[1] Of course, neither of these two generalizations will be what is usually called a 'psychological law'.

Let us examine the second generalization, and, in order to avoid confusion between it and the first one, let us assume for the moment that the agent himself is giving his reasons for his action after he has performed it. Then it may be objected that he is not committed to the truth of a generalization of the second type, since all that he needs to do is to give the main desire and belief from which his action issued. But such explanations are often very incomplete, and, the nearer they approach to completeness, the greater will be the certainty which anyone, spectator or agent, would have been justified in feeling, if he had predicted the action, inductively or immediately, from the state of desires and beliefs before it was performed. Suppose, for instance, that the main desire was opposed by another desire, and that it prevailed only because it was reinforced by a third desire. In that case anyone who only mentioned the main desire would not have given a complete explanation of the action, and, if he had predicted it before it was performed, he ought to have felt correspondingly uncertain of his prediction. If, on the other hand, the main desire prevailed without reinforcement, the same explanation would have been more complete, and, correspondingly, anyone who predicted it ought to have felt more certain of his prediction.

Most ascriptions of reasons for actions are meant only as incomplete explanations. There is nothing wrong with that. Nevertheless, we often can, and sometimes do make such explanations more complete. Could we make them absolutely complete? Or is the concept of an absolutely complete account of an agent's reasons for his action a Kantian idea of reason?

---

[1] This generalization need not be interpreted as an analytical statement. See p. 129, footnote 1.

These questions are unanswerable without a criterion of absolute completeness. A deterministic criterion would be this: an account of an agent's reasons for his action is absolutely complete if and only if anyone who gives it ought to have felt absolutely certain if he had used the same state of desires and beliefs in order to predict the action before it was performed. But this criterion is hopelessly unrealistic. For even the most elaborate and accurate account of the present pattern of the agent's desires and beliefs could not yield the degree of inductive certainty that is often justifiable when the prediction is about something that is not human. Various sources of uncertainty about predictions of human actions have already been mentioned. There might be an external impediment, or a change in the circumstances which produced a change of mind. Suppose, then, that we say that an absolutely complete account of his reasons will be one based on a state of desires and beliefs which would have given the highest degree of inductive certainty to the prediction that, if there were no such intervention from outside, he would perform the action. But even this is unrealistic. For, quite apart from intervention from outside, a person will not necessarily carry out the project that he favours most at the moment, even if he can do so, and knows that he can. There are also psychological impediments which are not opposing desires. So an absolutely complete account of an agent's reasons for an action would give the highest inductive certainty only to the prediction that he would perform the action, if there were no intervention from outside, and no psychological impediments of that kind. In short, this concept of absolute completeness only covers the system of the present desires and beliefs of the agent, and is not affected by adverse factors outside that system.[1]

Is anyone even then ever in a position to apply this concept to a particular account of an agent's reasons for his action? First, let us consider the spectator. If he cannot question the agent about the state of his desires and beliefs before the action, he will have to use a generalization of the first of the two types that I distinguished

---

[1] Of course we might use a non-deterministic criterion of 'absolute completeness'. We might simply say that an account of an agent's reasons for his action is absolutely complete if it covers all the desires that were at work, whether or not it yields a prediction with the highest inductive certainty. See pp. 130-1.

just now. But, even if we waive any difficulties about beliefs, generalizations of that type do not yield absolutely certain inferences of other people's desires. For, however well we may know a person, it does not seem possible to find reliable generalizations assigning precise and unvarying relative strengths to his desires. If this is impossible, there are many explanations of the impossibility. Even if people did not change, there is a limit to dependable discrimination in the vast field of objects of desire and aversion. But they do change, not only durably, but also momentarily and capriciously. Moreover, a person is aware of the pattern of his desires, and this too produces unpredictability in various complicated ways. Consequently, the spectator is often unable to collect the data from which an absolutely complete account of the agent's reasons would have to be extracted.

But perhaps the agent is in a better position to apply the concept of absolute completeness to his own account of his reasons for his action. Certainly at the moment of action he does not use the spectator's first generalization, since he knows immediately the state of desires and beliefs from which his action issues: nor is he committed to the truth of that generalization, since, given that favour can change from time to time, its falsehood is compatible with the truth of his account of his reasons. This removes one doubt that is often expressed about the thesis that I am advocating. It is supposed that, according to this thesis, the agent is at least committed to a generalization of the first type. But there is no such suggestion. It is only maintained that he shares the spectator's commitment to the second generalization, or rather to the following more fully developed form of it: whenever the same state of desires and beliefs recurs in him, he will perform a similar action, unless there is some specifiable intervention from outside, or some psychological impediment that is not a desire.[1] This is a very different

---

[1] This generalization need not be interpreted as an analytic statement. It would be analytic if, whenever a similar state of belief recurred in the agent, without any intervention from outside or any specifiable psychological impediment that was not a desire, the performance of the action were made a necessary condition of the recurrence of an equally strong desire for the same object. But, though object and strength of desire must sometimes be judged in this way, they need not always be. The agent himself is in a position to report them immediately without waiting until the moment for action arrives: and others can judge them from their general knowledge of his preferences, reinforced by his own report, which is unlikely to be mistaken, and which may be judged sincere by

commitment. It does not even imply that he really wanted to perform the action. For in the crucial period immediately before the action his reaction[1] may not agree with his true and settled preference. If, by using his advantageous position he can surprise a well-informed spectator, that may well be because his reaction is rather aberrant, so that his account of the desires that he felt in that particular situation will be less rich in implications about the rest of his life, and ought not to be used as evidence for a generalization of the first type.

Is his account of his reasons ever absolutely complete? Those who think that it can be must believe that he can sometimes survey the whole field of his desires and accurately assess their contributions at least at that moment. For, whenever he fails to do this, the generalization of the second type to which he will be committed will almost certainly be false.[2] Now there certainly are occasions when his survey of his desires or his assessment of their contribution will be deficient. For instance, he could hardly allow for the existence of unconscious desires. The only way to circumvent this difficulty would seem to be to deny that influences and impediments of that kind are properly called 'desires'. But this denial only reduces the importance of an absolutely complete account of reasons for an action by reducing the scope of the system of the agent's desires: so-called 'unconscious desires' would then have to be treated as enormously important psychological influences and impediments of the other kind. Moreover, even if no desires are omitted from his survey, his assessment of their contribution may well be mistaken. Everyone is familiar with the unnerving effect of this kind of mistake: one's assessment of the contribution of different desires to one's action in one situation does not square with

things that are independent of the sequel. Then the generalization will be a contingent statement.

The concept of strength of desire or favour is based on the high frequency with which such contingent general statements are satisfied by particular cases. But the concept conceals its own foundations by appropriating as working criteria the two things which are only contingently connected. See pp. 119-20.

[1] For the sake of simplicity, I sometimes speak as if he would always have a reaction at that time. But since desire is dispositional, it may only be true that he would have had one if he had paused to reflect.

[2] But there is the odd case in which he overlooks two desires which exactly cancel one another out.

one's actual desires in another slightly different situation; for, according to the original assessment, the slight difference in the situation ought not to have produced such a big difference in one's desires.

However, he may sometimes be able to produce an absolutely complete account of his reasons for an action. And, even if he never could, this concept of absolute completeness would still function as an idea of reason. It would be a point which made the structure of our conceptual system intelligible, even though it lay outside it. For our use of incomplete explanations based on states of desire and belief depends on the possibility of making them at least more complete. Perhaps we shall never discover an absolutely true generalization satisfied by a particular instance of desire and belief and action[1] unless we abandon psychology and adopt some entirely different system of descriptions. But it would not follow that an ascription of a reason for an action implies only that this instance satisfies some true generalization which may even be neurological. For the implied generalization can still be a psychological generalization about the agent's desires and beliefs, provided that we do not insist that it should be true without exception. Perhaps the exceptions will only be the result of our ignorance. For the pattern of a person's desires is very complex and difficult to make out, even if the person is oneself. Alternatively, it may be that the exceptions will be due to the nature of things. For even an account which covered all the desires that contributed to a particular action might still not be complete by the deterministic criterion. Whatever the explanation, it seems likely that this part of psychology will yield only approximate results.

If, deterred by the approximate character of these results, we maintain that the implied generalizations cannot be psychological, or at least cannot belong to this part of psychology, we shall be opening up a gap between the implications of these singular causal statements and the evidence on which they are based. But is such a gap objectionable? Ordinary singular causal statements are often based on very rough evidence, and the person who makes one often

---

[1] It is important to remember that the generalization would include the proviso that there must be no interventions from outside and no psychological impediments that are not desires. See p. 128.

has no inkling of the precise scientific generalization which could sometimes be included in the disjunction of generalizations which might be said to be implied by his statement. Moreover, psychological generalizations of the kind that are being discussed may not be necessarily approximate, and so they too may be included in the disjunctive implicate.

However, there are objections to this view. The disjunctive implicate is not fully specified, and therefore not falsifiable. Perhaps, if we did not insist that the generalizations should be true without exception, we might find a type of approximate generalization which could plausibly be said to be implied by singular ascriptions of reasons for actions. Now psychological generalizations of the kind that are being discussed may be necessarily approximate, and therefore not subject to knock-out falsification. But it is possible to collect overwhelming evidence against them. When this happens, it does sometimes lead to the retractation of a singular ascription of a reason.[1] Therefore, there is a strong case for saying that such psychological generalizations are implied by singular ascriptions of reasons, and are not merely included in a disjunctive implicate.

There is also another consideration which suggests that, whatever else a singular ascription of a reason implies, it must at least imply a psychological generalization of this kind. If the agent's state falls under a scientific description which yields a generalization which is true without exception, then there must be a general connection between the scientific description of his state and the ordinary description of it.[2] Now it is hard to see how this general connection could be established unless the ordinary description of his state could be elaborated until it yielded an explanation of his action which was at least more complete.[3] For, if he only gives the main desire which produced his action, it would be extravagant to hope for a straightforward general connection between his description of his state and some scientific description of it. That would be like hoping for a straightforward general connection between

---

[1] See pp. 130-1. The retraction mentioned there is retraction by the agent because he was mistaken. There is also retractation by the agent because he was insincere, and retractation by the spectator because he was mistaken.

[2] See p. 126, footnote 2.

[3] See p. 127.

the concepts of mechanics and the description of a single causal factor selected from the total cause of a particular physical event.

If we look back at the transition from desire through deliberation to selective favour, and perhaps to decision and action, it will be evident that the requirement that, when there are two ways of knowing that a statement is true, both built into its meaning, we must have some guarantee that they fit together, is met at every point. The spectator uses a generalization of the first type to infer the agent's desires and perhaps his decision in a particular situation, and the agent knows them immediately. The spectator uses a generalization of the second type to infer that the agent will perform the action, and the agent knows immediately that he will. At both these points we can rely on the fit between inductive and immediate knowledge. If, as I have been arguing, all the points in the transition are connected causally, then, if there were two ways of establishing the causal connections in particular cases, we would have to have some guarantee that they fit together.

This lecture has been devoted to describing and explaining the way in which inductive and immediate knowledge fit together at various points in the transition to action. The fit is very close and complex. Even when the agent takes the way of knowledge that is open to himself alone, he is depending on inductive psychological assumptions which figure as explicit premisses in the spectator's account. So, to revert to my opening topic, when the agent actually uses them as premisses, and predicts his own decision or action inductively, what is happening is that the underlying structure of the conceptual system of self-knowledge is showing through its finished surface.

'Will, therefore, is the last appetite in deliberating.'[1]

---

[1] Hobbes, *Leviathan*, pt. i, c. 6.

C. LEWY

G. E. Moore on the Naturalistic Fallacy

G. E. Moore's literary remains contain very little concerning ethics; but they include an unfinished draft (in manuscript) of what was intended to be a preface to the second edition of *Principia Ethica*. For various reasons it seems to me highly probable that this was written in 1920 or 1921; but in the end Moore abandoned the idea of a second edition, and in 1922 *Principia* was reprinted without any alterations, except for the correction of a few misprints and grammatical mistakes and the inclusion of a prefatory note of seven lines.

Owing to the fact that the draft is unfinished and in parts very fragmentary, the task of preparing it for publication would be a very difficult one, though I may possibly attempt it in the future. What I want to do today is first to give a synopsis, or rather a reconstruction, of what seem to me to be the main points of the unpublished preface (which from now on I shall simply call 'the Preface'), and secondly to discuss independently one particular aspect of the subject.

I

Moore begins by pointing out that there are several senses of the word 'good', and that in *Principia* he was concerned with only one of them. He does not now think, however, that this sense can be called *the* ordinary sense of the word, even if any one sense of it is commoner than any other. But he thinks that the sense in question can be specified by saying that it is *the* sense which has a unique and fundamentally important relation to the conceptions of right and wrong. *What* the relation in question *is*, he proposes, he says, to discuss later; but in fact no such discussion is included in the Preface.

He goes on to ask, however, what are the main things that he wished to say in *Principia* about the concept which is expressed by the word 'good', when the word is used in this sense. The first thing he wished to say, he continues, is that Good[1] is simple in the sense of being indefinable or unanalysable. Is this proposition true?, he asks. He still thinks it is probably true, but he is not certain, for it seems to him that possibly 'right' is unanalysable, and Good is to be analysed partly in terms of 'right'. But whether Good is analysable or not does not seem to him now nearly as important as it did when he wrote *Principia*. If Good *were* unanalysable, it would follow that it could not be identical with any such property as 'is desired' or 'is a state of pleasure', since these *are* analysable; but it would be a great mistake to suppose that, as he implied in *Principia*, the fact that Good is not identical with any such property *rests* on the contention that Good is unanalysable.

He says that in the passage in *Principia* (§§ 6–14) in which he asserted that Good was unanalysable, he made another assertion which must not be confused with it, though he did so confuse it, namely, the assertion '. . . good is good, and that is the end of the matter' (*Principia*, p. 6). What, he asks, did he mean by this? Clearly, he meant to assert about Good what Bishop Butler, in the passage which Moore quoted on his title-page, asserted to be true of everything, namely, that it is what it is, and not another thing. In other words, he meant to assert that Good is Good, and nothing else whatever.

But this, Moore now says, may mean *either* 'Good is different from everything other than Good' *or* 'Good is different from everything which we express by any word or phrase other than the word "good"'. The first is wholly trivial and unimportant; and that Good is unanalysable cannot possibly follow from it, since the property of being different from every property that is different from it, is a

---

[1] As Moore himself does in the Preface, I shall write *Good*, with a capital *G* but without quotes, when I talk about the concept, and not the word. But (again like Moore) I shall not adopt this device in connection with other concepts.

property which must belong to every property without exception, analysable and unanalysable alike. And for the same reason it cannot possibly follow from it that certain particular properties such as 'is a state of pleasure' or 'is desired' are different from Good. For even if Good were identical with, say, 'is desired', Good would still be different from every property which was different from it.

The second assertion, however—that Good is different from everything which we express by any word or phrase other than the word 'good'—is far from being trivial. If it were true, it would really follow that Good was different from any such property as 'is a state of pleasure' or 'is desired'. And also, if it were true, it would afford at least a strong presumption that Good was unanalysable. For 'where a word expresses an *analysable* property, that property is generally also sometimes expressed by a phrase, made up of several words, which point out elements which enter into its analysis, and, in that sense, "contain an analysis" of it'. So that if Good were analysable, it would probably be sometimes expressed by some such complex phrase—a phrase, therefore, different from the mere word 'good'. Indeed Moore thinks that this fact probably partly explains how he was led to identify such obviously different propositions as 'Good is Good, and nothing else whatever' and 'Good is unanalysable'. For we have just seen that if the former proposition be understood as asserting that Good is different from any property expressed by any phrase other than the word 'good', this proposition, if true, would at least afford a strong presumption that Good was unanalysable. And he may have supposed—he continues—that, conversely, from the fact that Good was unanalysable, it would follow that it could not be expressed by any phrase other than 'good'. He may have supposed so owing to his perceiving that if Good were unanalysable, it could not be expressed by any phrase which *contained an analysis* of it, but failing to perceive the distinction between expressing the meaning of a word in other words which *contain an analysis* of it, and expressing its meaning by giving a synonym.

But the fact that there is this distinction is fatal to the truth of the proposition we are now considering. It may be true that Good is unanalysable, and therefore cannot be expressed by other words which contain an analysis of it: but it is certainly not true that it cannot be expressed by any other words at all. For instance (quite apart from the obvious fact that there are languages other than English), the word 'desirable' is sometimes used as a synonym for 'good'.

Moore therefore concludes that the assertion 'Good is Good, and nothing else whatever' is either merely trivial or else obviously false.

But this is not the end of the matter. For Moore also thinks that the examples which he gave in *Principia* do suggest to most people's minds that what he really meant to assert was that Good was not identical with any property belonging to a *particular class*; and *this* assertion still seems to him both true and important. But what is the class in question? Moore says in effect that he can only describe this class by saying that it is the class of all those properties which are either natural or metaphysical; and what he really wanted to assert, he says, was that Good was not identical with any natural or metaphysical property.

He admits that in *Principia* he confused natural objects (or events) with a certain kind of property which may belong to them. He actually confused a particular event, which consists in somebody's being pleased, with the property which we ascribe to it when we say that it is 'a state of pleasure'—just as he confused a particular patch of yellow with the property of being yellow. And he also admits that he confused *parts* of natural objects with *properties* of such objects.

For these and other reasons his attempts to define a 'natural property' were, he says, hopelessly confused. The nearest he came to suggesting a correct definition in *Principia* was on p. 40, where he said that to identify Good with any natural property resulted in replacing ethics by one of the natural sciences (including psychology). This now suggests to him the following definitions. A 'natural' property is a property with which it is the business of the natural sciences or of psychology to deal, or which can be completely defined in terms of such. A 'metaphysical' property is a property which stands to some supersensible object in the same relation in which natural properties stand to natural objects.

Moore now points out that the proposition that Good is not identical with any natural or metaphysical property (as now

defined)—which is what he really wished to assert in *Principia*—
neither implies nor is implied by the proposition that Good is
unanalysable. For it might plainly be true, even if Good *were*
analysable; and, on the other hand, even if Good were *un*analysable,
Good might still be identical with some natural property, since
many such properties may be unanalysable. At the same time, he
says, if Good is not identical with any natural or metaphysical
property, it does follow that, if it is analysable at all, it involves in
its analysis *some* unanalysable notion which is not natural or metaphysical. That some unanalysable notion of this sort, he says, is
involved in ethics was certainly a part of what he wished to assert
when he asserted that Good was unanalysable. Only he did not see
that this was a far more important and less doubtful assertion than
that Good itself was the unanalysable notion in question.

Of course Moore realizes that his new definitions—and it would
perhaps be better to call them 'explanations' rather than 'definitions'—are still not fully satisfactory. It is clear that he intended to
return to the topic in a later part of the Preface; but he never in fact
came to write it.

There are, however, still some pages of the Preface which are of
considerable interest, and of special relevance to our subject. It
will have been noticed that so far the expression 'the naturalistic
fallacy' has not been introduced, although it is obvious that what
Moore meant by it is very closely connected with the propositions
we have been considering. But he now explicitly raises the question:
What *is* 'the naturalistic fallacy'? And he says that the most important mistake which he made in his discussion of the matter in
Principia was exactly analogous to the chief of those which he made
in his assertions about Good. In the latter case, as we have seen, he
confused the three entirely different propositions 'Good is not
identical with any property other than itself'; 'Good is not identical
with any analysable property'; and 'Good is not identical with any
natural or metaphysical property'. In the case of the naturalistic
fallacy, he goes on, he similarly confused the three entirely different
propositions (1) 'So-and-so is identifying Good with some property
other than Good'; (2) 'So-and-so is identifying Good with some
analysable property'; and (3) 'So-and-so is identifying Good with
some *natural or metaphysical* property'.

He points out that he sometimes implies that to say of a man that he is committing the naturalistic fallacy is to say (1) of him; sometimes that it is to say (2) of him; and sometimes that it is to say (3) of him.

But in addition to this, his main mistake, he also made, he says, two further mistakes. First, he sometimes talked (*Principia*, p. 14) as if to commit the naturalistic fallacy was to suppose that in, for example, 'This is good', the word 'is' always expresses identity between the thing called 'this' and Good. And secondly, he confused (A) 'To say that so-and-so is committing the naturalistic fallacy is to say that he is holding, with respect to some property of a certain kind, the *view* that that property is identical with Good', and (B) 'To say that so-and-so is committing the naturalistic fallacy is to say that he is *confusing* some property of a certain kind with Good'. But the operation mentioned in (A) is quite different from that mentioned in (B).

Finally, Moore admits that he feels doubtful whether either of these two operations could properly be called the commission of a fallacy, for the simple reason that to commit a fallacy seems properly to mean to make a certain kind of *inference*; whereas the mere confusion of two properties, or the holding of a view with regard to them, seems not to be a process of inference at all.

Moore ends this part of the Preface by saying that if he still wished to use the term 'naturalistic fallacy', he would define it as follows. 'So-and so is committing the naturalistic fallacy' means 'He is *either* confusing Good with a natural or metaphysical property *or* holding it to be identical with such a property *or* making an inference *based* upon such a confusion'. And he would also expressly point out that in so using the term 'fallacy' he was using it in an extended, and perhaps improper, sense.

This concludes my synopsis, or reconstruction, of the Preface, or rather of that part of it which it is possible to reconstruct, for the rest is in a very incomplete state indeed. And it will, I think, have been seen that many of the criticisms made of Moore's treatment of the naturalistic fallacy and related topics in the 1930s and 1940s were fully anticipated by him many years earlier.

II

I now wish to discuss independently one particular aspect of the subject. In the Preface, it will be recalled, Moore says that he still believes it to be true and important to assert that Good is not identical with any natural or metaphysical property. But he neither produces any new arguments for this assertion nor makes any comments on the arguments which he gave in *Principia*. I wish now to examine in some detail two passages in the book which contain such arguments. The first occurs in § 13 (pp. 15-16), and runs as follows:

The hypothesis that disagreement about the meaning of good is disagreement with regard to the correct analysis of a given whole, may be most plainly seen to be incorrect by consideration of the fact that, whatever definition be offered, it may be always asked, with significance, of the complex so defined, whether it is itself good. To take, for instance, one of the more plausible, because one of the more complicated of such proposed definitions, it may easily be thought, at first sight, that to be good may mean to be that which we desire to desire. Thus if we apply this definition to a particular instance and say 'When we think that A is good, we are thinking that A is one of the things which we desire to desire,' our proposition may seem quite plausible. But, if we carry the investigation further, and ask ourselves 'Is it good to desire to desire A?' it is apparent, on a little reflection, that this question is itself as intelligible, as the original question 'Is A good?' —that we are, in fact, now asking for exactly the same information about the desire to desire A, for which we formerly asked with regard to A itself. But it is also apparent that the meaning of this second question cannot be correctly analysed into 'Is the desire to desire A one of the things which we desire to desire?': we have not before our minds anything so complicated as the question 'Do we desire to desire to desire A?' Moreover anyone can easily convince himself by inspection that the predicate of this proposition—'good' —is positively different from the notion of 'desiring to desire' which enters into its subject: 'That we should desire to desire A is good' is *not* merely equivalent to 'That A should be good is good'. It may indeed be true that what we desire to desire is always also good; perhaps, even the converse may be true: but it is very doubtful whether this is the case, and the mere fact that we understand very well what is meant by doubting it, shews clearly that we have two different notions before our minds.

The second passage occurs a little later (p. 38). Moore there says that he will discuss certain theories which claim that only a single kind of thing is good. He thinks that such theories rest on the naturalistic fallacy, and goes on as follows:

That a thing should be good, it has been thought, *means* that it possesses this single property: and hence (it is thought) only what possesses this property is good. The inference seems very natural; and yet what is meant by it is self-contradictory. For those who make it fail to perceive that their conclusion 'what possesses this property is good' is a significant proposition: that it does not mean either 'what possesses this property, possesses this property' or 'the word "good" denotes that a thing possesses this property'. And yet, if it does *not* mean one or other of these two things, the inference contradicts its own premise.

It will have been noticed that Moore speaks in these passages as if he were showing that Good is not analysable at all; but what I chiefly wish to discuss is the question whether he has shown that Good is not identical with the property of being one of the things which we desire to desire—that is, with the property which he takes as an example in the first passage. Moreover, I cannot hope to say here all that ought to be said about these passages. In particular, I cannot consider all the different arguments which they contain and which are not clearly distinguished from each other. All I can do is to try to reformulate and discuss what seems to me to be the chief of these arguments.

I think I can do this most clearly with the help of an analogy. Let us suppose that we are concerned, not with Good, but with the concept of being a brother. Suppose that someone asserts that to be a brother is to be a male sibling—or, to use the terminology that Moore himself often used in later life—that the concept of being a brother is identical with the concept of being a male sibling. Now what follows from this proposition? So far as I can see, one thing which certainly follows from it is that the proposition 'John is a brother' is identical with the proposition 'John is a male sibling'. Similarly, in Moore's case, if to be good is to be one of the things which we desire to desire, it follows that any proposition of the form '*x* is good' is identical with the corresponding proposition of the form '*x* is one of the things which we desire to desire'. It follows, for instance, that the proposition 'A is good' (and we must now assume that 'A' is a name or description of a thing or state of things) is identical with the proposition 'A is one of the things which we desire to desire'.

Consequently, Moore could have argued against the identification of Good with the property of being one of the things which we desire to desire, by pointing out that even if at first it may seem plausible to suppose that these two propositions are identical, yet further reflection makes it apparent that they are *not* identical.

But this is not what he does. He obviously thought that he had a more complicated but more convincing argument. For what he asks us to consider are not the two propositions I have just mentioned, but the completely different propositions 'It is good to desire to desire A' and 'The desire to desire A is one of the things which we desire to desire'. And he says that it is apparent on reflection that *these* propositions are not identical.

Let me put the matter in terms of questions rather than propositions. Moore could have argued that the question (1) 'Is A good?' is quite different from the question (2) 'Is A one of the things which we desire to desire?' Yet if to be good is to be one of the things which we desire to desire, these questions are identical. But what he in fact says is that the question (3) 'Is it good to desire to desire A?' is quite different from the question (4) 'Is the desire to desire A one of the things which we desire to desire?'

But though the latter questions are more complicated than the former, they are no better. For on the view he is discussing, just as (1) and (2) are identical, so are (3) and (4). And it is no plainer that (3) and (4) are *not* identical than it is that (1) and (2) are not identical. Similarly, on the view in question, the proposition (3A) 'It is good that we desire to desire A' *is* identical with the proposition (3B) 'It is good that A is good' (and each of them is identical with the proposition 'We desire to desire to desire to desire A'). And again, it is no plainer that (3A) and (3B) are *not* identical than it is that 'A is good' and 'A is one of the things which we desire to desire' are not identical.

Did Moore, then, have at the back of his mind some other questions, even more complicated? I think that the second passage which I have quoted makes it fairly clear that he did, and that they were (5) 'Is A, which is one of things which we desire to desire, good?', and (6) 'Is A, which is one of the things which we desire to desire, one of the things which we desire to desire?' And I think that he confused (5) with (3), and (6) with (4).

Unfortunately, each of these last two questions—(5) and (6)— is capable of at least two totally different interpretations. Question (5) may mean *either* 'Is it the case that A is good if and only if it is one of the things which we desire to desire?'—where the expression 'if and only if' is used truth-functionally;[1] *or* 'Is it the case that to say that A is good is the same thing as to say that A is one of the things which we desire to desire?' More generally, the question of which (5) is merely a particular example may mean *either* 'Is it the case that a thing is good if and only if it is one of the things which we desire to desire?' (where the expression 'if and only if' is used truth-functionally); *or* 'Is it the case that to be good is to be one of the things which we desire to desire?' An affirmative answer to the *first* question would be given by the proposition 'It *is* the case that a thing is good if and only if it is one of the things which we desire to desire', which is logically equivalent to the proposition (α) 'A thing is good if and only if it is one of the things which we desire to desire'. An affirmative answer to the *second* question would be given by the proposition 'It *is* the case that to be good is to be one of the things which we desire to desire', which is logically equivalent to the proposition (β) 'To be good is to be one of the things which we desire to desire'.

Similarly, the question of which (6) is merely a particular example may mean *either* 'Is it the case that a thing is one of the things which we desire to desire if and only if it is one of the things which we desire to desire?' (where 'if and only if' is used truth-functionally); *or* 'Is it the case that to be one of the things which we desire to desire is to be one of the things which we desire to desire?' An affirmative answer to the *first* question would be given

<hr>

[1] That is to say, in such a way that the question can also be expressed by asking 'Are the two propositions "A is good" and "A is one of the things which we desire to desire" either *both* true or *both* false?'

by the proposition 'It *is* the case that a thing is one of the things which we desire to desire if and only if it is one of the things which we desire to desire', which is logically equivalent to (γ) 'A thing is one of the things which we desire to desire if and only if it is one of the things which we desire to desire'. On the other hand, an affirmative answer to the *second* question would be given by the proposition 'It *is* the case that to be one of the things which we desire to desire is to be one of the things which we desire to desire', which is logically equivalent to the proposition (δ) 'To be one of the things which we desire to desire is to be one of the things which we desire to desire'.

For the sake of simplicity, I will now again speak in terms of propositions rather than questions. The main point I now wish to make is that there is a fundamental difference between (α) and (γ) on the one hand, and (β) and (δ) on the other. For the truth-value (that is, the truth or falsity) of (α) would not be altered if we substituted for any expression which occurs in the sentence which I have used to express (α), another expression with the same extension (that is, another expression which applies to exactly the same things); and the same is true of (γ). But this is not true either of (β) or of (δ). In current logical terminology, whilst the sentences which I have used to express (α) and (γ) are *extensional*, those I have used to express (β) and (δ) are *not* extensional.

It is clear that at the time Moore wrote *Principia* (1903), he did not see this distinction; and he therefore failed to distinguish (α) from (β), and (γ) from (δ). But (α) *is* quite different from (β), and (γ) *is* quite different from (δ). Consequently, we get two different interpretations of Moore's argument.

First, we can interpret him as arguing that to be good is not the same as to be one of the things which we desire to desire, because, if it were, then (β) would be identical with (δ); and maintaining, further, that it is apparent on reflection that (β) is *not* identical with (δ). If interpreted in this way, the argument seems to me to be completely invalid. For in the same kind of way it would be possible to show with regard to any concept whatever that it is unanalysable—in other words, that it is simple. For instance, we could show that to be a brother is not the same thing as to be a male sibling, because, if it were, then the proposition 'To be a brother is to be a male sibling' would be identical with the proposition 'To be a male sibling is to be a male sibling'. Yet it is clear on reflection that these propositions are *not* identical.

In other words, Moore's argument, in this interpretation, would be a particular instance of what he himself later in life called the 'Paradox of Analysis'. He was never fully satisfied with any solution of it, and said different things about it at different times. But I have no doubt at all, on the basis of a large number of discussions which I have had with him on the subject over a period of many years, that his considered view was that whatever may be the *complete* solution, it was essential to hold that (in the example I have just given) to be a brother *is* to be a male sibling, and that yet the proposition 'To be a brother is to be a male sibling' is *not* identical with the proposition 'To be a male sibling is to be a male sibling'. And he therefore held that from 'To be a brother is to be a male sibling', the identity of these propositions does *not* follow. I think that this is right; and if so, then his *Principia* argument, in the interpretation I am now considering, is clearly invalid.

We must now, however, discuss my second interpretation. Here we should interpret Moore as arguing that to be good is not the same as to be one of the things which we desire to desire, because, if it were, then (α) would be identical with (γ); and maintaining, further, that it is apparent on reflection that (α) is *not* identical with (γ). Now *this* argument seems to me to be perfectly valid. For, although I once succeeded in so confusing myself as to deny it, I now think it undeniable that *if* to be good is to be one of the things which we desire to desire, then (α) *is* identical with (γ). Yet it is absolutely clear that (α) is *not* identical with (γ). And that (α) is not identical with (γ) follows from something which is also absolutely clear, namely, that it is logically possible to doubt (α) *without* doubting (γ); and each of these things follows from something which is also absolutely clear, namely, that whilst (γ) is a necessary proposition, (α) is a contingent proposition.

Moreover, it is *not* possible to use this kind of argument to show with regard to any concept whatever, that it is unanalysable. Indeed, if to be a brother is to be a male sibling, then the proposition 'A creature is a brother if and only if it is a male sibling' is identical with the proposition 'A creature is a male sibling if and only if it is a male sibling' (where in both sentences 'if and only if' is used truth-functionally). But *these* propositions *are* identical.

Of course, Moore's argument, in the present interpretation, may be said to be 'begging the question'. For a person who holds that to be good is to be one of the things which we desire to desire, may admit that if this is so, then (α) is identical with (γ); and he may then go on to assert that (α) *is* identical with (γ). This is true: but I think we can all see that a person who asserted *this*, would be mistaken.

It seems to me obvious that any theory which identifies Good with a concept which is not itself at least partially ethical, can be refuted in an analogous way. I think therefore that for all his mistakes, Moore can fairly be said to have found a means of refuting any such theory.

G. E. L. OWEN

The Platonism of Aristotle

Eight years ago, in a memorable Dawes Hicks Lecture to this Academy, Sir David Ross spoke of Aristotle's development as a philosopher. One theory of that development he singled out as having established itself in the fifty years since it appeared. It was pioneered in this country by Thomas Case and in Germany, with great effect, by Werner Jaeger. It depicts Aristotle, in Sir David's words, as 'gradually emerging from Platonism into a system of his own'. Aristotle's philosophical career began in the twenty years that he spent learning and practising his trade in Plato's Academy, and it ended in the headship of his own school. So it is tempting to picture him first as the devoted partisan, then as arguing his way free of that discipleship.

'Platonism' has become a familiar catchword in references to this theory. Case and Jaeger used it, and I have kept it in my title. Probably my argument will be reported as maintaining that we have been looking for Aristotle's Platonism in some wrong directions and proposing other directions to follow. But a warning is called for at the start. The catchword 'Platonism' will carry no independent weight in the argument. It is too often taken on trust, and too riddled with ambiguity to be trusted. Lest this seem to you either extravagant or truistic let me show its importance for the matter in hand.

Before you and I joined in a systematic search for Platonism in Aristotle—and this is a project far beyond the scope of one lecture—we should, if we knew our business, try to reach some understanding on Plato's own philosophical progress and achievements as well as on what Aristotle took those achievements to be. Then we should have to settle, at least *ambulando*, what kinds of agreement or sympathy with Plato were relevant—whether we were looking for affinities in large programmes as well as in special problems, for instance, in arguments and methods as well as in conclusions. Case and Jaeger both endeavoured to explain what they understood by 'Platonism'. But curiously little attention seems to have been paid to their answers to the questions I have just sketched. What Jaeger means by 'Platonism' differs at important points from what Case means, and this fact has not been advertised by those who hail them as co-founders of one theory. And what Jaeger means by the word commits him to giving a very odd answer to our questions: it depends upon a theory of Aristotle's procedure which is both radical to his interpretation and, I think, mistaken. Clearing up the mistake will be a first step towards some positive conclusions. That it has excited so little comment seems largely due to the muffling effect of the blanket-word 'Platonism'.

Aristotle's debts

Aristotle remained a member of Plato's Academy for nearly twenty years. He joined it as a student when he came to Athens about the time of his seventeenth birthday, and when Plato died in the spring of 347 he left the city. Thereafter, according to Jaeger, he gave up his practice of publishing works in which he wrote simply as the philosophical partisan of Plato. Those twenty years were to be the longest time he spent in Athens, and there can be no doubt of their importance either for Aristotle or for Plato himself. For Plato they seem to have been a time of immense activity, in which political disappointments were far outweighed by philosophical achievements. He wrote, *inter alia*, the *Theaetetus* and the *Parmenides*, the *Sophist* and the *Statesman* and the *Philebus*, dialogues in which he showed a new preoccupation with philosophical method and with what his successors classified as problems of logic. These were the years in which logic was born in the Academy; the dialogues must have partly fomented, partly reflected the impulse towards that subject which seized Speusippus and Aristotle and their contemporaries, and sent them seeking criteria for synonymy and homonymy and settling the rules of definition and division. So Jaeger was right to say, at the beginning of his study of the subject, that if we are to understand Aristotle's relationship with Plato it is on this period of the Academy and of its founder's career that we must concentrate.

Yet of those later dialogues, and of the whole context of logical discussion in the Academy which Aristotle records in his *Topics*, Jaeger had disappointingly little to say. During these years, he insisted, Aristotle was a faithful spokesman of Plato's theories. The proof was to be found primarily in fragments of the pupil's writings that could be dated to the last five or six years before Plato died. But the Plato that Jaeger detected behind some of these fragments was the Plato of the *Phaedo* and the *Symposium* and the *Republic*, dialogues which on Jaeger's own view were already classic when Aristotle reached Athens and already under fire in the Academy long before the fragments in question were written. Some of this fire came from Plato himself, in the *Parmenides* and *Sophist* and *Philebus*; some of it can be heard in Aristotle's handbooks of Academic debate, the *Topics* and *De Sophisticis Elenchis*. Yet in the *Eudemus*, a dialogue which Aristotle wrote after the death of a friend in 354 B.C., Jaeger discovered the Theory of Forms and the view of personal immortality which had been propounded in the *Phaedo*; and he himself held that neither of these survived without change or challenge in Plato's later writings.

Still worse, Aristotle wrote a dialogue, the *Sophist*, which Jaeger dated to the time of his dependence on Plato and (in default of any direct evidence) held to have been just as faithful in conforming to Plato's dialogue of the same name as the *Eudemus* was faithful to the *Phaedo*. Yet Plato's *Sophist* contains a powerful attack on the metaphysics of the *Phaedo*.

So this feature of the 'Platonism' that Jaeger discerned in Aristotle's lost works certainly called for comment, namely the hospitable impartiality of his metaphysical borrowings. The problem need not exercise those unitarians who suppose that Plato never changed his mind or conceded an objection. Case may have been one of these, so far as Plato's published writings are concerned, though he held that during Aristotle's membership of the Academy Plato turned to other theories which are not represented in the dialogues. But Jaeger, like most later scholars, was no unitarian. He represented his account of Aristotle's development as an overdue attempt to do for Plato's pupil what had already, and successfully, been done for Plato. So the supposed jackdaw borrowings cried for some explanation.

.The explanation that Jaeger found was striking. He divided Aristotle's philosophical theories from his studies in logic and philosophical method, and claimed that in the Academy the second proceeded quite independently of the first. He appealed to fragments of the *Eudemus* to show that Aristotle worked out much of his logic, and in particular his account of substance and the categories, without letting himself recognize that it implied the rejection of important parts of Plato's metaphysics as that had been developed in, for instance, the *Phaedo*. Later, after Plato's death, he was to press this implication at every turn. But so long as he was under Plato's spell he was content to take his conclusions from his master's writings and to draw on his own logic merely to provide these with new and sharper arguments.

So the answer to those questions we raised about 'Platonism' is clear and surprising. 'Platonism' becomes a matter not of arguments but of theorems, not of philosophical method but of doctrinal conviction. Aristotle 'was already a master in the realms of method and logical technique at a time when he was still completely dependent on Plato in metaphysics'; and Jaeger concludes that 'this dependence was obviously rooted in the depths of Aristotle's unreasoned religious and personal feelings'.

If this were true it would explain more than Aristotle's supposed readiness at this time to draw doctrine from any part of Plato's work. It would certainly explain that; for 'unreasoned religious and personal feelings' can accommodate a good deal of inconsistency, so long as they are not made answerable to 'method and logical technique'. But it would also explain the relative neglect of Aristotle's logic in Jaeger's impressive sketch of his philosophical progress. Thomas Case could appeal to Plato's analysis of true and false statements in the *Sophist* in order to explain the 'Platonism' of some of Aristotle's early moves in logic. But here his difference from Jaeger is fundamental. For Jaeger the Platonism is not to be sought in the logic.

At the same time Jaeger's explanation put a premium on a certain method of interpretation, a method to which Jaeger himself allowed little force when he turned to Aristotle's extant works. If doctrines are to be removed from their parent arguments and taken for independent agents, they need other means of identification. The readiest method then of picking them out in other philosophical contexts is by the occurrence of particular idioms and turns of phrase which accompanied their appearance in the original, canonical, context. This popular device is exploded by Aristotle's own writings. There is a set of idioms in which he is accustomed to portray Plato's theories, and when he does so he is liable to denounce the idioms as vacuous or misleading. They include the expressions 'idea', 'paradigm', 'participation', 'the one beside the many'. But elsewhere in his work they turn up, clean and ready for use, where the context shows that they carry no reference to the rejected theories.[1]

This preamble may serve to show that the word 'Platonism' is not to be taken without scrutiny as a key on the interpreter's ring. But it leads to a more substantial point. The divorce that Jaeger thought he had made out between the logical and metaphysical partners in Aristotle's early philosophizing was fictitious. There is no good evidence for it, and strong evidence against it. And the evidence against it is positive support for the different approach that I shall sketch later. Let us start at the negative pole of this argument.

Categories and Forms in the Eudemus

The topic of Aristotle's lost dialogue, the *Eudemus*, was the immortality of the soul. It was not one of those dialogues in which Aristotle is reported to have introduced himself as a speaker, so some scholars have urged that we cannot be sure whether a given view derived from the work would have been endorsed by its author. But the argument with which we are concerned does not call for this scepticism. It can safely be credited to Aristotle, not because it reinforces an argument in Plato's *Phaedo* but because in his later

---

[1] 'Idea', Bonitz, *Index. Arist.* 338^{b}34-48; 'paradigm', *Phys.* 194^{b}26, *Met.* 1013^{a}27, *Top.* 151^{b}20-21; 'participate', Bonitz, op. cit. 462^{b}36-43; 'one beside the many', *An. Post.* 100^{a}6-9, Alexander *in Met.* 79. 16-17.

work *De Anima* Aristotle is still attacking the same theory against which our argument is levelled.

The theory under attack is that the soul, the principle of life, is nothing but a 'harmony', that is to say a proper co-ordination of elements in the body. When the co-ordination breaks down the life and therefore the soul is at an end. In the *Eudemus* Aristotle is said to have countered this by saying: 'Harmony has a contrary, disharmony. But soul has no contrary. So the soul is not a harmony.'[1] Another authority, earlier but not therefore better, fills out the argument. 'Soul has no contrary, *because it is a substance.*'[2] This expansion is one of the pivots on which Jaeger's interpretation turns. He recognizes that it is almost certainly a gratuity from the commentator, Olympiodorus, who puts similar stuffing into other Aristotelian and Platonic arguments in the same context. But in this case Jaeger thinks that the expansion merely brings out an implication that was present though tacit in the original. For if Aristotle said that soul has no contrary he must have had in mind the proposition which appears in the *Categories*, that substance has no contrary. White has a contrary, black; in Aristotle's account of the categories this is enough to prove that white and black are not substances. They are qualities, or species of quality. Man is a species of substance, and there is no logical contrary to man. So, if Aristotle's argument in the *Eudemus* presupposes that the soul is a substance, it presupposes the analysis of substances *vis-à-vis* other categories that is proprietary to Aristotle's logic.

But now for the other arm of Jaeger's interpretation. In the *Phaedo*, and again in the fifth book of the *Republic*, Plato had proposed his own candidates for the title of *substance* or *ousia*, namely the Forms. In the *Phaedo* he gives as examples of such Forms the Equal, the Beautiful, the Good, the Just, the Greater, the Less. All of these have contraries, and in the *Republic* he expressly argues to the unity of a Form from its having a contrary, and seems to say that the same argument holds good of all Forms.[3] So these Forms cannot satisfy Aristotle's definition of a substance. Nor does Aristotle think that Plato is using the word 'substance' simply in a

---

[1] Fr. 7 Ross (Philoponus *in de an.* 144. 22-25).
[2] Fr. 7 Ross (Olympiodorus *in Phaed.* 173. 20-23).
[3] *Phaedo* 75 c, *Rep.* 475 e-6 a.

different sense from his own: he consistently reproves Plato for putting up candidates for the status of substance which fail to meet the basic requirements for that grade. So it is unsettling to find Jaeger arguing, as the other limb of his account of the *Eudemus*, that in that dialogue Aristotle accepted the Theory of Forms as it had been formulated in the *Phaedo*. It is by combining these two theses that he is able to conclude that at this time Aristotle was wholly dependent on Plato for his metaphysics but quite independent of him in his logic, namely in his theory of categories. He does not seek to palliate, nor even expressly recognize, the paradox that in Aristotle's view this would commit him to accepting a class of substances which is expressly debarred by the logic he deploys. For my part I find this degree of philosophical *akrasia* incredible.

. Fortunately, we need not believe it. Neither arm of Jaeger's interpretation holds firm. That the doctrine of the *Categories* had been worked out during Aristotle's years in the Academy seems to me certain, and I shall try to show how it came about. But given that doctrine, there is no inference from the statement that the soul has no contrary to the presupposition that the soul is a substance in Aristotle's sense. For the *Categories* lays it down that the lack of a contrary is characteristic not only of substances but of the members of various other categories: all quantities, some qualities, some relatives. The argument works very well as it stands: it operates by a simple appeal to a distinction in current usage, and this is wholly appropriate to the form of dialogue that Aristotle is writing: possibly a piece of consolation-literature, certainly not a systematic treatise.

It remains a question whether, and if so in what sense, the soul was argued to be a substance in the *Eudemus*. Evidently Aristotle wrote the work with the *Phaedo* in mind: part of the discussion was concerned with the possibility of the soul's existence before and after its incarceration in the body, a possibility for which his mature psychology leaves no room. On the other hand, part of the discussion is said by Simplicius to have depicted the soul as a 'form' ($\epsilon\hat{\iota}\delta\acute{o}s\ \tau\iota$), a use of the word which is familiar enough in the mature psychology but makes small sense within the Platonic Theory of Forms.[1] In

---

[1] Fr. 8 Ross (Simplicius *in de an.* 221. 28–30); cf. Arist. *Met.* 1077^a 32–33 and Cherniss, *Aristotle's Criticism of Plato and the Academy*, i, pp. 506–12.

brief, the evidence is too equivocal to saddle Aristotle himself at this date with a theory that the soul is a separate substance transiently and painfully housed in a body; and even if it were not, it would not commit him, as Jaeger claims in the second arm of his interpretation, to postulating Plato's transcendent Forms for the disembodied soul to contemplate. Jaeger himself allows that the lost dialogue 'On Philosophy' seems to have given a sympathetic hearing to the first theory but rejected the second, and it would be natural for Aristotle to hold them apart: the immortality of the soul was a matter of tradition, the Theory of Forms a philosopher's invention. When Aristotle discusses the views of 'the many and the wise', it is the second party that gets the shorter shrift.

What evidence then is there that the Forms of the *Phaedo* still haunt the *Eudemus*? There is a mythological description of the soul's passage from Hades, in which the soul is said to forget 'the sights yonder';[1] but comparison of other texts from the same source shows that these 'sights' were probably not the desiderated Forms but merely Styx and Lethe and the conventional paraphernalia of the underworld. What part this and other myths played in the dialogue we cannot tell, but plainly they are not to be confused with metaphysical argument. Nor again can Aristotle's beliefs be deduced from a report discovered in the Arabian philosopher al-Kindi, to the effect that Aristotle discussed an anecdote in which the soul of a Greek king departed to contemplate 'souls, forms and angels'.[2] The myth of Plato's *Phaedrus* must stand behind the anecdote, but what use Aristotle made of the myth is not on record.

I shall not pursue this hunt for the Platonic Forms into the fragments of Aristotle's *Protrepticus*, where Jaeger thought to find them. The fragments have been well beaten in recent years, and the quarry was not there. What evidence remains? Aristotle set up to teach rhetoric in the Academy in rivalry to Isocrates. Worse, he seems to have tried to capture some of Isocrates' own field of political patronage in Cyprus. Henceforth he was a fair target for Isocrates' school. An historian of the fourth century A.D. records that one of Isocrates' pupils wrote against Aristotle and remarks,

---

[1] Fr. 5 Ross (Procl. *in Remp.* ii. 349. 13–26), fr. 4 in context (Procl. *in Tim.* 323. 16–4. 4).

[2] Fr. 11 Ross (cf. *Select Fragments*, tr. Ross, p. 23).

with astonishment, that Aristotle was attacked as representative of Plato's best-known theories and in particular of the Theory of Forms. But the more we learn of the conventions of ancient rhetoric the less weight there seems to be in this evidence. It is matched by the polemic of another contemporary, Euboulides, in which Aristotle was accused of destroying his master's writings and being absent at his master's death;[1] these charges too seem to have been first levelled at Plato and then ritually transferred to his pupil, much as in comedy and public and forensic oratory the misdemeanours of the parent or patron were visited on the dependent.[2] Such a polemic is not even evidence that the polemist did not know Aristotle's own views, though in itself this is likely enough.

Still it may be felt that philosophical piety would be the natural posture for Plato's pupils and associates, at least during the great man's lifetime. We know that it was not: the best of the others, Eudoxus and Speusippus, challenged and tried to reform the Theory of Ideas. Nor would simple acquiescence be encouraged by those later dialogues in which Plato subjected his own earlier metaphysics to an unsentimental appraisal. The debates charted in Aristotle's *Topics* are enough to prove that his criticisms of Plato would not estrange him from the rest of that argumentative school. More positively, it can be shown that Aristotle's own account of substance and the categories, so far from being the autonomous growth required by Jaeger, was born and bred in these controversies of the Academy. So far from seeming reconcilable with the Theory of Forms it presupposed and was evolved from a celebrated criticism of that theory.

Before turning to this point it may be worth while entering two disclaimers. First, there are of course many signs of Plato's influence to be found in Aristotle's early works, including the fragments of his lost writings, other than the putative signs I have been questioning. To some of these I have called attention elsewhere; others, notably in Aristotle's cosmology, have often been discussed.[3] Nothing in my argument makes against the importance of detecting

---

[1] See I. Düring, *Aristotle in the Ancient Biographical Tradition* (1957), p. 374.
[2] See W. Süss, *Ethos* (1910), pp. 247–54.
[3] Recently by F. Solmsen, *Aristotle's System of the Physical World* (1960); I. Düring, 'Aristotle and the Heritage from Plato' in *Eranos*, lxii (1964).

F

and exploiting these clues in interpreting Aristotle. I have been concerned only with one, the most celebrated and influential, account of Aristotle's 'Platonism', and with a curious thesis on which that account turns. And I have been questioning this not from the joy of battle but because, as I shall try to show, it obstructs the use of genuine clues to Aristotle's philosophical progress.

Next, in saying that Aristotle's logic was bred of discussion in the Academy, I do not imply that it was a donation from his colleagues. There used to be a myth, promoted by Burnet and Taylor, that the theory of categories was a commonplace of the Academy, derived from scattered hints in Plato's writings. This myth was exposed, not simply by the obvious lack of system in the supposed hints, but by the fact that no other Academic known to us endorsed the theory and that Xenocrates, Plato's self-appointed exegete, denounced it as a pointless elaboration and went back to a simpler distinction derived from Plato's *Sophist*. Nor again do I mean that Aristotle's logic had come to full maturity before Plato's death. The division of the categories, and probably the general theory of the syllogism, had been worked out by then; but Aristotle continued to review and develop these doctrines in his later work. The same is true of his theory of definition and, more generally, his theory of meaning. What is beyond question is that these theories were developed in practice and not as an independent exercise. The theory of definition was modified to keep pace with the work of a biologist who had once held that a definition could be reduced to a single differentia and then found himself, when he set out to define any natural species, faced with a set of competing criteria. The theory of meaning, of synonymy and homonymy, was enlarged to allow a value to philosophical inquiries which had been earlier denounced as trading on an equivocation. At every stage Aristotle's logic had its roots in philosophical argument and scientific procedure: it would be an anachronism to think otherwise. So what arguments lie at the root of his early account of substance and the categories?

Substance and the criticism of the Forms

Aristotle brings a great variety of arguments against the Theory of Forms, and the variety reflects the faces and phases of that theory as well as Aristotle's shifting interest in it. But the objection to which he recurs most often is that which the Academy dubbed 'the Third Man'. It makes an ambiguous appearance in Plato's *Parmenides*, and it was set out schematically in Aristotle's early essay *On Ideas*.[1] It is the argument behind Aristotle's stock complaint that when Plato invented his Forms he made a mistake about predicates: he took any predicate-expression to stand for some individual thing instead of for some sort of thing.[2] Thereby, Aristotle held, he committed two faults: he failed to explain how we use predicates to classify and describe actual individuals, and he cluttered the scene with other individuals which were fictions.

Here it is important to be clear on Aristotle's use of 'predicate' and 'predication'. If I say 'Socrates is old' or 'Socrates is a man', what I predicate of Socrates is not old age or manhood but simply *old* or *man*—or, in English, *a man*. Its linguistic expression must be an appropriate filling for 'Socrates is . . . (or is a . . ., or is a kind of . . .)'. Greek lacked, what English enjoys, an indefinite article; and Greek philosophers had not come to see the cardinal importance of quotation marks, or of the clumsier devices that served for such marks. But though this sometimes clouds the interpretation of what Aristotle says about predicates it does not blunt the point of his objection to Plato.

The point is this. Plato is accused of misconstruing the logic of such a statement as 'Socrates is a man' by making two incompatible assumptions about it. He thinks (*a*) that what is predicated, in this case *man* (not the expression but what it stands for), is always something different from the subjects of which it is predicated; for if it were identical with its subjects these would become identical with each other. Plato is a man, Socrates is a man: if these statements have the form of '*a* = *c*, *b* = *c*', *a* will be *b* and Plato will be Socrates. But also Plato thinks (*b*) that what is predicated is itself a subject of that same predicate; for it seems undeniable even if truistic that *man is man* or *a man is a man*. We can borrow the indefinite article and recast the point. Plato had said: 'When I call *A* a man and *B* a man, what does this common label "a man" stand for? Not for the

---

[1] *Parm.* 131 e-2 b (the argument in 132 c-3 a with which later writers from Eudemus onward conflated it is a different objection); *De Ideis*, fr. 4 Ross (Alexander *in Met.* 84. 21-85. 12).

[2] e.g. *de soph. el.* 178^{b}36-9^{a}10, *Met.* 1038 34-9^{a}3.

individual subject I apply it to, else it would stand indifferently for any such subject; but *A* and *B* cannot both be the single common thing we are after. So "a man" stands for some third thing.' But then, it is objected, *ex hypothesi* this third thing is *a man*. And thus we have three men where we began with two, and by similar manipulations we can generate a fourth and fifth *ad infinitum*.

The two premisses (*a*) and (*b*) set out by Aristotle were recently rediscovered and entitled the Non-identity Assumption and the Self-predication Assumption. I am not now concerned with the fairness of the objection that Aristotle bases on them, only with the moves by which he constructs a theory of predication that is immune to the paradox. There is a familiar and somewhat reach-me-down diagnosis of the Third Man regress, to the effect that it showed the error of construing every predicative statement as relational—of analysing 'Socrates is a man' as mentioning two objects and reporting some relation between them. Plato had said, 'There is Socrates, and there is Man, and we have to determine the connection between them: participation, resemblance, or whatever. No doubt Aristotle has seen something of this when he accuses Plato of taking the predicate-expression to signify a 'this' instead of a 'such-and-such', an individual instead of a sort or kind. But for two reasons he could not propound this as a final diagnosis. One is that he is scarcely clearer than Plato on the nature of relations. He has no word for 'relation' in the modern sense, and his nearest approach to the idea is in fact a survey of incomplete or relative predicates such as *father, slave, bigger*.[1] The second and more important reason is that he came to think his first short reply—that what is predicated of an individual is not another individual—as much of an over-simplification as the theory it was meant to rebut. His own positive account of the matter, and therewith his first move towards a new theory of predication and the categories, came when he considered which of the two premisses of the regress must be given up, and characteristically refused to give one general answer. For the question assumes that one account will hold good of all predicates, and Aristotle tried to show that this was false.

He countered it by drawing a sharp contrast between two sorts of predicate. One sort is represented by 'man', the other by 'white':

[1] As in *Cat.* vii, *Met.* Δ xv.

these remained his favourite illustrations. 'Man', he points out, is used in the same sense whether we use it to describe Socrates or to speak of the kind or species under which Socrates falls. For suppose we ask what man is: the answer to this general question (say, 'a featherless biped') will be equally applicable to the particular man Socrates. But with 'white' it is different. To say that Socrates is white is to say that he is coloured in a certain way; but if we go on to ask what white is, we shall have to say, not that white is coloured in a certain way, but that white is a certain colour. In the *Categories* Aristotle puts this contrast by saying that when we use 'white' to describe someone or something we cannot predicate of our subject the *definition* of white; we can predicate only the word 'white'. But when we call someone 'a man' we can go on to predicate of our subject the definition of man.[1] Elsewhere he puts it by saying that a man cannot be *what white is*.[2]

With the Third man in view the moral of this is obvious. There is one sort of predication that does not seem to imply the Self-predication Assumption: white is not white in the sense in which Socrates is white. But there is another sort, represented by the predication of *man*, which for convenience I shall call 'strong predication'; and this sort does seem to imply this Assumption.

If this is so we can expect Aristotle to tolerate the Non-identity Assumption in the first case but to repudiate it, on pain of a regress, in the second. And this he does: not indeed in the early *Categories*, which resorts to an older way of disarming strong predication, but in other works which build on the *Categories*. The first sort of predication, he says, is one in which the subject is something *different from* the attributes ascribed to it (ἄλλο κατ' ἄλλου λεγόμενον, ἕτερόν τι ὂν λευκόν ἐστιν, κτλ). But the second is one in which there is no such difference: *man* is just what Socrates is. 'Man' and 'white' remain his stock examples.[3]

The *Categories* is at an early and interesting stage of these ponderings on the Third Man. It has seized the difference between the two sorts of predicate, but it has not yet swallowed all the implications. It is still at the stage of disarming strong predication by the old plea that 'man' does not stand for any individual thing. So it

---

[1] 2ᵃ19-34.   [2] e.g. *An. Post.* 83ᵃ28-30, *Met.* 1007ᵃ32-3.
[3] *An. Post.* 83ᵃ24-32, *Met.* 1030ᵃ3-5, 11.

can still speak of such a predicate-expression as standing for something different from its subject.[1] And thereby it avoids the embarrassments into which Aristotle is later due to fall when he decides to reject the Non-identity Assumption outright in such predications. Some of the perplexities of *Metaphysics Z* stem from this rejection; for it leads him to argue that, if we take any primary subject of discourse (καθ' αὐτὸ λεγόμενον) and say just what it is, we must be producing a statement of identity, an equation which defines the subject. And this in turn helps to persuade him that the primary subjects of discourse cannot be individuals such as Socrates, who cannot be defined, but species such as man.[2] In the *Categories*, on the other hand, the primary subjects are still the individual horse or man or tree. Aristotle seems at this early stage to be much more hostile than he later becomes to Plato's treatment of the species as a basic and independent subject of discourse. So it becomes tempting to think of this element in *Metaphysics Z* as a return to, or a renewal of sympathy with, Plato. Perhaps it is, but it is the outcome of pressing a powerful objection to Plato's theories. It is a philosophical position, hard-won and (as Aristotle insists) hard-beset. If this is Platonism there is nothing of pious discipleship in it.

To return to our division of predicates. We have already enough evidence to prove that Aristotle's criticism of Plato led him to draw some distinctions in his account of predication. It is not yet enough to prove that that criticism lay at the root of his theory of predication and the categories. If Aristotle had left his contrast here it would have remained both parochial and perplexing. Its importance came from his use of it to make a far more radical distinction. Namely, it enabled him to divide all the predicates of any individual into two groups: those which hold good essentially or *per se* of their subject, as *man* does of Socrates; and those which merely happen to be true of their subject, as *white* does of Socrates. What Socrates happens to be is what he could also cease to be without ceasing to exist: after such descriptions of the subject it makes sense, even if it is false, to

---

[1] 3*b*10-19, 1*b*10.
[2] That this is one thesis that Aristotle takes seriously in *Metaphysics Z* needs no arguing: it is already afoot when 1030 6-14 is read with *Z* 6. How much of it survives the argument of the later chapters is another matter.

add 'but only sometimes'.[1] But it would be absurd to say that Socrates merely happened to be a man. If Socrates were still in existence it would be the same man in existence, whatever had happened to his colour or shape. So *man* is the kind of predicate that shows what the individual is, whereas to call Socrates 'white' is (as Aristotle can finally put it, after reflecting on the Third Man) to introduce something different from the subject, a colour that happens to belong to or be found in Socrates.[2]

Now notice one consequence of drawing the contrast in this way. We have given pride of place to the *noun* 'white' over the adjective, and this primacy of the noun was engineered by stressing the question *what white is*. The same result follows when the noun and the adjective differ in verbal form: it is 'brave' that is derived by change of inflection from 'bravery' and not vice versa, according to Aristotle in the *Categories*,[3] for to say 'X is brave' is to invite the question what bravery is; and thus again the situation comes to be represented as the presence of bravery in X. But with 'man', Aristotle says, it is different. Yet why not perform the reduction here too? Granted, as Aristotle points out, we cannot say 'There is man (or a man) in Socrates' as we can say 'There is bravery in Socrates'. But—shelving other objections to this curious test of status—why not coin one more abstract noun, say 'humanness' (since 'humanity' and 'manhood' have been pre-empted for other jobs), and let this replace 'man' in the first sentence? Why not 'There is humanness in Socrates'? And then, for all this criterion shows, being a man will be just as much something that merely happens to be true of Socrates as being brave or white. All alike will be attributes present in a Socrates who remains *ex hypothesi* different from them all.

It is not hard to piece together Aristotle's answer. It is no accident that there are predicates like *man* which form no abstract noun in current use. Not all predicate-expressions can be analysed as introducing attributes which are merely present in some individual; for there must be an identifiable individual to possess

---

[1] *Top.* 102 4–26, cf. *An. Post.* I. xxii, *Met. Δ* xxx and *E* ii.
[2] As in the stock descriptions of accidental predication, ἄλλο κατ' ἄλλου λέγεται, ἕτερόν τι ὂν τοιόνδε ἐστι, κτλ.
[3] I 11–15.

or contain them, i.e. a subject identifiable on different occasions as the same *so-and-so*, as Socrates is identifiable as the same *man*. To say baldly that something is 'the same' is, in Aristotle's view, to say something that either has no determinate sense or else requires different interpretation for different sorts of subject. So the distinction holds firm between what the individual is, as a matter of strong predication, and what else may turn up as an attribute in the individual.

Now it is notoriously this distinction that Aristotle takes as the basis of the general theory set out in his *Categories*. Reflection on the Third Man had thrown up two morals. One was that to say 'Socrates is a man' is to mention one individual and not two. But this would remain nebulous until more light was thrown on the idea of an individual. So Aristotle asked, What is it to distinguish a particular X from X-in-general? Can one answer to this be found to cover all values of X, particular virtues or times or places as well as particular men? In the *Categories* he tackled these questions by applying the second moral derived from the Third Man, the distinction we have just made out between what can be said of the individual as a matter of strong predication and what attributes may turn up in the individual.

By manipulating the first arm of the distinction Aristotle contrives to distinguish individuals from the species and genera under which they fall; in strong predication the predicate-expression never introduces an individual, always a species or genus. And then by using the second arm he is able to cross-divide these partitions so as to mark off substances from non-substances. A substance can never turn up as an attribute in some other subject in the way that, for instance, a colour or a virtue does. Meditation on the Third Man has borne fruit. And the anti-Platonic provenance of the whole account is further certified by the examples that Aristotle gives of substance in the 'strictest, primary sense': mutable things such as a man or a horse, able to house contrary attributes at different times, but never identical with the contraries they house. The substance itself—the mutable man, or horse, or tree—has no contrary. When Jaeger borrowed this proposition from the doctrine of the *Categories* he was drawing upon a logical system that could not have been constructed before Aristotle had rejected the classical Theory of Forms.[1]

This is enough to upset our confidence in the 'Platonism' postulated by Jaeger. But in lifting us off a false trail it puts us upon a true one. Aristotle's philosophical relationship to Plato had better be plotted, not by cutting off his studies of logic and method from his philosophical and scientific thinking, but by watching the interplay of the two in the Academy. So let us take Aristotle back again to his seventeenth birthday and ask: what philosophical interests, and what associated methods, could a new student expect to find in the Academy if he joined it in 367? To this the dialogues of Plato's middle period, together with the evidence of Aristotle and his pupils, give a sufficiently clear answer.

The Academy: (i) *the autonomy of the sciences*

Briefly, the student could expect to find two major and conflicting interests at work. Plato had professed to reconcile them, and the nerve of Aristotle's early work is his exposure of the conflict.

In the first place the Academy housed a great deal of activity in exact science which played no part in, for instance, the rival school of Isocrates. Greek mathematics had made huge progress since its beginnings in the sixth century. Arithmetic, impeded by a clumsy notation and bewildered by the discovery of irrationals, was becalmed; but geometry flourished. Already in the three-quarters of a century before the founding of the Academy so many theorems had been (at least notionally) proved that it became a question how to connect them in a family tree—that is, how to axiomatize the science of isolating the fewest independent assumptions from which these and further discoveries could be validly derived. This project held the attention of Plato and the Academy and issued in more than one handbook of mathematical 'elements'. Two generations later Euclid is said to have built his own canonical system of Elements on the work done in Plato's circle. Here Aristotle would meet the principal mathematicians of the day, resident or visiting; and there

---

[1] Jaeger himself held that the *Categories* in its present form is not an early work by Aristotle, but he took its doctrines to be both early and Aristotelian. His reasons for doubting the authenticity and earliness of the work (or at least its first nine chapters) were weak (*Aristotle*, p. 46, n. 3).

is some thin evidence, often quoted, that the best of them, Eudoxus, was deputizing for Plato when Aristotle arrived.

So when in the first book of the *Posterior Analytics* Aristotle sets out what he takes to be the general logical structure of a science it is naturally to mathematics and especially to geometry that he looks for his model. His picture of a systematic science probably belongs to his Academic years or shortly after, and its debt to mathematics is a commonplace; but the debt is general and not particular. It is in devising and adapting the details that he shows his hand.

Thus it is mathematics that provides him with the expository (or what he often calls 'didactic') form in which the science is to be cast. In nearly all the surviving productions of Greek mathematics traces of the workshop have been systematically removed; proofs are found for theorems which were certainly first reached by other routes. It is mathematics too that shows him the anatomy of such a science: knowledge is demonstrable, save when it is of the sort presupposed by all demonstration, and demonstration calls for an axiomatic system in which theorems are derived by valid forms of argument from principles basic to the science. It may have been mathematics that gave him his division of these principles into hypotheses, definitions, and general rules of inference. But it is when he goes beyond his mathematical brief, setting himself to analyse the logical form of the proofs and the nature and derivation of their ultimate premisses, that the philosophical interest of his account begins. The theory of syllogistic argument is his own, and he has obvious difficulty in fitting a mathematical proof into this form.[1] His long discussions of definition in the second book of the *Posterior Analytics* are designed partly to show how the mathematical model is to be adapted to the procedures and explanations of natural science.[2]

Indeed if one considers the influence of the mathematical model on his other writings it is this remaking of the ingredients that seems to matter, far more than the general recipe for a science. The recipe plays small part in his scientific and philosophical inquiries just because it is not a model for inquiry at all but for subsequent exposition of the results of inquiry. Nevertheless there remains one

---

[1] *An. Pr.* 48^{a}29-39.
[2] Cf., e.g., *An. Post.* 94^{b}8-95^{a}9 with *Met.* 996^{a}21-^{b}1.

point at which the influence of the favoured science on Aristotle's philosophizing was radically important.

The drive to axiomatize mathematics and its branches had one implication which Aristotle seems to have pressed far harder than his contemporaries: it was a drive for autonomy. The domestic economy of one field of knowledge was to be settled by fixing its frontiers. The premisses of the science were to determine what questions fell within the mathematician's competence and, not less importantly, what questions did not. Thus a cardinal section of *Posterior Analytics* I is given up to the problem what questions can be properly put to the practitioner of such-and-such a science. Other parts of the work, trading on the rule that one science studies one class of objects, denounce arguments which poach outside their own field—which try, for instance, to deduce geometrical conclusions from arithmetical premisses. Even when an axiom is applied in both arithmetic and geometry the formula has a different use in each science: the analogy between them may be recognized, but for Aristotle 'analogy' is compatible with the formula's retaining not even the most generic identity of sense. He allows that sometimes one science may take over and apply the arguments of another; but these are the exceptions. The impulse throughout the first book of the *Posterior Analytics* is towards establishing what he later calls 'exact and self-sufficient sciences'.[1]

It is the same impulse that leads him to map the field of knowledge into its departments and sub-departments.[2] Such mapwork was not his prerogative in the Academy, Plato among others took a hand in it, as an exercise in generic division. But for Aristotle the rationale was supplied by the hard-won independence of the axiomatic system; and this ran quite counter to Plato's interests and apparently to those of his contemporaries, including Speusippus.[3] When in the *Posterior Analytics* Aristotle presses for 'universality' in the theses of a science he means just that *within the given science*

---

[1] *Eth. Nic.* 1112^{a}34–^{b}1.

[2] Even in the well-known fr. 5a of the *Protrepticus*, or rather in that version of the fragment which E. de Strycker proved to contain the original argument (*Aristotle and Plato in the Mid-fourth Century*, pp. 76–104), what is remarkable is not so much the parallel which Aristotle sets up between an ethical and a physical argument as the care with which he distinguishes the two and assigns them to separate sciences.

[3] Diog. Laert. iv. 2, but the sense of this remains uncertain.

the premisses should have a given form: the subjects should be classes and not individuals, and the predicates should hold true necessarily of all and only the members of the subject class.[1] Plato had tried to engage his colleagues in a very different search for universality. The second strand that we have to trace in Aristotle's early philosophizing is his rejection of this attempt.

The Academy: (ii) *dialectic*

Under Plato mathematics could not be the sole or even the primary concern of the Academy. The *Republic* had argued for a grounding in the exact sciences as a valuable propaedeutic to philosophical inquiries, valuable because philosophy deals chiefly with a world of Forms which is not the physical world, and the numbers and exact figures and angles treated in mathematics are themselves evidently not physical objects but part of the furniture of the non-physical world explored by philosophers. But, though valuable, the mathematical sciences were not in Plato's view the highest form of inquiry; and his prime reason for demoting them is just the drive for independence which so impressed Aristotle. Mathematicians, Plato complains, argue from hypotheses which they do not step back to explain or justify. But, he goes on, there is one form of inquiry which is designed to examine people's assumptions, in mathematics or in morals or wherever: the inquiry or family of inquiries that Plato calls 'dialectic'. This alone is qualified to play governess to all the departmental sciences and to aim, by contrast with them, at a synoptic account of reality. Earlier, in the *Euthydemus*, Plato had claimed that any mathematician in his senses would hand over his discoveries to the dialectician to use; later, in the *Philebus*, 'dialectic' is still the name of a master-science which takes precedence in 'truth and exactness' over mathematical studies. A student as impressed as Aristotle by the mathematicians' drive for autonomy would have to take a stand on these issues. He would hardly be put off by the solemn recommendation in the *Republic* that young men under thirty should not be taught dialectic. Whether or not the Academy offered him any training in the subject there was enough evidence at hand to show what Plato had meant by dialectic, enough written evidence

[1] $73^{b}25-74^{a}3$.

on which to assess his claims. So what, on the evidence, would those claims come to?

Dialectic at its simplest is what Socrates and other speakers do most of the time in Plato's earlier dialogues. Someone asks, What is courage? or, Can we be taught to be good? And various answers are tried out and either brought to grief by Socratic arguments or else, supposing they can be defended from the inquisition, accepted at least provisionally as true. The propositions handled in the argument are the stock material of philosophical discussion, generally matters of common conviction or usage, sometimes the minority views of intellectuals. Aristotle in his own account of dialectic calls them 'things accepted by all men or by the majority or by the wise'.

With time, as Plato becomes more self-conscious over his methods, the devices at the speaker's command become more sophisticated. The objections turn decreasingly on trapping an opponent into self-contradiction, increasingly on serious paradoxes of the sort developed in the *Parmenides*, *Theaetetus*, and *Sophist*. There is a new insistence on the risks of over-simplification. The old Socratic hunt for the unitary definition of some general idea gives way to the attempt, reinforced by the use of generic division, to show that such an idea embraces a family of specifically different and sometimes contrary ideas. In the *Theaetetus* Socrates is still insisting as strongly as he had in the *Meno* on seizing some highly generic concept, such as knowledge or virtue, in a single definition, discounting the various forms that knowledge or virtue can take. Later, in the *Philebus*, he warns his interlocutor against generalizing irresponsibly about pleasure or wisdom before he has meticulously listed and compared the varieties of both. And the same insistence on considering all the possibilities bearing on a topic produces the recommendation in the *Parmenides* to work out the implications of denying as well as of asserting an hypothesis, and to work them out for other things as well as for the formal subject of the hypothesis. Significantly, Parmenides addresses his recommendation to the young Socrates, who has been dashing into the business of defining Goodness and Beauty and Justice without any adequate training for the job. The faults of over-simplification against which Plato is now producing his safeguards are the faults of Socrates in the earlier dialogues. It is Socrates, or Plato the Socratic, who has generalized hastily from a few favoured instances, Socrates whose trust in the telling counter-example has led him to trust the would-be telling example. Now Plato is taking precautions.

Many of these safeguards were introduced in dialogues which appeared during Aristotle's years in the Academy. All reappear in his own dialectical exercises. The impulse behind them is central in his own thinking: his standard complaint against other philosophers is that they over-simplify. Like Plato, they rely on one model of predication to explain predicates of very different types. Or they fail to realize that the same state of affairs can usually be explained in many different ways (Aristotle reduces them to four). Or they try, like Plato's Socrates, to manufacture a single definition for an expression that can be shown to have many senses: we shall come to an important example of this shortly. So it is tempting to suggest that here, at least, and in another sense than Jaeger's, Aristotle shows himself a Platonist. The methods which come to bulk large in Plato's later dialogues are Aristotle's methods. But in the circumstances we are not entitled to this claim. What may be part of the Platonism of Aristotle may equally be part of the Aristotelianism of Plato.

In any event Aristotle accepts dialectic on these terms and codifies its procedures in the *Topics*, not merely as a device for intellectual training or casual debate but as essential equipment in constructing the sciences. Yet, as he insists, the material of dialectic remains common convictions and common usage, not the self-evident truths which his admiration of mathematics persuades him are characteristic of science. Nor are the methods of dialectic confined to systematic deduction. So how could Plato claim more certainty and exactness for such discussions than for geometry? In outline the reply seemed clear, though the detail varied with time. Dialectic took its authority from its proprietary connection with the Forms. Its successes were neither arbitrary nor confined to corrigible personal agreement because it was the sole method competent to identify and map those stable realities of which Plato in his middle dialogues had argued the physical world to house only deceptive reflections.

So when Aristotle came to the Academy there would seem to be two principal strands in Plato's large claims for dialectic. One was the thesis that above the special sciences struggling for autonomy there stands a quite general survey of what there is, a master-science without whose authorization the work of the rest is provisional and insecure. The other was the Theory, or Theories, of Forms. Aristotle came to think that dialectic itself was competent to undermine both these claims. Recent controversy over the question whether he was a 'Platonist' in his earlier years has focused on his handling of the second claim. We have said enough of that. The originality of his position in the Academy will be clearer if we consider his rejection of the first.

Return or Advance?

This is a twice-told tale,[1] and I need not dwell on it before discussing its moral for our inquiry. Aristotle in his earlier works turned two principal arguments against Plato's master-science. One was drawn from his own model of a science. A master-science, he urged, must set out to prove the premises of the others, that is, to establish by deduction from its own quite general axioms the requisite special truths on which the departmental sciences were based. But no such proof can be given. Nor can any general proof be given of the rules of inference applied in these sciences, such as the law of excluded middle. If Plato had attended to the actual procedures of those disciplines whose independence he deplored he would have been saved from this piece of logical *naïveté*.

The other argument was one more accusation of over-simplifying. There cannot be a single synoptic science of all existing things because there is no such genus as the genus of existing things; and one, though not the only, reason for this is that the verb 'to exist' (strictly, the verb 'to be' in its existential role) is a word with many senses. For a cat to exist is for it to be alive, and alive in more ways than a vegetable. For a patch of ice to exist is for it to be, *inter alia*, hard and cold; when it ceases to be these things it melts and ceases to exist. At the most general level, for a substance to exist is one thing, for a quality to exist is another, for a quantity it is yet another. Plato had not drawn these distinctions when he engaged in his hunt for the common elements or

---

[1] The evidence for what follows is discussed in 'Logic and Metaphysics in some earlier works of Aristotle', in *Aristotle and Plato in the Mid-fourth Century*, pp. 163–90; and 'Aristotle on the snares of ontology', in *New Essays on Plato and Aristotle*, pp. 69–95.

principles of all existing things, στοιχεῖα τῶν ὄντων. He was the dupe of one multivocal word.

When we turn to *Metaphysics Γ E* all is changed. There is, after all, a single and universal science of what exists. If those who looked for the elements of all existing things were on the track of this science, their enterprise was respectable. In the previous book of the *Metaphysics* Aristotle has made a good deal of the first objection to any such general science; now that objection is quietly dropped. The new science is not an axiomatic system; and lest it seem curiously like those non-departmental inquiries which Aristotle has previously dubbed 'dialectical' or 'logical' and branded as un-scientific, dialectic is quietly demoted to one department of its old province so as to leave room for the new giant.[1] It is the second objection to the programme that is triumphantly disarmed. The verb 'to exist' is not to be dismissed as a mere source of puns: the simple dichotomy 'univocal or multivocal, synonymous or homony-mous' is not sophisticated enough to catch such a word. It is, cer-tainly, a word with a great range of senses, but these senses are systematically connected. They can be sorted into one which is primary and others which are variously derivative from the first. The primary sense is that in which substances, the ultimate subjects of reference in all discourse, exist; and this sense will reappear as a common element in our analyses of the existence of non-substances such as colours or times or sizes. Their existence must be explained as the existence of some substance or substances having them as attributes. Given an understanding of this reduction, an inquiry into substance will be an inquiry into all existence.

So the search for the 'elements of existing things' is reinstated, and it is tempting to say that in his metaphysics Aristotle has come back to Platonism rather than moved from it. But, again, 'Platon-ism' in what sense? The old questions must be pressed. Certainly Aristotle seems prepared to represent his broad programme as conceived in the tradition of Plato's metaphysics, and certainly the methods by which he begins to carry it out are descended from Plato's dialectic and not from the axiomatic systems which he had taken for a model in the departmental sciences. This is why he can inaugurate it by arguing dialectically for logical axioms which, as

[1] Cf. 1004^{b}17-26 with *de soph. el.* 169^{b}25, al.

he has always insisted, cannot be axiomatically proved without begging the question. But what lies at the heart of the new enterprise, including the discussion of the axioms, is Aristotle's analysis of substance. And that analysis is not intelligible except as the product of his criticism of Plato.

It may be argued, on the other hand, that the device by which he turns an inquiry into substance into a survey of all that exists is a conscious debt to Plato or to the partisans of Plato's metaphysics. For the idea that an expression has *focal meaning*, that is to say that it has a primary sense by reference to which its other senses can be explained, seems to have been first clearly set out and exploited in an argument for Plato's Forms. The argument was retailed by Aristotle in his essay *On Ideas*,[1] and that essay is earlier than the earliest criticisms of Plato in our text of the *Metaphysics*. But then it becomes a puzzle why Aristotle took so long to appreciate the value of this device. True, the illustration of it in the original argument was one which he evidently found unacceptable. He had to work out his own examples, and he pitched on the expressions 'medical' and 'healthy' as favourite illustrations. It is medical skill that is called 'medical' in the primary sense; a medical knife is a tool required for the exercise of that skill, medical treatment is the regimen prescribed in the exercise of that skill, and so forth. But dissatisfaction with the original illustration scarcely explains, what the evidence shows to have been the case, that Aristotle was at one time content to work with the simple dichotomy 'univocal or multivocal' and saw little if any virtue in the *tertium quid*. It may then seem plausible to suggest that, as he renewed his sympathy with Plato's metaphysical programme, so he came to see new virtue in a technique that had been evolved in support of that programme.

This explanation will not do. Aristotle's appreciation of focal meaning seems to have increased steadily in his work, as can be seen from an analysis of the strata in his philosophical lexicon, *Metaphysics Δ*. And for this a different explanation suggests itself. There are two very different impulses in his philosophy which do not naturally mesh together. In the use of focal meaning he found himself, with increasing confidence, able to mesh them. One of these we have already seen. He is occupationally sensitive

[1] *De Ideis* fr. 3 Ross (Alexander *in Met.* 82. 11–83. 17).

to expressions with more than one meaning. In the Academy he and Speusippus worked out methods of showing the different senses carried by a single word, methods which come down finally to finding a different paraphrase for the word in its different roles. For Aristotle, this is one more expression of the conviction that he shared with J. L. Austin, that 'it is an occupational disease of philosophers to over-simplify—if indeed it is not their occupation'.

But when he turns to the positive business of explaining one of his own key-terms, a different method comes in view. Now he is liable to start from some special, favoured situation of use. Given this starting-point there are likely to be uses of the expression which do not match up to the favoured conditions, and with these uses he deals in various ways. Sometimes he discounts them; sometimes he stretches and weakens his description of the basic situation to cover them; finally he sees a better way of accommodating such deviant forms.

These manœuvres can be readily illustrated. The first is familiar from his reply to Zeno's paradox of the flying arrow.[1] He cheerfully concedes Zeno's claim that nothing can be said to be moving at an instant, and insists only that it cannot be said to be stationary either. He is so preoccupied with the requirement that any movement must take a certain time to cover a certain distance (and, as a corollary, that any stability must take a certain time but cover no distance) that he discounts any talk of motion, and therefore of velocity, at an instant. He takes no account of the fact that in Greek, as in English, one can ask how fast a man was running when he broke the tape, i.e. at an instant. Yet he could have accommodated this derivative use of expressions for motion and velocity admirably by recourse to focal meaning, and his failure to do this spoilt his reply to Zeno and bedevilled the course of dynamics.

The second manœuvre can be seen in his analysis of change in the first book of the *Physics*. In the fourth and fifth chapters of that book he argues that any change implies a swing between contrary attributes—either from one to the other, or somewhere on a spectrum between the two. In the sixth and seventh chapters he argues that there must be something to make the swing, that is, something

---

[1]   *Phys.* 239^a 23–^{b} 9, 30–3; cf. 'Zeno and the Mathematicians', *Proceedings of the Aristotelian Society*, lviii (1958), pp. 216–22.

which changes but survives the change. His first illustrations show the typical situation from which he argues: something expanding or contracting, or something that is light turning dark. But he stretches his analysis of this situation to cover an instrument going out of tune, the building of a house from a jumble of bricks, the shaping of a statue from unformed bronze; and in the process the two basic ideas, of a *contrary* and of a *subject*, are also inevitably extended. A contrary attribute may now be a nameless state of affairs which is identified only by its lack of the positive marks which could, in some sense of 'could' which Aristotle proposes to explain, have been present. He cites as examples the unsculptedness of bronze, the disorder of bricks that could be a house. The idea of a subject is similarly enlarged to take account of situations which are not at all a matter of contrary states succeeding each other in some separately identifiable subject. Among such situations he mentions the birth of a plant or an animal. The subject, the 'matter', is no longer required to secure its identity by satisfying some categorical description, answering to some such classification as 'a man' or 'a tree'; for the man and the tree are the outcome, and not the residual subjects, of such processes as these. So, with each step away from the original situation, something seems to be dropped or weakened: some condition for the central or typical use of the expressions concerned.

I am not saying that this is a bad procedure: it is a familiar and valuable procedure. Without it we could not speak as we do of the feelings and thinkings of other kinds of animal than men. I cite it to illustrate Aristotle's inclination to start from the favoured case in explaining some important expressions and then move outwards.[1] But there are hazards. In the second book of the *Physics* Aristotle argues that natural processes have as much right to be explained in terms of ends and purposes as the products of any skilled artificer. The reader acquiesces when he points out that we speak of spiders

---

[1] There is a wealth of other instances. One of the best known is his description of the terms in the syllogism. In all figures of the syllogism he calls the predicate of the conclusion the *larger* or *major*, and the subject of the conclusion the *lesser* or *minor*; but these descriptions, and his explanation of them (*An. Pr.* 26 ^{a} 21–3), are appropriate only to the first figure. Similarly with his description and explanation of the middle term (25^{b}35–6). See W. and M. Kneale, *The Development of Logic*, pp. 68–71, G. Patzig, *Die arist. Syllogistik*, ch. iii.

spinning their webs or swallows building their nexts 'for a purpose', but he starts to squirm when Aristotle goes on: 'As one proceeds in this way step by step one can see that with plants too things happen for some end—leaves are grown to shade the fruit, roots are sent down to get moisture.' As he proceeds step by step, Aristotle progressively disengages our talk of purposive behaviour from the idea of having skills or being able to think out steps to an end, and it is not clear where the process is to stop. Now we hanker for Aristotle's other approach, the readiness to detect and delimit the different senses of one multivocal expression. It is a relief, and an achievement, when he marries this second technique to his interest in setting out from some central, paradigm situation of use. They are wedded in the concept of focal meaning, and we need not talk of Platonism in order to explain Aristotle's steadily increasing appreciation of this fertile device.

'Platonism', to be sure, is a slippery term. But we might have looked in many other directions for signs of Plato's influence on Aristotle and, given due care, brought home the booty. We took this direction because the others, in physics and psychology for instance, have been and continue to be well explored, whereas in logic and metaphysics the hunt seemed to get off to a false start. So long as the logical and metaphysical strands in Aristotle's thinking were taken to be initially separate, his progress in both became unintelligible.

It seems possible now to trace that progress from sharp and rather schematic criticism of Plato to an avowed sympathy with Plato's general metaphysical programme. But the sympathy is one thing, the concrete problems and procedures which give content to Aristotle's project are another. They are his own, worked out and improved in the course of his own thinking about science and dialectic. There seems no evidence of a stage in that thinking at which he confused admiration with acquiescence.

P. T. GEACH

Some Problems about Time

When I was invited to give this philosophical lecture and was considering which subject to talk about, I found my mind turning towards a great philosopher, a Fellow of this Academy, who died just forty years ago: John Ellis McTaggart. I consider myself very lucky to have been introduced to McTaggart's work early in my philosophical life; McTaggart sets high standards of clarity, rigour, and seriousness for a young philosopher to try to live up to. I suppose McTaggart is little read nowadays; he was a metaphysician, and metaphysics is not in fashion; even those who stridently call out for metaphysics to be done do not produce any themselves, and ignore the one British metaphysical work of genius in this century. But I make bold to put into McTaggart's mouth the words of one of his favourite poets:

> But after, they will know me. If I stoop
> Into a dark tremendous sea of cloud,
> It is but for a time; I press God's lamp
> Close to my breast; its splendour, soon or late,
> Will pierce the gloom: I shall emerge one day.
> (Browning's *Paracelsus*)

I shall be talking about a subject that was of central concern for McTaggart—the problems of time. I begin by examining a view of time that is now widely held in one form or another. In its crudest form, this view makes time out to be simply one of the dimensions in which bodies are extended; bodies have not three dimensions but four. An instantaneous solid is as much a mere artificially abstracted aspect of a concrete thing as a surface without depth is; photographs of a man at different ages represent different three-dimensional cross-sections of a four-dimensional whole. Time is only subjectively and relatively distinct from the other dimensions in which things are extended. We may illustrate this by the simile of horizontal and vertical; though at any given point on the Earth's surface a unique vertical direction can be picked out, there is no cosmic distinction of horizontal and vertical, and people at different places on the Earth will take different directions to be vertical. Or again, as Quine says: 'Just as forward and backward are distinguishable only relative to an orientation, so, according to Einstein's relativity principle, space and time are distinguishable only relative to a velocity'; and he speaks of 'an hour-thick slice of the four-dimensional material world . . . perpendicular to the time axis'.[1]

Since Einstein, indeed, this sort of view has been very popular with philosophers who try to understand physics and physicists who try to do philosophy. Some of the arguments used in its favour are decidedly odd. Thus, it is supposed to be supported by the fact that we can represent local motion in a graph with axes representing space and time; the line drawn on the graph-paper is taken to represent a 'world line' or 'four-dimensional worm' stretching through a 'space-time continuum'. We might as well be asked to believe that the use of temperature charts requires the physical existence of 'world lines' in a 'temperature-time continuum'. Obviously the two axes of a graph, though themselves magnitudes of the same sort, may represent quite heterogeneous magnitudes.

Another odd argument is that modern formal logic, in particular quantification theory, can be applied to propositions about physical objects only if these objects are regarded as four-dimensional. This is not at all true. In Quine's *Methods of Logic*, for example, we learn from his precept and practice how to apply modern formal logic to propositions of ordinary language; there is no obstacle to such application, he points out, in the sort of ambiguity that is resoluble by considering 'circumstances of the argument as a whole—

[1] *Word and Object*, p. 172.

speaker, hearer, scene, date, and underlying problem and purpose';
all that we really need is that the sense and reference of expressions
should 'stay the same throughout the space of the argument' (op.
cit., p. 43). In a later work, *Word and Object*, Quine does indeed
pay lip service to the need of four-dimensional talk; but the parts
of his book essentially involving such talk could easily be cut out;
the great majority of the sentences given as logical examples are in
a streamlined version of English, not in four-dimension-ese; and
Quine's discussions almost all relate to the mode of significance of
terms and the structure of propositions in this near-vernacular
language. Thus it is not open to Quine to maintain that if we are
to be 'serious about applying modern logic to temporal entities',
in particular if we are so to apply quantification theory, then we
need 'the four-dimensional view' as 'part and parcel' of what we
are doing.[1]

Logic would not be much use for arguments about concrete
realities if we had to hold that, outside pure mathematics, logic
applied only to a language yet to be constructed, one that nobody
talks or writes. Logic was a going concern, and was applied to
inferences about concrete matters, long before anyone ever dreamed
up four-dimensional language. If all these past applications of logic
had to be written off as misconceived, we could not have high hopes
for future applications to an as yet non-existent language. Quine is
certainly not himself prepared to write off so much of logic's past.

Nor ought any logician to try to accommodate his doctrines to
demands made in the name of contemporary physics. Logic must
be kept rigid, come what may in the way of physical theories; for
only so can it serve as a crowbar to overthrow unsatisfactory theories.
Lavoisier remarked that the phlogistonists ascribed different and
indeed incompatible properties to phlogiston in order to explain
different experimental results; what a good thing there were not
then logicians prepared to bend logic in the interests of the phlogiston theory—to say that these were 'complementary' accounts of
phlogiston, both true so long as you did not combine them!

The view that time is merely a fourth dimension in which

---

[1] 'Mr. Strawson on Logical Theory', *Mind*, October 1953, p. 443. On the previous page
of the same article, Quine had quoted the very passage from his own *Methods of Logic* that
I quoted just now!

things extend is in any event quite untenable. On this view, the variation of a poker's temperature with time would simply mean that there were different temperatures at different positions along the poker's time-axis. But this, as McTaggart remarked, would no more be a *change* in temperature than a variation of temperature along the poker's length would be.[1] Similarly for other sorts of change. A man's growth would be regarded as the tapering of a four-dimensional body along its time-axis from later to earlier; but this again would no more be a change than is a poker's tapering along its length towards its point. We thus have a view that really abolishes change, by reducing change to a mere variation of attributes between different parts of a whole. But, as McTaggart again remarked, no change, no time; the view we are discussing countenances talk of a *time* axis, but such talk is inappropriate on these premises.

The view really commits us to saying that time is an illusion. In Absolute Reality there is a changeless arrangement of four-dimensional solids; in Present Experience certain aspects of this arrangement appear to our perceptions as changes of three-dimensional bodies. McTaggart too thought that time was an illusion—though he had a very different account to give of the Absolute Reality that we misperceive as changeable bodies. But time cannot be an illusion; and certain arguments of McTaggart's own, ironically enough, are readily adapted to prove this.

The arguments in question show that certain features other than time in our experience cannot possibly be illusory. Thus, there really must be error in the universe; for there appears to be error, and if this appearance is false, then again there is error.[2] Parmenides and Mrs. Eddy alike are in a quandary what to say about the 'error of mortal mind'. Again (as mention of Mrs. Eddy reminds me) there is plain incoherence in the optimistic doctrine that misery is only an 'error of mortal mind': if my 'mortal mind' thinks I am miserable, then I am miserable, and it is not an illusion that I am miserable.[3] (Of course, so far as this goes, it might still be true that our misery would vanish if we all perceived things without illusions; McTaggart could consistently hold that, as he in fact did.) But

---

[1]   *The Nature of Existence*, vol. ii, sections 315-16.
[2]   Ibid., section 510.
[3]   Ibid., section 857.

now, quite similarly, even if my distinction between past, present, and future aspects of physical things is a fragmentary misperception of changeless realities, it remains true that I have various and uncombinable illusions as to which realities are present. I must therefore have these illusions not simultaneously but one after another; and then there is after all real time and real change.

One might perhaps hold that time and change are only in the mind, in the sense that only a mind lives through time and undergoes change; in this sense, misery is 'only in the mind'. But this sense of the phrase must be sharply distinguished from the sense in which a thing's being 'only in the mind' implies its unreality. A man can no more 'only think' he has changing impressions of the world than he can 'only think' he is unhappy.

McTaggart tried to show that there was a difference between error and misery, on the one hand, and time on the other. A state of error or misery cannot be just illusory, because to be under such an illusion would be a state of real error or misery; but a state of self-consciousness that presents itself as temporal need not, he argued, be on that account really temporal.[1] This distinction is sound, so far as it goes; however, it misses the point that temporal appearance requires the existence of diverse *and uncombinable* impressions as to what is present. I am not arguing that *each single* state of self-consciousness must really be temporal because it presents itself as temporal; I am arguing that the *variety* of states each person experiences must really be, as it appears to be, a change in his experience, because these states are combinable only in succession, and not simultaneously.

However, we might try modifying the view of a four-dimensional and changeless *physical* reality by allowing that there is real change in the world of experience. There would then be a set of observing minds each of which continuously 'moved on' from one part of the four-dimensional physical world to another; though the ordered cross-sections of four-dimensional bodies would then appear to an observing mind as earlier and later, they would not really stand in temporal relations—only in the experiences of the observing minds would there be real time and change.

To make this story consistent, the observing minds must be

[1] Op. cit., section 511.

supposed incorporeal and physically dimensionless; otherwise there would, contrary to hypothesis, be real change in the physical world. How then can mind be said to *move*? We need not make heavy weather of this; a simple analogy may help us out. The order of printed words on a page is an unchanging spatial order; but it appears as a temporal order to a reader whose attention moves on from word to word and from line to line—and surely nobody will have felt a difficulty over my use of 'moves on' in this context.

The theory I have just sketched is *one* theory of time to be found in the opening discourse of the Time Traveller in Wells; and it is a theory that lends itself to speculative developments. Why should we assume that an observing mind's attention must always travel on in one direction like that of a slow, plodding, reader? Even normal minds may sometimes slip back to a part of the physical continuum that their attention has already scanned; Wells in fact gives us this 'explanation' of vivid reminiscence. And why should not a practised observer learn a skill like that of the practised reader, of looking before and after, seeing, for example, by anticipation those parts of the physical continuum that he would observe only later on by the normal movement of his focus of observation?

This whole theory, though, is open to the gravest objections. It incorporates an extreme form of Cartesian dualism: the human body is a changeless four-dimensional solid, the human mind a changeable dimensionless entity that reads off data for its *cogitationes* along one dimension of this solid. The theory is thus exposed to all the general arguments against Cartesian dualism; and also, to certain special objections. Though admitting an inability to understand the mind's power to move the body, Descartes did not venture to deny this power; even the Occasionalist disciples of Descartes, who did deny such a power to the mind, held that God would miraculously tamper with our normally automatic bodily machinery so that within limits it should move as we wish. On the theory we are now considering, there is no time or change except in minds; the four-dimensional physical world is an absolutely fixed order, not to be altered by any will, human or divine. The mind just cannot interfere with what will physically come to be; in fact, the very phrase I just used is only a loose manner of referring to those regions of the changeless four-dimensional world which a given mind is next going to observe.

Such a view would reduce the will of man to an impotent chimera, buzzing in a void and feeding upon second intentions (in the words of the perhaps legendary medieval conundrum). It may be beneath the dignity of philosophy to say 'We know our will is free, Sir, and there's an end on't'; but we do know that our plans and purposes radically alter our physical environment, and there's an end on't; any contrary theory, however plausibly argued, just has to be false.

The view that our decisions cannot bring about physical changes may be called *fatalism*. Fatalism has a bad name among philosophers, like solipsism; arguments in favour of either will be dismissed as ingenious sophistries, and a reduction of a thesis to either counts as checkmate in the philosophical game. Determinists are mostly anxious to repudiate fatalism: to maintain only that human designs are predictable from causes, not that they do not have effects. I think this defence is open only to some varieties of determinist; other determinists evade fatalism only by a sort of doublethink; indeed, it sometimes looks as though doublethink were being deliberately advocated as a way out of free-will puzzles. Be that as it may, fatalism naked and undisguised has a strong imaginative and emotional appeal for many people. John Buchan was such a person; in his admirable novel *The Gap in the Curtain* he worked out the consequences of that purely mental 'time-travel' into the future which, as we just saw, would be allowed as a theoretical possibility by the theory of mental observers' scanning an unchanging physical world. I will not spoil this novel, for those of you who have not read it, by giving away the plot; I will just remark that the fatalism is consistently upheld. Buchan's characters merely get a glimpse of the future, with no power to change it; as in Oriental tales of Fate, what is to be comes to pass regardless of man's designs.

We find it easy to imagine the future as a country into which we are travelling and which is there before we travel into it; a country of which we might get a Pisgah sight through a break in the clouds before we actually get there. Here it is interesting to notice the change of meaning that has happened to the phrases 'the next world' or 'the world to come'. They originally meant the *age* to come, *vitam venturi saeculi*, which is to follow the return of Messiah; nowadays, to many people, they suggest some other *place*, as when one calls Mars 'another world'.

The fundamental difficulty about this picture is quite different from the obvious one. At the price of adopting dualistic fatalism, one can, as I have shown, make some kind of sense out of this talk about travelling; it is not the travelling that raises the real difficulty, but the destination. What *is* (say) the England of 1984? Is there really such an object *in rerum natura*, distinct from the England of 1965?

It is very natural to talk this way: very natural to think of the successive phases in an object's history as ordered parts of the object itself—somehow like the segments of a worm's body. I shall here borrow an example from McTaggart; he, of course, did not believe in Time, but his example suits well enough for recent statements of this view, for example, by Quine and J. J. C. Smart. The phrase 'St. Paul's in the nineteenth century' would designate an individual, and so would, for example, 'St. Paul's in 1801'; and these must be two distinct individuals, for many predications that are true of St. Paul's in (the whole of) the nineteenth century are false of St. Paul's in 1801 and vice versa. Moreover, 'St. Paul's in 1801' will designate a part of the whole designated by 'St. Paul's in the nineteenth century'; and if we take the individuals designated by 'St. Paul's in 1801', 'St. Paul's in 1802', up to 'St. Paul's in 1900', they will together include all the content of the individual designated by 'St. Paul's in the nineteenth century'.[1]

I think this account involves an erroneous analysis of propositions into subject and predicate. Let us consider one sort of predications that might be used to discriminate the individuals designated by phrases like 'St. Paul's in 1856': if you were answering the question 'How many visitors were there?' you might have to give a different answer for each year of the nineteenth century and of course a different answer again for the century as a whole. We

---

[1] *The Nature of Existence*, vol. i, section 163. It is of no present concern that McTaggart chose to use the word 'substance' where I use 'individual'. He was clearly assuming that the Christian era begins on 1 January A.D. 1, so that the nineteenth century runs from 1 January 1801 to 31 December 1900.

can certainly consider a proposition: 'There were *n* visitors to St. Paul's in 1856', as a predication about St. Paul's; I have chosen this example to show that the problem I am raising does not arise from superficial grammatical considerations, for here we have in any case a logical subject of predication that is not a grammatical subject.[1] The question is whether we can also analyse the same proposition as a predication about St. Paul's in 1856; as attaching to the subject 'St. Paul's in 1856' the predicate: 'There were *n* visitors to . . .'. This analysis is not excluded because the other is possible; we may surely analyse 'Queen Anne's hat was red' equally well as predicating of Queen Anne's hat that it was red and as predicating of Queen Anne that she had a red hat; similarly, it could be argued, our example *both* predicates something of St. Paul's *and* predicates something of St. Paul's in 1856. But I think the second analysis can be excluded on other grounds; phrases like 'St. Paul's in 1856' cannot be taken as logical subjects at all.

Let us shift to another example: 'McTaggart in 1901 was a philosopher holding Hegel's dialectic to be valid, and McTaggart in 1921 was a philosopher not holding Hegel's dialectic to be valid.' If we regarded 'McTaggart in 1901' and 'McTaggart in 1921' as designating two individuals, then we must also say they designate two philosophers: one philosopher believing Hegel's dialectic to be valid, and another philosopher believing Hegel's dialectic not to be valid. To be sure, on the view I am criticizing the phrases 'McTaggart in 1901' and 'McTaggart in 1921' would not designate two philosophers, but two temporal slices of one philosopher. But just that is the trouble: for a predicate like 'philosopher believing so-and-so' can of course be true only of a philosopher, not of a temporal slice of a philosopher. So if our example, which is a plain and true[2] empirical proposition, were construed as a conjunction of two predications about temporal slices of McTaggart, then it would turn out necessarily false; which is an absurd result.

[1] Anyone disturbed by this sort of subject-predicate analysis may be reminded that it has an Aristotelian precedent. Aristotle analyses 'There is a single science of (a pair of) contraries' into subject '(pair of) contraries', predicate 'there being a single science of them'; and he explains this as meaning, not that contraries *are* there being a single science of them, but that *it is true to say of them* that there is a single science of them. (*Analytica Priora* 48*b*4 ff.)

[2] Cf. *The Nature of Existence*, vol. i, sections 48–50.

The absurdity does not come about just for my chosen example; it arises equally for Quine's example 'Tabby at t is eating mice';[1] for a cat can eat mice at time t, but a temporal slice of a cat, Tabby-at-t, cannot eat mice anyhow.

The friends of temporal slices will no doubt here pray leave to amend the examples so that they contain predicates fitting temporal slices, instead of predicates like 'philosopher believing so-and-so' or 'cat eating mice', which fit living beings and not temporal slices of living beings. But we ought not to grant them leave to amend. The whole ground for treating, for example, 'McTaggart in 1901' and 'McTaggart in 1921' as designating two distinct individuals was that we seemed to find predicates true of the one and false of the other. But now we find that such predicates as appear in ordinary empirical propositions are often of a kind that could not be true of temporal slices; so the ground for recognizing temporal slices as distinct individuals has been undercut; and we ought to reject temporal slices from our ontology, rather than cast around for new-fashioned predicates to distinguish them by.

I conclude that temporal slices are merely 'dreams of our language'. It is no less a mistake to treat 'McTaggart in 1901' and 'McTaggart in 1921' as designating individuals than it would be so to treat 'nobody' or 'somebody'. If we take the name 'McTaggart' as logical subject of both clauses in our example, no such troubles arise; for, on the face of it, the predicates we are attaching to this subject are a compatible pair, namely 'philosopher believing in 1901 that Hegel's dialectic is valid' and 'philosopher not believing in 1921 that Hegel's dialectic is valid'.

Predicates of this sort, in which dates are mentioned, are a long way above the most fundamental level of temporal discourse. Our ability to keep track of the date and the time of day depends on a set of enormously complicated natural phenomena; such phenomomena, serving 'for signs and for seasons and for days and for years', might easily not have been available. We can easily imagine rational beings, living on a cloud-bound planet like Venus, who had no ready means of keeping dates or telling the time, and were too well endowed by Nature with the necessities and amenities of life to feel any need to contrive such means. Clearly, such creatures might

[1] *Word and Object*, p. 173.

still speak of one thing's happening at the same time as another, or after another, and might have past, present, and future tenses in their language. This is grass-roots temporal discourse; it is perverse to try to analyse it by means of the vastly more complex notions that are involved in saying 'in 1901' or 'at time *t*'.

In particular, it is definitely wrong to analyse an unsophisticated simultaneity proposition, like 'Peter was writing a letter and (at the same time) Jenny was practising the piano', in terms of what happened at some one time *t*—'For some time *t*, Peter was writing a letter at *t* and Jenny was practising the piano at *t*.' Such a use of 'at the same time' as we have here does not involve any reference to an apparatus or technique for telling the time (and still less, a reference to Absolute Time). On the contrary, telling the time depends on knowing some of these primitive simultaneity propositions to be true. Telling the time by an ordinary clock involves observing that the long hand points (say) to the 12 and the short hand *at the same time* points to the 6; clearly we do not need another clock to verify that it *is* at the same time. A physicist may protest that he simply cannot understand 'at the same time' except via elaborate stipulations about observing instruments; his protest may be dismissed out of hand, for he could not describe the set-up of any apparatus except by certain conditions' having to be fulfilled *together*, i.e. simultaneously, by the parts of the apparatus.

Simultaneity is involved in empirical statements; but it is not an empirical relation like neighbourhood in space. The natural expression for simultaneity is not a relative term like 'simultaneous with', but a conjunction like 'while' joining clauses; it is an accident of English idiom that 'at the same time' seems to refer to a certain *time* that has to be *the same*, and the words for 'at the same time' in other languages—Latin *simul*, Greek ἅμα, Polish *razem*—have no such suggestion.

These conjunctions joining clauses no more stand for a proper relation than, for example, 'or' does. If I say I can see with my myopic eyes something over there that is *either* a hawk *or* a handsaw, I do not claim to observe a hawk in the act of being an alternative to a hand-saw; to try to conceive a relation of alternativeness between such concrete objects would soon land us in paradoxes. Like alternativeness, simultaneity is not a relational concept, but is one of those concepts called transcendental by the medievals, formal in Wittgenstein's *Tractatus*, and topic-neutral by Ryle; the last term is the most informative of the three—it shows us that these concepts are not departmental but crop up in discourse generally.

Because of this topic-neutrality, 'at the same time' belongs not to a special science but to logic; its laws are logical laws, like the so-called De Morgan laws for 'or'. Physicists may have interesting things to tell us about the physical possibilities of synchronizing clocks by the transmission of electromagnetic signals; but this information is wholly irrelevant to the logic of basic simultaneity propositions. Our practical grasp of this logic is not to be called in question on account of recondite physics; for without such a practical grasp we could not understand even elementary propositions in physics, so a physicist who casts doubt upon it is sawing off the branch he sits upon. And a theoretical account of this logic must be given not by physicists but by logicians.

I remarked just now that the natural, primitive, way to speak of simultaneity is to use a conjunction joining clauses, rather than a relational term like 'simultaneous with'. In general, I think we need to get events expressed in a propositional style, rather than by using name-like phrases (what Kotarbiński has called 'onomatoids'). We need, that is to say, propositions like 'Wellington fought Napoleon at Waterloo after George III first went mad', rather than 'George III's first attack of madness is earlier than the Battle of Waterloo'.

Some years ago philosophers were all the while talking of people and things as being 'logical constructions out of events'. This was a topsy-turvy view: nobody ever has talked or is going to talk a language containing no names of people or things but only names of events, and the claim that our language could in principle be replaced by such a language is perfectly idle. On the other hand, any sentence in which an event is represented by a noun-phrase like 'Queen Anne's death' appears to be easily replaceable by an equivalent one in which this onomatoid is paraphrased away; we could use instead a clause attaching some part of the verb 'to die' to the subject 'Queen Anne'. Any ordinary sentence, that is, will allow of such paraphrase; philosophical sentences like 'Queen Anne's death is a particular' may resist translation, but we can get on very well without them. On the other hand, 'Queen Anne's death is a past event' goes over into 'Queen Anne has died' (or 'is dead'), and 'The news of Queen Anne's death made Lord Bolingbroke swear' goes over into 'Lord Bolingbroke swore because he heard Queen Anne had died'. Cutting out the onomatoids in this way, we get a manner of speaking in which persons and things are mentioned but events do not even appear to be mentioned; so far from its being people and things that are logical constructions out of events, events are logical constructions out of people and things.

McTaggart's proof that time is unreal has often been criticized on the score that it essentially depends on treating 'past', 'present', and 'future' as logical predicates in propositions like 'Queen Anne's death is past'. I think I could show that this is too easy a way of dismissing McTaggart; some at least of his arguments could be restated so as to avoid the criticism. Anyhow, the critics have oddly failed to see that if the ostensible predicate 'past' in 'Queen Anne's death is past' is not to be parsed as a logical predicate, then equally the phrase 'Queen Anne's death' is not to be regarded as being, or even going proxy for, a logical subject.

In his lectures on Logical Atomism, Bertrand Russell forcibly argued that a phrase like 'the Kaiser's death' is not even a description, let alone a name, of an object nameable by a proper name, but rather goes proxy for the corresponding proposition 'The Kaiser is dead'. For example, people might in 1918 assert or deny or doubt the Kaiser's death; this shows that the onomatoid 'the Kaiser's death' goes proxy for a clause 'The Kaiser is dead'. (Observe that it would be nonsense to speak of asserting or denying the Kaiser's *spiked helmet*—this phrase *is* a description of a nameable object.)

To be sure, later on in the same course of lectures Russell tells us that a person or thing is 'a series of classes of particulars, and therefore a logical fiction'.[1] This often happens with a work of Russell's: you pays your money and you takes your pick. I have no hesitation which of the two views I should pick. For the first, there are sound logical reasons; for the second, there is only an ontological prejudice of Russell's—'the things that are really real last a very short time'.[2]

[1] *Logic and Knowledge* (Allen & Unwin, 1956), pp. 186–9.
[2] Ibid., p. 274.

G

There is more than this wrong with Russell's treatment of persons. He is trying to ride two theories of classes at once: the no-class theory (that classes are fictions) and what we may call the composition theory (that classes are composed of their members and series of their terms). Only the composition theory, *plus* the segmented-worm idea of a person's temporal parts, can make it plausible that a series of classes is what a person is; Russell then concludes that, being a series of classes, a person is a fiction, by jumping over to the no-class theory. I doubt the staying power of either horse; to try to ride both at once is really desperate.

If my own arguments are sound, time-order and space-order are radically different. We can indeed verbally use such forms as '*A* is between *B* and *C*' for either sort of order; but I think this only leads to confusion. Spatial order relates individual objects: Bill is between Tom and Joe. We can get grammatically similar sentences about time-order by using onomatoids like 'the Battle of Waterloo'; but the logically perspicuous way to represent time-order is a complex sentence whose sub-clauses *report* (not name) events, these clauses being joined by temporal conjunctions like 'and then', 'and at the same time', 'while', etc. Such conjunctions, which form narrative propositions out of simpler ones, are of course quite different in category from relative terms that form propositions out of names or name-substitutes; and time 'relations' are not to be spoken of in the same logical tone of voice as space relations.

If in '*x* adjoins *y*' we replace the schematic letters by names or descriptions of bodies, the resulting proposition will not be even a description, let alone a name, of something that can itself adjoin a body. On the other hand, if we replace the letters in '*p* and then *q*' by narrative propositions like 'Queen Anne died' or 'Wellington defeated Napoleon', the result is again a narrative proposition reporting a course of events; and this can be used to build up more complex narrative propositions, of such forms as 'while *r*, (*p* and then *q*)'. Nothing analogous to this is possible for propositions describing spatial order: '*x* is between (*y* is above *w*) and *z*' gives us mere gibberish if we replace the schematic letters by names.

Miss Anscombe has raised an interesting objection to this

argument. She rightly remarked that from a grammatical point of view 'where' will serve as a conjunction forming sentences out of sentences just as well as 'when' will. To give an example: we may join 'The Dome of the Rock was built' and 'Solomon's Temple was built' either with 'when' or with 'where' so as to make sense; the 'when' proposition is of course false, but that is no objection to it as a logical example. Some medieval logicians did in fact class both conjunctions as means of forming 'hypotheticals', i.e. complex propositions, out of simpler propositions; there were temporal hypotheticals and local hypotheticals. But without going into the analysis of local hypotheticals, we can quickly see that their logic does not run at all parallel to that of temporal hypotheticals. For, as I just now remarked, a temporal hypothetical '*p* and then *q*' can be used as a clause in a more complex one such as 'while *r*, (*p* and then *q*)'. We can play no similar tricks with local hypotheticals: 'where *r*, (*p* to the south-east of where *q*)'—e.g. 'Where the Dome of the Rock was built, (the Pyramids were built to the south-east of where the Parthenon was built)'—is just not an intelligible build-up for a proposition. The Pyramids just *were* built to the south-east of where the Parthenon was built; this just *is* so, and there's no sense in trying to say *where* it was so. The more we try to assimilate space and time, the more we shall find ourselves logically impeded from doing so.

I am strongly inclined to maintain that the rules for our grass-roots employment of temporal conjunctions—not only 'at the same time', but also 'before' and 'after'—belong to the domain of formal logic. This claim is highly disputable, and I can here only sketch my reasons for it. They derive from the branch of logic called modal logic—the logic of necessity and possibility. Tie-ups between modal logic and our elementary temporal discourse might well have been suspected; for is not the future precisely the domain of unrealized possibility? Arthur Prior was a pioneer in these researches, and further work has been done by a band of younger logicians, including Hintikka, Dummett, Lemmon, and Kripke. The March 1965 number of the *Journal of Symbolic Logic* contains an important article on the adequacy of certain modal-logic calculi for dealing with temporal order.[1] I feel confident that much progress

[1] R. A. Bull, 'An Algebraic Study of Diodorean Modal Systems'.

will be made in these researches; I am not invoking anyone's authority, but you can see that the idea of clearing up time problems with tools of modal logic is not just a programme vaguely sketched by me here and now. Nor would it be fair to say that calling these researches 'logic' is an arbitrary bit of nomenclature; modal logic is traditionally a part of logic, from Aristotle onwards; and the systems now being used in tense logic are based on modal systems originally devised by Lewis and Langford with no such application in mind.

People have long felt inclined to ascribe to some truths about time the same necessity as logical truths have: one could as easily describe a world in which *modus ponens* broke down as a world in which time was two-dimensional or the past was changeable. If I turn out to have been right in my conjecture about the possibility of reducing to modal logic the rules that govern temporal discourse, then this feeling will have been a divination of the truth. Geometrical truths, as is well known, are not necessary in this way; we can describe without contradiction a world whose geometry is non-Euclidean just as well as a Euclidean world. But if these basic truths about time are logical, then a world differing from ours in regard to them is a mere chimera.

However this may be, it is certain that there is a category-difference between space and time order, between events and individuals; and this can be brought out in quite ordinary language. But sometimes important things are too close to us to be clearly visible, or are concealed like faces in a puzzle picture; the labour of bringing them into plain view is then not wasted. And mistakes and confusions about this sort of thing are both common—witness the reams of nonsense about time you can find in bookshops—and of some practical importance. Squandering vast sums on foolish enterprises is an everyday occurrence; we may yet be witnesses of a 'time race' between East and West. Will the U.S. time explorer get back and eliminate Lenin before his Russian rival gets back even earlier and eliminates George Washington? In a few years the world may be anxiously waiting for the answer. If such spectacular folly once gets under way because governments have been convinced of some nonsensical theory, a logician will not waste effort on protests that will certainly go unheeded; he need not, after all, lose any sleep about who is going to succeed, and he could be glad that destructive efforts were directed where they would only squander human resources in a silly way.

One does what one can, though, against the Kingdom of Darkness; and perhaps less spectacular follies can be cured by exposing them to the light. Let me just instance a sophistry often used on one side of a current controversy. Some people are wont to say that it cannot make any significant moral difference whether you avoid something you wish to avoid by interposing a spatial barrier or by interposing a temporal barrier. If we do not let ourselves be fooled by the merely verbal assimilation of temporal and spatial barriers, the principle is really not a bit plausible; we need only test it on a case that rouses nobody's passions.

Let us suppose that it is my duty to organize a meeting in Cambridge. I fix a date for the meeting; then I suddenly realize that that ass Smith, whose presence would be disastrous, is coming to Cambridge for the day on that date, and will certainly attend given this opportunity. I may avoid this disaster either by changing the date of the meeting—'interposing a temporal barrier'—or by locking Smith in his hotel room—'interposing a spatial barrier'. It really is not morally indifferent which of these methods I adopt.

When we find writers copying from one another the false moral principle I have just attacked—particularly when we find one of them supporting it with talk of 'space-time'—we may be pretty confident what the trouble is; here we have, to use Hobbes's phrase, Darkness from Vain Philosophy. It is not for me here and now to enter upon a discussion 'of the Benefit that proceedeth from this Darkness, and to whom it accrueth'.

BERNARD WILLIAMS

Imagination and the Self

I start with a notorious argument of Berkeley's.

Phil. But (to pass by all that hath been hitherto said, and reckon it for nothing, if you will have it so) I am content to put the whole upon this issue. If you can conceive it possible for any mixture or combination of qualities, or any sensible object whatever, to exist without the mind, then I will grant it actually to be so.

Hyl. If it comes to that, the point will soon be decided. What more easy than to conceive a tree or house existing by itself, independent of, and unperceived by any mind whatsoever? I do at this present time conceive them existing after that manner.

Phil. How say you, Hylas, can you see a thing which is at the same time unseen?

Hyl. No, that were a contradiction.

Phil. Is it not a contradiction to talk of *conceiving* a thing which is *unconceived*?

Hyl. It is.

Phil. The tree or house therefore which you think of, is conceived by you.

Hyl. How should it be otherwise?

Phil. And what is conceived is surely in the mind.

Hyl. Without question, that which is conceived is in the mind.

Phil. How then came you to say, you conceived a house or tree existing independent and out of all minds whatsoever?

Hyl. That was, I own, an oversight; but stay, let me consider what led me into it—it is a pleasant mistake enough. As I was thinking of a tree in a solitary place, where no one was present to see it, methought that was to conceive a tree as existing unperceived or unthought of, not considering that I myself conceived it all the while. But now I plainly see, that all I can do is to frame ideas in my own mind. I may indeed conceive in my own thoughts the idea of a tree, or a house, or a mountain, but that is all. And this is far from proving, that I can conceive them *existing out of the minds of all spirits*.

Phil. You acknowledge then that you cannot possibly conceive how any one corporeal sensible thing should exist otherwise than in a mind.

Hyl. I do.

First Dialogue between Hylas and Philonous

It is not very difficult to refute this argument. I shall not rehearse a number of the considerations that might be brought against it. Yet it seems to have something in it which is not utterly implausible; the difficulty is to pin this down. A first step to doing this is to recall the familiar Berkelian insistence on the connection of thinking and images, and to take him to mean by 'conceiving' a thing, having an image of it or—to concentrate on the leading case—visualizing it. Not, of course, that this interpretation will save the argument for the very ambitious purpose to which, as I suppose, Berkeley assigned it, that of showing that an unperceived object is logically impossible. For one thing, in the sense of 'conceive' in which what is conceivable is logically possible, and what is not conceivable is not logically possible, conceiving and visualizing are clearly different things; as Descartes explicitly and correctly remarked. Indeed, Berkeley himself had to concede this for the case of minds, and in particular of God, but then they were not the sorts of things that could be perceived at all; for things of such a sort that they could be perceived, to think of them is for him (roughly) to visualize them. This is a mistake, and inasmuch as the argument rests on it, it fails. But if we jump over that mistake, and inspect the ground on the further side of it, we meet a much more interesting question: whether we can visualize something that is not seen. At least here, it might seem that Berkeley has a good point—not indeed to establish his idealism, but a good point nevertheless. For it is plausible to say that if I visualize something, then I think of myself seeing it; and that I could think of myself seeing something which was not seen does look as though it involved a contradiction. Does it indeed do so?

There is one sense, certainly, in which it does not, and this must be got out of the way first. This is the sense in which the relative clause, 'which is not seen', is taken in a purely extensional manner: that is to say, that in which the statement 'A thinks of himself seeing x, which is not seen' is equivalent to the bare conjunction, with external quantification, 'A thinks of himself seeing x, and x is not seen'. Such a conjunction can obviously be true: the fact that someone in the nineteenth century visualized the South Pole had no tendency to anticipate the feat of those who first saw that place. This rather blank consideration is enough to dispose of Berkeley's argument for his idealist purpose, I think, even with respect to visualization; if at least he really wants to 'put the whole upon this issue'. It would only be if we had already accepted his earlier arguments about the status of the objects of sense that we might find the considerations drawn from visualization persuasive for idealism.

This extensional sense, however, constitutes only one way of taking a relative clause of this type and it is of limited application. The question of taking the statement in this way would seem to arise only in those cases in which what I visualize is something that actually exists; only in this case can we quantify over the statement 'A thinks of himself seeing x' and conjoin it with the statement 'x is not seen'. But the fact that what is visualized is an actual object, while it may allow the extensional interpretation, certainly does not demand it. For—to change the example for the moment—the statement 'He thought of himself seeing the Queen, who was riding a bicycle' admits, as well as the extensional interpretation, an intensional interpretation by which it means the same as 'he visualized the Queen riding a bicycle'; under this latter interpretation the statement is not equivalent to a conjunction of the previous type, and not falsified by its being the case that the Queen was not at that time, or indeed at any other time, riding a bicycle.

I said just now that it was only with the visualization of actual objects that the extensional interpretation could even present itself; if that is true, with imaginary objects only an intensional one is available. I gave as a reason for this claim the consideration that only with actual objects could one make the quantification

required for the bare conjunction which is the mark of the extensional interpretation. I think that this is right, but there is a complication about it that I shall explore a little since it will be relevant
to the argument later on.

The complication emerges if we consider the following case. A
man is invited to visualize an ideal girl friend; and he visualizes a
girl who turns out to be exactly like Claudia Cardinale. We might
report this state of affairs by saying, 'Asked to visualize his ideal
girl, he visualized a girl just like Claudia Cardinale.' At first glance
we may be inclined to take the expression 'just like Claudia Cardinale' here in the same way that we took the expression 'riding
a bicycle' in the earlier example 'he visualized the Queen riding a
bicycle'. But this could be misleading. For in that former example,
the phrase 'riding a bicycle' represents an essential element of
what he visualized: if he were to give as exact an account as he
could of his thought he would tell a story in which the Queen was
described as riding a bicycle. Now this *could* be the case with the
man who visualized a girl just like Claudia Cardinale; Claudia
Cardinale might occur essentially in his account of what he visualized—if he constructed his ideal girl to the specification of Claudia
Cardinale, as it were. But this does not have to be so. It might
merely be that he visualized a girl, and that that girl happened to
be just like Claudia Cardinale—he may, indeed, never have heard
of Claudia Cardinale, and no reference to her would appear in his
description of the girl he visualized. Since, in these circumstances,
the description 'just like Claudia Cardinale' does not occur essentially in the characterization of what he visualized, it is tempting
to revert to the bare conjunction analysis and represent the state of
affairs by saying, 'He thought of himself seeing a certain girl;
and that girl was just like Claudia Cardinale.' But this of course
will not do, since it keeps the description 'just like Claudia Cardinale' out of the content of his thought only if we read it fully
extensionally, with a quantifier external to the whole thing, so
that it comes to saying that there is a certain girl of whom it is
true both that he thought of himself seeing her, and that she is
just like Claudia Cardinale: which is of course false. Recoiling
from this, we may seem to be left with no option but to put the
description 'just like Claudia Cardinale' straightforwardly into the

account of his thought; which obscures the fact that this was not in the present case an element of his thought, but an *ex post facto* comment on it.

I think that in this present case a solution might be achieved on the lines of representing the statement 'He visualized a girl just like Claudia Cardinale' as 'He visualized a girl of a certain sort; and Claudia Cardinale is a girl of that sort'—that is to say, as indeed a conjunction, but a conjunction that does not rest on quantifying over individuals. However, even if such a solution might do here, I think that there will prove to be a wider range of problems of a similar kind, which may well require other sorts of treatment. They concern more generally the role that a man's knowledge and beliefs may play in relation to what he visualizes, imagines, and so forth; and if we take a further look at this we shall see that the complication introduced by the present example goes deeper than this example by itself reveals. I have discussed this example in terms of a contrast between what is essential to what the man visualized, as he visualized it, and what comes into a description of it only via an *ex post facto* comment—an external fact, as we might say. But if we now take a case that introduces not merely ignorance (in the sense that the previous man had not heard of Claudia Cardinale), but false belief, we shall see that the phrase 'essential to what he visualized' is not merely vague (as it evidently is) but also in an important way ambiguous.

Suppose a man imagines assassinating the Prime Minister; and that his imagining this takes the form of visualization. Suppose, further, that being rather radically misinformed about political developments, he supposes Lord Salisbury to be the Prime Minister. What is it in fact that this man imagines? It seems difficult to deny that he does imagine assassinating the Prime Minister, since that is the act—let us suppose him to be a violent anarchist —which he sets himself to imagine. Nevertheless it would be very misleading just to say without qualification that he had imagined assassinating the Prime Minister, since it would naturally imply that he had been imagining the assassination of Mr. Wilson: in the fact that this could be misleading we see an illustration of the difficulty of keeping intensional contexts pure. At the same time, if his mistaken belief was operative in this piece of imagining, it will also be that he imagined assassinating Lord Salisbury. Elements drawn from Lord Salisbury will occur in his visualizing; his image of the fallen Prime Minister will be an image of Lord Salisbury.

Another way of putting the situation here, which will be useful to us later on, is to introduce the notion of the story that the man would ideally tell if telling what he imagined. I do not mean by this a genuine autobiographical story, rehearsing for instance the sequence of his images, but rather the story, as full as possible, of what, as he imagined it, happened—a piece of fiction, which in this case might start off 'I was standing in front of 10 Downing Street, the gun in my pocket . . .'. Such a story I shall call—merely using the term as a label and no more—the *narration*. In this present case, if indeed the man's mistake about the Prime Minister's identity was operative in his imagining, the narration will introduce Lord Salisbury—very possibly by name. In this sense, the introduction of Lord Salisbury is essential to the account of what the man on this occasion imagined, in a way in which the introduction of Claudia Cardinale was not essential to the account of what the man in our first example imagined; in that case, we made an addition for him in telling the tale, in this case not. Yet, while Lord Salisbury is in this way essential to the account of what the man imagined, it may not be that Lord Salisbury is essential to what he was really trying to imagine—and if it at all depends on false belief, as we are supposing, he is probably not essential in this second sense. For it may be that precisely what this man wants to do is to imagine assassinating the Prime Minister *whoever he may be*; and when his mistake is pointed out to him, he regards the Salisbury elements in his previous act of imagining as at best an irrelevance, at worst an embarrassment.

In this sense of 'essential'—the sense in which an element is not merely essential to the account of what I do imagine, but is essential to my particular imaginative *project*—the Salisbury element will be essential, not to a man who is imagining the assassination of the Prime Minister and merely believes that Lord Salisbury is the Prime Minister, but rather to a man who is imagining the assassination of the Prime Minister and also *imagining Salisbury as the Prime Minister*. For such a man, it will be a misunderstanding to point out, with respect to his narration, that Salisbury is not the Prime Minister; it is part of the point of his imaginative tale that Salisbury should occur in it in this role.

The point about the different nature of the project in the two cases seems not merely to *emerge* in the difference of the treatments which would be appropriate to the narrations, but in some more basic way to be characterized by that difference. For if we take the two men I have described, one of whom merely thinks that Salisbury is the Prime Minister, the other of whom is, as part of his imagining, imagining Salisbury as the Prime Minister, it is surely obvious that there need be no difference at all in the *content* of their respective narrations. Exactly the same story could come from either; similarly, on the purely psychological level, the same visualizings, the same images, could surely occur in both cases. The difference lies rather in how the story is meant.

Let us now go back to the problem of whether one can visualize an unseen object. We saw earlier on that if what is in question is a real object, together with a purely extensional interpretation of the statement that it is not seen, there is evidently no difficulty at all. We then broached an intensional interpretation, and have been pursuing a complication that attended getting clearer about what was involved in intensional interpretations. Using a distinction we have made in the course of that, we may now consider the case of visualizing an object—let us say a tree—where the idea that it is not seen by anyone is intensionally contained and is essential in the strongest sense: that is to say, the idea that it is not seen is essential to the imaginative project (it was such a project that Hylas was invited to undertake, presumably, in the original Berkeley argument).

Consider now two possible narrations. One goes roughly: 'A tree stands on an utterly deserted island; no one has ever seen it or will see it. It is a green deciduous tree, flowers on one side of it, etc., etc.' The second goes: 'I see in the middle distance a tree. As I get nearer I see that it is green. Moving round, on the far side I glimpse some flowers. This tree has never been seen by anyone and never will be.'

The first of these two narrations would surely be that of a man whose project it was *to imagine an unseen tree*. If that was his project, his narration reveals him as having succeeded in it. Notice that the narration does not contain any incoherence; nor does any incoherence arise from the fact that he is able to give this narration. A difficulty of this latter kind *would* arise if what we were considering were not an imaginative narration, but a description which claimed to be factually true of the world; for in that case, one could of course ask, 'If what you are saying is true, how do you or anyone else know that it is?' But since it does not claim to be factually true, but is a product of imagination, no such question can arise. It is *his* story. So we can coherently *imagine* an unseen tree: but, remember, we knew that already. Our question is about visualization.

The second narration would seem to be that of a man whose project it was to *imagine himself seeing a tree*. And in his narration, surely, there is something incoherent. For the last element in it, that the tree was not seen by anyone, really does clash with the rest of the narration, which is precisely a narration of his seeing it. Thus there does seem to be some incoherence in imagining oneself seeing an unseen tree, unless—boringly—this merely meant that one imagined oneself seeing a tree never seen by anyone else.

Now how are we to take the claim that it is impossible to *visualize* an unseen tree? One way of taking it would perhaps be this: that a man who was a visualizer, who did his imagining by way of visual images, would be bound in honesty to give the second type of narration and not the first. If he visualized this tree, he would by that fact be *imagining himself seeing a tree*; and that, as we have seen, does appear incoherent with an element in what he imagines being that the tree is unseen. Hence a visualizer, on this view, cannot imagine an unseen tree; he can only imagine himself seeing a tree, and that tree cannot be unseen. But if this is what the claim about visualization means, it is patently absurd. For if, as has been said, there is a coherent project of imagining an unseen tree, how can the fact that a man is a visualizer debar him from carrying it out? The narration—which is the fullest account of what he imagined—makes no reference to anything being seen, and is coherent. How could such a narration be in some way impugned by the discovery that the man was a visualizer?

Well, it may be said, what this shows is that the correct thesis about the relations of imagination, visualization, and the unseen is not *that* thesis, namely that one who does his imagining by way of visualizing is incapable of imagining an unseen tree. The correct thesis will rather be this: that although a man may imagine an unseen tree, and do it by visualizing, he cannot do it by *visualizing an unseen tree*. For visualizing, it was suggested earlier, means 'thinking of oneself seeing': and to think of oneself seeing an unseen tree is (the thesis claims) a nonsense, in much the same way as (we have already seen) imagining oneself seeing an unseen tree is. So we cannot visualize an unseen tree; though we can imagine one, and possibly by way of visualizing.

If this is the thesis, what now is the relation between what I imagine and what I visualize? It is tempting to say that if I imagine by visualizing, then what I visualize is what I imagine, or at least part of it; but clearly this temptation must be resisted, if the present thesis is to stand up. But perhaps there is a way of doing this, in terms of the distinctions I made earlier. We recall the man who imagined assassinating the Prime Minister, and who suffered at the time from a false belief that Lord Salisbury held that office. There were Lord Salisbury elements in his visualizing which, I suggested, were not essential to his imaginative project. Now it might be the case that a man who visualized found himself visualizing various elements which he realized were unsuitable to his imaginative project, and correspondingly left them out of his narration.

Thus suppose a man to be imagining a bath, and that he indeed visualizes a bath. Having been recently much at the Bonnard exhibition, he finds himself unable to visualize a bath without a woman in it. However, the woman being irrelevant to his imaginative project, he leaves her out of the narration. If, moreover, his imaginative project positively demanded the absence of the woman—if he were required to imagine an empty bath, for instance —he would *have* to leave her out.—But, it may be objected, the narration was said to be the fullest account of what he imagined; and if he leaves out these elements in what he visualizes, surely it is not the fullest account?—Yes, it can still be the fullest account of what he *imagined*; what it is not, is the fullest account of what he *visualized*. What this means is that, for certain purposes at least, and for certain applications of 'imagine', we can properly make the determinant of *what he imagined* his imaginative project, and not what he visualized, if he visualized anything. There seems to be a strong case for this in the example of the man and the bath; for it seems insane to say that this man could not imagine an empty bath, while it is perfectly true that in his present state he cannot visualize one.

Thus even when we imagine by way of visualizing, we can properly be said to imagine something lacking an element which is present in what we visualize. The suggestion I am now considering is that this is how things are with imagining and visualizing the unseen; it is like the bath example, with the man precisely setting out to imagine an empty bath, but with this difference: that the inseparability of the woman from the bath is a contingent fact about this man's present visualizings, whereas the inseparability of *being seen* from the objects of visualization is a necessary and ubiquitous feature of them. Thus on this account, a man can imagine an unseen tree, and by way of visualizing a tree; but he does not, and cannot, visualize an unseen tree, and the reason why what he visualizes is different from what he imagines is that he is allowed to discard elements from his visualization incompatible with the essentials of his imaginative project.

One merit of this cumbrous proposal is that it at least seems to leave a place for something like the visual in visualizing, without jeopardizing the truth that visualizers are not debarred from imagining the unseen. Moreover, the idea which it introduces of a man constructing his narration to suit his imaginative project fits well what I take to be a fact, that a man who vividly visualizes may be incautiously drawn on into a narration which actually does not suit his imaginative project. Thus the bath man, narrating a scene supposedly with an empty bath, might make a lunge in his narration into suggestions of the presence of the woman. Rather similarly, the man who was a visualizer giving the narration of the tree, while he is unlikely to move off into talking about his own perceptual activities, as in the second narration I considered before, might very well find himself saying things like this: 'A tree stands on a deserted island. On this side there are green leaves, round towards the back some flowers. To the right, a cactus plant . . .'—a narration not incoherent like the one before, but which, as a narration of an unseen tree, gives grounds, let us say, for disquiet.

But not for ultimate disquiet; and we shall now see that the cumbrous account I have just been considering made too many concessions. The fact that the narration just given introduces something like a perceptual point of view may well reveal something familiar about visualization; visualization is (at least usually, and if vivid) visualization of an object as seen from a point of view. The object may well be as though seen from one side rather than another. But this does not in fact mean that any imagined seeing is going on *in* the visualized scene. Even if we accept the description of visualizing as *thinking of oneself seeing*—and we shall come back to that later—this still does not mean that an element or feature of what I visualize is that it is being seen; as it was an element or feature of the visualized bath that it contained a woman. I as perceiver do not necessarily belong inside the world that I visualize, any more than I necessarily do so in the world that I imagine; or the painter in the scene that he paints; or the audience in the world of the stage. The cumbrous account I have been considering was wrong in treating the 'seeing' element in visualizing as an element in what is visualized. Let us then abandon that account—though not, I hope, everything that was said in the course of formulating it—and see what sense we can make of what is surely nearer the truth here, that we can in fact even visualize the unseen, because the fact that in visualization I am as it were seeing is not itself necessarily an element of what is visualized.

We may start with the analogy of the stage; and I shall consider, begging a large number of interesting questions which revolve around this point, only what may be called very vaguely the illusionist stage, problems of alienation and so forth being left on one side. The audience at such a play are spectators of a world they are not in. They see what they may well describe as, say, Othello in front of a certain palace in Venice; and they see that from a certain point of view—not meaning by that that they see it from a certain seat in the theatre, but rather that what they are presented with is a certain view of that palace, e.g. a view of

its front. But they are not themselves at any specifiable distance
from that palace; unlike Othello, who may be (thus he may be
just about to enter it).

They are, of course, at a certain specifiable distance from certain
pieces of scenery, as is Sir Laurence Olivier, and they again at
a certain distance from him. It is also true that they would not
be seeing Othello unless they were seeing Sir Laurence or another
real man moving around in such an area, nor would they be seeing
the palace, unless they saw some such scenery. But we must not
say that the reason why, in seeing Sir Laurence, they see Othello,
is that Sir Laurence *is* Othello: at least if that 'is' is the 'is' of
identity. For if Sir Laurence *is* Othello, then Miss Maggie Smith,
or whoever, *is* Desdemona, and since Othello strangles Desdemona, it would follow that Sir Laurence strangles Miss Smith,
which is false. What Sir Laurence does to Miss Smith is (something like) pretending to strangle her: but Othello does not pretend
to strangle Desdemona, and it would be a very different play if he
did. This lack of formal identity between actor and character holds
also, of course, for the relations of scenery and setting: when in a
play someone sets fire to the palace, they do not, hopefully, set
fire to the scenery. It is just because of these failures of identity
that we can sensibly say that we are, as spectators, at a certain
distance from the scenery and the actors, but not from the palace
or from Othello; if identity held, we should, in being 150 feet
from Sir Laurence, be just that distance from Othello.

Although this is, of course, only the crudest gesture towards a
complex and fascinating subject, it is enough perhaps to contri-
bute some of the content to saying that we as spectators are not *in*
the world of the play itself; we—in a sense—see what is happening in that world, but not in the same sense as that in which we
see the actors, nor as that in which the characters see one another
or events in the play. For if I see Othello and Desdemona, then I
see Othello strangle Desdemona; but that will not entail that I,
as part of my biography, have ever seen anyone strangle anyone.
Nor need the actress who plays Emilia ever see a dead body; but
Emilia does, for she sees the dead body of Desdemona. These
points suggest a particular consideration relevant to our argument,
that things can happen in the play unseen; not just in the sense,

obvious enough, in which things can happen on the stage unseen
(as when an actor skilfully conceals from us a prop left over from
the last act), but in that sense in which the playwright can provide
the direction, 'Enter First Murderer unobserved', and yet still
consistently hope that his piece will have an audience, an audience
who will indeed see this unobserved murderer.

The cinema provides more complex considerations of the same
sort. Here the point of view from which things are seen moves.
This point of view, relative to the actors and to the set, is in fact
that of the camera. What is done artistically with this point of
view can, of course, vary very greatly. It can in some rather unusual films be itself, in the film, the point of view of a camera:
that is to say, when the scene presents straight on the front of a
mirror, what we see in it is the lens of a camera. In many films
for some of the time, and in at least one film for all of the time, it
is the point of view of a character: when it is directed to a mirror,
we see the face of that character, and when that character is struck,
a fist grows larger until it fills the screen, and so on. In most conventional films most of the time, it is neither of these things. What
then is it? We cannot say, at least without great care, that it is *our*
point of view; for we are not, in the usual case, invited to have the
feeling that we are near to this castle, floating towards its top, or
stealing around these lovers, peering minutely at them. This effect
can be created, sometimes unintentionally—but in the general
run, it is not. One thing, in the general run, is certain: *we* are not
there. Nor, again, can we say in any simple way that this point of
view is the director's, though this suggestion does not entirely
fail to make a point. We cannot quite simply say it, since we are
no more invited to think of Griffith or of Antonioni floating up
towers or creeping around lovers. It is his point of view only in
the derivative sense that he is directing our attention to this and
that by showing it to us as it appears from that point of view. In
the standard case, it is not anyone's point of view. Yet we see the
characters and action from that point of view, in that sense, or
near it, in which we saw Othello. Thus once more, and very obviously, we can see in this way what in terms of the action is unseen.

That there are clues to be found in the dramatic and visual
arts to the problems of visualization is, I suppose, obvious and

unsurprising. If, however, what we are concerned with is the *nature* of visualization, these clues notoriously run out at the crucial stage. One reason that they run out is that in both theatre and cinema we really see *something*—something which we might say (coming out into the open a bit more than I have done so far) *represents* the characters and action. But in visualization nothing is really seen—and this is a big difference. It is a big enough difference to defeat, I think, Sartre, who seems to hope (in *L'Imaginaire*) that he has acquired enough impetus from the representational cases to convey him through the air to visualization, where our 'intention', in his terminology, is not sustained by any matter at all. But the impetus does not seem sufficient.

Yet even if these analogies leave us baffled, as they certainly leave me baffled, about the nature of visualization, they seem to provide sufficient clues to relieve us of puzzlement at least about visualizing the unseen. For even if visualizing is in some sense thinking of myself seeing, and what is visualized is presented as it were from a perceptual point of view, there can be no reason at all for insisting that that point of view is of one *within* the world of what is visualized; any more than our view of Othello is a view had by one in Othello's context, or the cinematic point of view is necessarily that of one stealing around the characters. We can, then, even visualize the unseen.

But now—if we are impressed at all by these analogies, and in particular by the cinematic analogy, should we remain satisfied with this formula: visualizing is thinking of myself seeing? Why does it have to be *myself*? The cinematic point of view, I suggested, did not have to be anyone's point of view; what is the ground for insisting that the point of view in visualization must be mine? Berkeley perhaps—to revert to him for the last time—was struck by a consideration that this point of view did not need to be distinctively mine. This may help to explain an extraordinary feature of his argument, that Hylas is not supposed to conclude from his thought-experiment, as one might suppose, that he cannot conceive an object unperceived by himself; he is supposed to conclude that he cannot conceive an object unperceived by any mind.

At this point we must distinguish some different kinds of visual

imagery in relation to myself; something that we have so far not
needed to do. The first is that which we have just been discussing
at some length, that in which I merely visualize something, without myself being in the visualized world at all. The second is
contrasted with this: that in which I visualize a world in which
I am acting, moving around, seeing things, and so forth—a form
of imagery involving, very often, kinaesthetic imagery of various
sorts. This second sort is, of course, possible and frequent; in
what I said earlier, I was not denying that I *could* be in my imagined
scene, I was merely denying that I had to be. In terms of imagining,
it is natural (though not inevitable) to associate the first sort of
imagery with imagining a certain thing, the second with imagining
(myself) doing, seeing, etc., certain things.

But the expression 'imagining myself doing, etc.' could cover
also a third possibility for imagery, which constitutes not really
a distinct third kind, but a special application of the first: namely
that of visualizing from the outside a figure who is myself doing
the things in question. This sort is capable of alternating quite
happily with the second—as we might say, *participation*—type:
thus, if I am prone to fantasies of being a world champion racing
driver, this could involve kinaesthetic imagery of tension, hands
clasped on the steering-wheel, and visualization of wet tarmac
as seen through an oil-spattered windscreen, and so forth; and,
also, at some different point, some visual image of myself, as
though in a newspaper photograph, having a garland hung around
my neck.

All these types of imagery are familiar, of course, from dreams,
as well as from fantasy in waking life. Dreams present also further
possibilities, less common perhaps in waking life; notably that
of an uncomfortable half-way house between the first type, in
which I am not in the scene, and the second or participation type;
that in which I am there, in the same space as the happenings,
but am, for no apparent reason, a transfixed and impotent observer
of them. Still more painful is that case in which all this is com-
pounded with the third type of imagery, and the happenings of
which I am a transfixed observer are happenings which I can see
happening to me. The complexities of dream-dissociation, however, we may leave.

Now in a great deal of fantasy and imagination of the second, participation, type, there is no great problem concerning the *me* that the fantasy is about: it is the actual empirical me, or more or less so. This does not mean, of course, that in order to entertain this fantasy of myself as a champion racing driver I have to engage in an elaborate work of intercalating racing-driving activities hypothetically into my past career, or extending hypothetically my future career so as to embrace them; I do not have to join the imagined activities in any determinate way on to my actual history. Nevertheless, I am, very often, putting quite a lot of my actual self into it, and where not consciously doing this, am prepared, as it were, to accept a lot of my actual self in the fantasied scene. It is, for instance, relative to my real wants, ambitions, and character that the imagined happenings are, to me in them, satisfying or upsetting.

Again, in the third type, very often, there is no problem about the figure that I visualize being me; at least no more problem than there is anyway about any imaged figure being someone in particular: the problem, for instance, that it looks as though an image I have of someone can be an image of that person only because I *mean* it to be so, and yet at the same time there is such a thing as *recognizing* an imaged figure. These problems I shall not pursue. The present point is that there is no special problem about the visualized figure being myself; he looks, for instance, like me (or at least like what I think I look like).

In the sense in which these types of imagining involve myself, simple visualizing—type one—does not involve myself, except as the person who, as a matter of simple biographical fact, does the visualizing. I indeed, at a certain point in my empirical history, visualize, say, a tree; but I do not occur in this operation again, as that person concerning whom, when I visualize a tree, I think that *he* sees a tree. So, bearing in mind those other relatively straightforward cases, it is misleading to say that straight visualizing is thinking of myself seeing something. It may indeed have actually misled people; for instance, Schlick. Schlick famously claimed that survival after death must be a contingent matter, because he could imagine watching his own funeral. In order to make good this claim, Schlick would have had to give a coherent account of how, as a participant at his own funeral, he could be himself, Schlick; all the problems of continuity, personal identity, and so forth are called up. It is no good trying to rest the case for this logical possibility merely on the alleged possibility of imagining oneself watching one's own funeral. In default of an independent argument that this is a coherent description of anything, we have only too readily to hand another account of the experience which, I suspect, was the one that Schlick reported in this way: namely, that he was not imagining himself watching his own funeral, he was *visualizing his own funeral*. And what that proves in the way of logical possibility, if it proves anything, is only the logical possibility *of his funeral*, which is not in dispute.

However, it is obviously not enough merely to eliminate from the discussion at this stage any reference to a 'myself' which is not the actual, empirical myself. I have said only that a *lot* of imagery about myself is recognizably about my actual self as—roughly—I am. But it looks as though some imagery, and in particular participation imagery, can be about myself, and yet precisely involve the elimination of my actual characteristics. I can imagine, in particular, being somebody else. It is with some remarks about this sort of possibility, which involves perhaps the most intimate relations between the imagination and the self, that I shall end.

'I might have been somebody else' is a very primitive and very real thought; and it tends to carry with it an idea that one knows what it would be like for this 'I' to look out on a different world, from a different body, and still be the same 'I'. To start at the easiest place, we know perfectly well that a great deal of what we are, in terms of memory, character, and bodily development, is the product of accidental factors which we can readily conceive to have been otherwise: 'if my parents had, as they considered doing, emigrated when I was two . . .'—yet it would still have been me. Suppose, further, that I had had different parents, who had borne me in a different year, a different century, even. . . . Such speculations can retain a grip on the imagination only up to a certain point, perhaps; and it is a significant fact that the point at which the grip slips, as it were, will differ with different people. For instance, it may well be the case that many people would

find the first line of speculation I just imagined, about the emigra-
tion of one's parents, much more compelling than the second,
concerning one's parents' identity; and I suppose this to be not
because of some beliefs about the overwhelming importance of
heredity in the formation of character (which may well be false,
and are dubiously relevant), but because in our form of society
parents play such a large part in one's early history, one is emotionally involved with them, and so forth. In the Guardian class
of Plato's Republic the difficult supposition would not have been
that one might have had different parents (since one was not to
know who they were, anyway), nor yet that one might have been
born years earlier (since the state was supposed to go on without
historical social change), but rather that one might have been born
somewhere else, and not be a Platonic Guardian at all. One's sense
of identity involves one's identifications.

Nevertheless, it is an important fact that, whatever the limits,
one seems to be able to carry on these speculations about *oneself*
in a way in which one cannot about other people. 'I might have
been . . .' is a form of thought that holds up much longer than
'he might have been . . .', although the latter, too, does better if
there is identification, in the sense for instance of a close emotional
attachment. In general, if we carry speculations about him very
far, there soon comes a point where it is vacuous to say that we are
talking about *him* at all—we are just imagining some arbitrary
historical figure. In thinking that I might have been . . ., it is not
like this; or not so soon.

If we press this hard enough, we readily get the idea that it is
not necessary to being *me* that I should have any of the individuat-
ing properties that I do have, this body, these memories, etc. And
for some of them, such as the body, we may think that it is not
necessary to have one at all; and, quite readily, we might not have
any memories. The limiting state of this progress is the Cartesian
consciousness: an 'I' without body, past, or character. In pursuing
these speculations to this point, we do not so far meet any obvious
dilemma or paradox—at most, there is a sense of strain, an increasing attenuation of content. A dilemma or real philosophical
obstacle occurs, however, when one adds to these speculations
another consideration: that it must also be true that I might not

have existed. This we certainly want to agree to—few will be persuaded that their own existence is a necessary feature of the universe. Now it is clear that, if we admit the previous speculations, the 'I' of 'I might not have existed' must be the same attenuated 'I' that seemed to emerge from those speculations. For suppose we took 'I might not have existed' to mean (as it might naturally be taken to mean) that there might not have been someone who had such and such a history, such and such an appearance, etc., filling this out with a list of one's actual empirical properties. If the previous speculations in fact made sense, then this filling-out cannot be an adequate account of what it means to say 'I might not have existed'. For if, on the line of the previous speculations, I had been someone else, lived at a different time, and so forth, then it might well be true that there would not have existed someone with just the properties I actually have, and yet not be true that I did not exist—I would exist, but not with those properties. The same point can be approached from the opposite end: it looks as though we might admit that someone could exist with just those empirical properties of history, appearance, etc., that I as a matter of fact have, and yet that person not be me. So, by these arguments, 'I might not have existed' cannot mean 'there might not have existed a person with just this specification', where the specification is that of the properties I actually have. Nor will any other specification of properties do better. So it looks as though the 'I' of this statement must again be the attenuated 'I', the Cartesian centre of consciousness. But if this is so, what can 'I might not have existed' possibly mean? For it now looks as though there is absolutely nothing left to distinguish any Cartesian 'I' from any other, and it is impossible to see any more what would be subtracted from the universe by the removal of *me*.

Once the difficulty has presented itself in this form, it works back to the original set of speculations. For suppose I conceive it possible that I might have been Napoleon—and mean by this that there might have been a world which contained a Napoleon exactly the same as the Napoleon that our world contained, except that he would have been me. What could be the difference between the actual Napoleon and the imagined one? All I have to take to him in the imagined world is a Cartesian centre of consciousness; and that, the real Napoleon had already. Leibniz, perhaps, made something like this point when he said to one who expressed the wish that he were King of China, that all he wanted was that he should cease to exist and there should be a King in China.

Thus we seem to reach an impasse: on the one hand, we have a type of speculation which can, perhaps rather compulsively, seem to make sense; on the other hand, considerations which show that the speculations must fail. The way out of this impasse lies, I think, in diagnosing an illusion that lies in the speculations. This illusion has something to do with the nature of the imagination.

If the activity of imagining being Napoleon involves in any important way imagery, it is bound, I think, to involve participation imagery. Images of myself being Napoleon can scarcely merely be images of the physical figure of Napoleon, for they will not in themselves have enough of me in them—an external view would lose the essence of what makes such imaginings so much more compelling about myself than they are about another. They will rather be images of, for instance, the desolation at Austerlitz as viewed by me vaguely aware of my short stature and my cockaded hat, my hand in my tunic.

Consider now the *narration*, to revert to the model we used earlier, appropriate to this sort of imagination. It is going to be of the general form: 'I have conquered; the ideals of the Revolution in my hands are sweeping away the old world. Poor Maria Walewska, I wonder where she is now' and so on and so on, according to whatever knowledge or illusions I possess about Napoleon. Now suppose that we actually heard someone saying things like this. In general, when we hear utterances in the first person, there is only one question to be asked relative to the identity of the 'I' involved: 'Who is the speaker?' But in the case of utterances as unlikely as this, there are two questions: 'Who is the speaker?' and 'Who is it that he either believes that he is, or is pretending to be?' In the present case, the latter alternative is in question: a man engaged in an imaginative narration like this would be a man pretending to be, or playing the role of, Napoleon. The 'I' of his discourse is to be taken as an 'I' uttered by Napoleon; who it stands for, if it stands for anybody, is Napoleon. But, of course, this being the playing of a role, the actual utterer is someone else, who in the next moment may use 'I' in its ordinary way with respect to his ordinary self.

Now this narration does not, of course, have to be actually produced. I am using it, as I was using it before, as a model to display what the man is imagining; some of his imaginative activity may actually take the form of saying some of these things to himself, but much of it may take such forms as imagery of his doing and seeing things, of which this narrative merely represents the ideally best verbal expression. But what is true, as we have seen, for the public verbal performance is true also for the private fantasy; what I am doing, in fantasy, is something like playing the role of Napoleon. In this respect, if not more generally, I agree with Professor Ryle's association, in *The Concept of Mind*, of the imagination with pretending. In the description of this activity, only two people need figure: the real me and Napoleon. There is no place for a third item, the Cartesian 'I', regarding which I imagine that *it* might have belonged to Napoleon. To suppose that such an entity is involved seems, in some part at least, to follow from a confusion of two modes of the imagination: that of imagining with regard to a certain thing, distinct from myself, that it is such and such; and that of imagining being such and such.

I have used several times in this lecture the formula 'imagining myself doing, being, etc., such and such'. Where this 'myself' is, roughly, my ordinary self, as in the case of the racing driver fantasy I discussed before, there is no great harm in this formula. But where the question is of imagining being, for instance, Napoleon, the formula 'imagining *myself* being Napoleon' is possibly misleading. It draws us near to a formula that may also be used, and which may be even more misleading—though misleading, of course, only when I start reflecting on it: the formula 'imagining that I am (or was) Napoleon'. For with regard to this formula, we may feel bound to ask what this 'I' is that turns up inside the expression of what I imagine. If it is the ordinary empirical me, as I am, what I imagine seems to be straightforwardly self-contradictory, which stops me in my tracks; and this will not do, for I know that, in imagining being Napoleon, I am not stopped in my tracks. Impressed by the fact that I am not stopped in my tracks, I may come to embrace the only apparent alternative: that this 'I' is a Cartesian one. The same sort of alternatives may seem to present themselves with the formula 'imagining myself being Napoleon', when we ask about the identity of the *myself*.

The mode of imagining appropriate to these fantasies, when they are not stopped in their tracks, is least misleadingly expressed as 'imagining being Napoleon': what this represents, the fantasy enactment of the role of Napoleon, is the only mode that has the power to sustain the speculations we have been discussing at all. And this mode, properly understood, does not introduce a further 'me' to generate these difficulties: there are only two persons involved in this, as I said, the real me and Napoleon. It is as unproblematic that I can imagine being Napoleon as that Charles Boyer could act the role of Napoleon.

It is perhaps in some such way, then, that we can explain why it is that although I can certainly imagine being Napoleon—or if I cannot, this is a limitation of mine—I still do not understand, and could not possibly understand, what it would be for me to have been Napoleon. For the fact that I can, in the only way that arouses my interest, imagine being Napoleon has no tendency at all to show that I can conceive, as a logical possibility, that I might have been Napoleon; any more than the fact that Charles Boyer can be Napoleon on the screen enables us to understand (in any serious sense) what it would be for Charles Boyer to have been Napoleon. Here we meet yet once more something that, in different ways, we have met twice before in this lecture, once with Berkeley and once with Schlick; that at least with regard to the self, the imagination is too tricky a thing to provide a reliable road to the comprehension of what is logically possible.

G. J. WARNOCK

The Primacy of Practical Reason

'Two things fill the mind with ever new and increasing admiration and awe, the oftener and more steadily they are reflected on: the starry heavens above me and the moral law within me.'[1] These words, which occur in the 'Conclusion' of Kant's *Critique of Practical Reason*, are of course very familiar, and have often been respectfully cited as a succinct expression of his intense and highly characteristic feeling for the sublimity of Nature and of the Moral Law. They have, I think, less often been critically considered. That the starry heavens are a proper object of admiration and awe is a proposition which I do not intend to discuss on this occasion, though it is, no doubt, discussable; but about the Moral Law there are questions, seldom raised, which I think may prove of interest. In a word, my question is this: why was Kant thus awestruck? Why did he, in this and other passages of similar tone and topic, present the Moral Law as pre-eminently, indeed uniquely, a proper object of reverence, respect, and veneration? I do not particularly wish to suggest that he was wrong to do so, but only to seek to understand why he did.

·The interest of this question is by no means purely historical. For in our own day most, if not all, philosophers who discuss the

[1] This and subsequent quotations from Kant are taken from *The Critique of Practical Reason and Other Writings in Moral Philosophy*, translated and edited by L. W. Beck, University of Chicago Press, 1949. The passage here cited is to be found at p. 258 of that volume.

nature of morality appear to agree with Kant in the opinion that, where moral considerations are relevant to some problem of conduct, they must certainly be accorded preponderant weight over all others; but very seldom is anything said as to why this should be so. There are indeed ethical theories which yield the implication that a man's moral views are, simply by definition, those which regularly preponderate in his practical decisions; but if, as I think is clear, such theories are mistaken—if, that is, the question what moral considerations are is logically separable from the question what weight they should carry, or do in fact carry for this person or that—then the question arises why moral considerations should be accorded the preponderant weight or authority which, by pretty general consensus, is actually and often tacitly ascribed to them. It would surely be impossible to go further than Kant did in insisting upon the overwhelming authority of the demands of Duty on our obedience; it is of particular interest, accordingly, to consider in his case on what foundation this tremendous authority was supposed to rest. He, if anyone, might be expected to have clear and definite views on this matter. I am not primarily raising here the psychological or genetic question of how or why Kant came to have the feelings that he did towards the Moral Law; that question, in the answer to which the special character of his early upbringing, and particularly his religious upbringing, would doubtless bulk large, is neither unimportant nor irrelevant, but is not here in issue or really within my competence. I shall in fact have occasion to allude to it, very briefly, in my conclusion, but my main and prior question is: does Kant's theoretical account of what the Moral Law is, taken along with his views on other related matters, justify, make reasonable or appropriate, the peculiarly awestruck attitude towards it which he so readily adopted and so frequently avowed?

What then did Kant find so tremendous, so uniquely deserving of respect, in the Moral Law? One might be inclined to think that in general there are three, not mutually exclusive, possibilities here. First, it might be held that the special respect-worthiness of the Moral Law derives from its source—for example, as some would hold though Kant of course did not, its source in the nature or will of a supreme law-giver and creator. Second, one might seek to derive the 'worth' of the Law from some valuable end which its promulgation and general observance would be calculated to promote. And third, one might argue that its claim to peculiar respect rests upon, and can be substantiated by, consideration of its own nature, of what it itself is. Now it could, I think, be said truly enough that Kant rests his case on considerations of each of these three kinds; but then it must be added that, in one way or another, for him all these seemingly diverse considerations boil down to the same thing. He is indeed anxious, in certain passages, to insist that the Moral Law subserves, and moral action aims at, no end at all—that the worth of moral action, and the respect-worthiness of the Law, do not consist in anything which either produces, or has as an actual or probable consequence. But in another and less ordinary sense moral action does have, he holds, an end—namely, human nature or, more strictly, *rational* nature; that is, that element or capacity in human beings which makes them capable of moral action and proper subjects of moral judgement. 'Rational nature exists as an end in itself', and has in itself 'absolute worth'.[1] But then 'rational nature' is taken also to be the source of the Moral Law; for Kant's celebrated doctrine of the autonomy of the will is exactly the contention that the obligations of morality are (and necessarily are) self-imposed by any rational being in virtue of his rationality; being rational is the condition, both necessary and sufficient, of being a self-legislating member of the 'Kingdom of Ends', bound, equally with all others, by laws of one's own making. And then, finally, it is for Kant another way of saying the same thing to say that the Law demands respect simply because of what it is—namely, an Imperative categorically pronounced by, and unconditionally binding upon, every rational being in virtue of his rationality, of the instantiation in each such being of 'rational nature'. 'Rational nature' is thus at once the source, and end, and essence of the Moral Law; and the peculiar respect-worthiness of the Law is not so much derived from, as indissolubly united with, the 'absolute worth' of rational nature.

Now these are high words, and words not without their attendant and more or less familiar obscurities. But my concern at the moment is with the content, rather than with the merits or adequacy, of

[1] Beck, op. cit., p. 87.

Kantian doctrine—with the question what he is saying, rather than with the question whether what he is saying is right. And what he is saying, I think, is really plain enough. He is saying that there is something in human beings (and possibly, or at any rate conceivably, in other beings too) which itself is, and in virtue of which they are, of pre-eminent value, of 'absolute worth'; and this is *reason*. But reason necessarily involves—this is his contention—recognition of and subjection to the Moral Law; such recognition and subjection is in a sense the distinctive characteristic of a rational being; and thus, in revering the demands of the Moral Law, one is really paying due reverence to that in oneself and others, namely reason, which has, and alone has, value for itself, real and unconditional 'worth', a proper claim to be not merely admired, or liked, but 'respected'.

But why, one may now ask, does Kant see reason in this light? Let us suppose, for the sake at least of the present argument, that he is successful in deriving the Moral Law from the concept of 'rational nature', and so in attaching to one the awe-striking properties, if any, of the other; but why is 'rational nature', why is reason, so peculiarly to be valued? Why should one be so particularly, and indeed uniquely, struck by it? The answer that Kant offers is sufficiently plain. It is simply that reason is itself unique. Reason is not valuable, he holds, for any good that it does; that the sedulous employment of reason contributes, for example, to the happiness and well-being of human beings is, he believes, far from certainly the case. Besides, even if that were the case, it would be a purely contingent fact that it was so, and perfectly conceivable that the good produced might have been secured, as effectively or more so, in some different way, for instance by the operation of sheer, blind instinct. That would not make instinct in any way particularly worthy of respect; while by contrast, even if the use of reason were to yield no particular benefits, its worth would thereby not be diminished in any degree. It is what reason *is* that counts—its being, in itself, unique in the universe. In the inanimate world, Kant believed (and believed that he could prove), there can be no occurrence that is not the law-determined resultant of antecedent occurrences and states; in the case of animals, and of men also to the extent that they are animals too, there is a determined, quasi-mechanical succession of 'inclination' and action not essentially different from the operation of physical causes in and on inanimate things. It is only in rational beings that anything different is to be found; and this is precisely the capacity to exercise reason, independently of, and sometimes in opposition to, physical or psychological influences, sensory stimuli, or 'inclinations'. This capacity, in Kant's view, raises 'rational nature' entirely above the natural order; here alone do we find an exception to, and independence of, that natural, law-governed sequence of causes and effects which prevails in all the rest of creation. In this, then, we find what he calls 'the sublimity of our own nature' and, derivatively but inseparably, the sublimity of the Moral Law which reason, freely and yet necessarily, prescribes for itself.

But at this point a further question very naturally arises. Is there not, one may think, a puzzling disparity between the argument Kant thus offers and the conclusion he draws? He insists, repeatedly, eloquently, emphatically, upon the uniqueness, the astonishing, awe-inspiring, absolute uniqueness, of reason; he insists correspondingly upon the uniqueness in creation, and so the sublimity and 'absolute worth', of rational nature or, as he sometimes expresses it, of personality. But how, we may ask, does he effect the transition from this—why, indeed, does he seem scarcely aware of making any transition—to his impassioned avowals of respect for the Moral Law? For surely there is a transition of some magnitude here. Let us suppose, as before, that Kant is wholly successful in his argument that any rational being is, as such, unconditionally bound by the Moral Law, that *qua* rational he can and must act as Duty requires; yet this, plainly, is not all that a rational being can do. Let us grant that there is, employed in moral deliberation and action, what Kant calls 'practical reason'; but then, there is 'theoretical' reason as well, and all its manifold doings. Indeed, on Kant's own insistence, there are not really two faculties of reason, one practical and the other theoretical; if there were, we might have asked why Kant should have regarded the former as somehow more awe-inspiring (almost more unique!) than the other. But rather, as he says himself, 'in the final analysis there can be but one and the same reason which must be differentiated only in application';[1] and if so, then we may

[1] Beck, op. cit., p. 54.

well be inclined to ask all the more insistently why Kant should have regarded, as he evidently did, *one* application of reason, namely its application in moral thought and action, as peculiarly respect-worthy. He seems, indeed, quite often to forget about theoretical reason altogether in this connection, and to locate the 'worth' of rational beings in their capacity for practical reasoning alone; or, put otherwise, he seems often to write as if practical reasoning, which for him is identical, at least in its pure form, with moral thinking and decision, were the only kind of reasoning there is.

It is, I think, a pleasing curiosity in the history of philosophy to observe here how closely, for a moment, Kant's course approaches to that of Aristotle, and then how widely, and as yet unex-plainedly, they ultimately diverge. Each seems clearly to employ uniqueness as a sign, or even as a proof, of distinctive worth; for each, the question what is distinctively valuable in man is to be answered by finding that respect in which man is unique; and, though Aristotle of course does not share Kant's belief in the strict determinism of nature in general, they agree in the conclusion that reason, 'rational nature', is what really distin-guishes men from all other beings—at least from all other ter-restrial beings. But at this point Aristotle finds it natural to conclude that theoretical reasoning must be the highest of human activities; for, though reason is indeed employed in practical matters, he thinks it plain that the timeless, incorruptible, non-sensuous objects of theoretical contemplation provide a wor-thier field for reason's activity than the humdrum situations and predicaments with which practical deliberation has, often in-conclusively, to do. But Kant, so far unaccountably, turns the other way; the theoretical employment of reason is by him given scant regard, and is never, I think, spoken of in the exalted, awe-struck tones which he so regularly feels to be appropriate to practical reasoning. But why, we may ask, did Kant not draw Aristotle's conclusion, having reasoned so far as he did along substantially the same line?

It is both true and, as I shall suggest in a moment, highly sig-nificant, that this is a question of which Kant was only flicker-ingly aware. The primacy of pure practical reason, and so of the Moral Law, impressed him so forcibly that he was conscious

H

only occasionally of any need to account for it; and such accounts as he offers may well be found perfunctory and unconvincing.

There is one passage of the second *Critique* in which Kant addresses himself formally and explicitly to argument for the 'primacy' of practical reason; but before considering that I would like to mention another matter which carried, I believe, some weight with him on this issue. Kant frequently observes, in a manner which implies that the observation is peculiarly striking, that reason in its practical use can 'determine the will'. He regards it, with some justice, as a distinctive feature of moral decision, at least in human beings, that such decisions can be and often are made independently of and often contrary to 'inclination'; and indeed the capacity so to decide seems to be for him just what the possession of a 'will' consists in. Now he is, I think, clearly of the opinion that in the use of theoretical reason no such thing is to be found; there is absent here the peculiarly striking capacity of reason to determine the will, so that, in this respect, practical reason is much the more extraordinary and distinctive phenomenon of the two. I believe, however, that this supposed contrast, by implication so much to the advantage of practical reason, actually vanishes if one examines more closely what it is taken to consist in. We must note that, in the practical employment of reason, it is 'the will' that reason is said to 'determine'; Kant is not saying, and it seems indeed that he could not consistently with his own principles have said, that reason can 'determine' physical happenings, for example, movements of the limbs in human action. We may say, then, that it is the inner, intellectual performance of decision, or of resolution, which is determined by reason; and if so, what Kant is saying is that, in the practical employment of reason, we are able to decide in the light of what we take to be reasons for so doing, and do not merely pass quasi-mechanically from thought to action as would creatures governed solely by 'inclination' or reaction to stimuli. But if so, it seems no longer at all clear in what respect this exercise of reason is to be regarded as essentially different from, and much more striking than, its purely theoretical exercise. For in the exericse of theoretical reason also we are, or at least we are no less inclined to suppose that we are, able to think, to believe, or argue, to conclude, in the light of what we take to be reasons for so doing, and do not merely slide, as it were, from thought to thought in sequences capable only of causal description and explanation. It is true that, outside the context of practical reasoning, we do not naturally, or not often, speak of the will as being involved, but there seems to be nothing in this point that would serve Kant's turn. For one thing, if practical reason determines our decisions rather than our actions, it is not clear in any case that Kant can properly speak of it as determining the will; for one might reasonably hold that, if the notion of a 'will' is to be employed at all, it should be supposed to be employed at the point at which decisions are put into execution, rather than in the process of arriving at decisions; practical reasoning, one may think, terminates in a practical conclusion, and it is only after that point, in the executive rather than the deliberative phase, that 'the will' takes over. Alternatively, if 'the will' is taken to be exercised merely in reasoning independently of, and perhaps contrary to, the influence of 'inclinations', then it would seem pertinent to point out that we may, for reasons, reach non-practical conclusions, just as we may reach practical conclusions, that may run counter to our inclinations. We may be reluctant to believe things no less than to do things. Just as we may find that there are reasons for doing what we would much prefer not to do, we may find that there are reasons for thinking what we would much prefer not to think.

However, Kant's explicit case for the 'primacy' of practical reason is not made to turn on the notion of the will. In a somewhat contorted passage of the second *Critique* which deals with this issue he writes in part as follows:

If practical reason may not assume and think as given anything further than what speculative reason affords from its own insight, the latter has primacy. But suppose that the former has of itself original *a priori* principles with which certain theoretical positions are inseparably bound but which are beyond any possible insight of the speculative reason (although not contradictory to it). Then the question is: Which interest is superior? It is not a question of which must yield, for one does not necessarily conflict with the other. . . . But if pure reason of itself can be and really is practical, as the consciousness of the moral law shows it to be, it is only one and the same reason which judges *a priori* by principles, whether for theoretical or for practical purposes. Then it is clear that, if its capacity in the former is not sufficient to establish certain propositions positively (which however do not contradict it), it must assume these propositions just as soon as they are sufficiently certified as belonging imprescriptibly to the practical interest of pure reason.[1]

What does this amount to? Kant's argument could fairly be summed up as follows. The power of reason in its speculative employment is, as the whole of the first *Critique* had been directed to establishing, strictly limited. It is not the case indeed, as Hume had contended, that nothing whatever about the world can be established *a priori*. Nevertheless, it can be shown, Kant thinks, that by theoretical arguments nothing whatever can be established about the world except as an object of 'possible experience'; and this implies, as the 'Dialectic' in the first *Critique* seeks to show in detail, that the traditional grand objects of metaphysical ambition are in principle unattainable by speculative reasoning. No valid argument from known premisses, set out in intelligible terms, can have as its conclusion that there is a God; that the soul is immortal; that the will is free; or can tell us anything at all of the world as it is 'in itself'. But the case, he holds, is otherwise with the practical employment of reason; here we do find, at least, reason to believe at least some of these speculatively indemonstrable propositions. For some of these propositions are, as he calls them, 'postulates' of pure practical reason; they are not exactly proved by, but nevertheless must be accepted as the basis or condition of, practical reasoning. 'These postulates are those of immortality, of freedom . . ., and of the existence of God.'[2] Briefly: we must believe that the soul is immortal since we are conscious of the requirement to achieve moral perfection, and have no prospect of doing so in the course of any finite existence; we must believe that the will is free since only on that supposition is morally assessable action, indeed *action* of any kind, a reality; and we must believe that there is a God since the 'highest good', an ideal coincidence of happiness with desert, can be supposed to be attainable only if a beneficent Creator has designed that sooner or later it should be attained.

[1] Beck, op. cit., pp. 194–5.
[2] Beck, op. cit., p. 235.

But these are propositions which, by the purely speculative exercise of reason, we could find no reason to believe, and which indeed could be shown to be theoretically indemonstrable; if, therefore, in the exercise of practical reason and the implications of that exercise, we do find reason, and indeed the necessity, to believe these propositions, then it must be concluded, in Kant's submission, that practical reason has, in this very crucial respect, the edge. It would not do, indeed, for the postulates of practical reason to conflict with anything that can be theoretically demonstrated; but since these are topics on which speculative reason is necessarily quite silent, we may be sure that that is not the case here.

Such is Kant's central argument for the primacy of practical reason, and hence for the peculiar veneration with which he regards the Moral Law; and it is fairly evident, I think, that it does not amount to much. It is, for one thing, very far from clear that what he offers as the indispensable 'postulates' of practical reasoning have any very serious claim to be so regarded. That the will is free, at least in some sense or other of that profoundly obscure and perplexing phrase, no doubt is presupposed in our attitudes towards and beliefs about the actions of others and, perhaps most importantly, of ourselves; but the two other supposed 'postulates' would probably be regarded by many as singularly dispensable. It may well be the case that moral perfection, as perhaps for that matter perfect physical health, is not attainable in the course of any finite span of terrestrial existence; but why is it necessary to believe that it is attainable at all? If it is said that its being attainable is implied by the proposition that we ought to attain it, we may reply that that implication is easily avoided by substituting the proposition that we ought to *strive* to attain it, a proposition which seems to have just as good a claim to express the substance of the moral conviction in question. Similarly, it is far from clear that it is necessary to believe that the 'highest good' is actually attainable; and if so, then it is not necessary to believe in any supernatural arrangements for its realization.

But let us suppose, again for the sake of the present argument, that these allegedly necessary 'postulates' really are necessary; even so, I believe that it can quite readily be seen that argument on this basis for the primacy of practical reason is far from conclusive, and may, indeed, be regarded as positively double-edged. Much turns, it seems to me, on the question in exactly what terms the argument is set out. Kant would wish to put it in this way: in the 'practical use' of reason we find grounds for accepting those important propositions which are its postulates, but which speculative reason is demonstrably powerless to establish. This seems to say that practical reason yields, so to speak, a bonus or dividend not procurable by any other means. But some might feel disposed to express the matter in this way: in the 'practical use' of reason, we find ourselves obliged to accept as its pre-conditions propositions which cannot conceivably be shown to be true, and which otherwise we have no reason whatever to believe. And this seems to say that reason in its practical use lies under the logical disability of leaving, so to speak, intellectual loose ends, of constraining us to accept what we cannot possibly show to be true. What is the real difference between these two ways of expressing the matter? They do not differ structurally, or logically; in each case it is said—and this is the substance of Kant's argument—that certain propositions which cannot be theoretically established play the role of 'postulates' in the employment of reason in practical matters. The difference is that our hypothetical anti-Kantian takes it to be a bad thing to be committed to accepting what cannot be established as true, whereas Kant very evidently regards it as a good thing that at any rate these propositions should be accepted. But why is it a good thing? It seems that his answer would be that acceptance of these propositions is morally and spiritually salutary, and that this 'interest' far outweighs any speculative, rationalistic discontent that might thereby be occasioned. But this, of course, is to assume the conclusion of his own argument—namely that, at any point of divergence between the practical and theoretical uses of reason, it is to its practical use that 'primacy' is to be accorded. It seems clear that, if the argument does not begin with this tacit conviction, it can quite naturally be read as establishing the opposite position—the position, namely, that the theoretical use of reason is more admirable, more impressive, more fully satisfactory than its practical use, since it does not, as the latter does, lie under the dialectical disadvantage of committing its practitioner to mere assumptions for which no support is conceivably forthcoming.

I believe that in fact one must now say, without further beating about the bush, that Kant's convictions on this matter really cannot be adequately supported, or even explained, within the confines of his own theory of morals. It is the fundamental contention of that theory that, to exhibit man as a moral being, nothing further is required than the supposition that man is a *rational* being; the source, and indeed the content, of the Moral Law is to be located in or extracted from 'concepts of pure reason' alone. It is thus inevitable that sentiments of 'respect', or even of awe, towards the Moral Law should have to be explained in terms of the peculiar respect-worthiness of reason; and this poses for Kant the difficulty, from which in my submission he does not escape, that while he does not really wish to accord such respect to reason in general, this is actually what his own theory would require him to do. He might have made a case, and indeed does make something of a case, for the idea that the faculty of reason is, when considered in a certain light, peculiarly striking, perhaps quite unique, very crucially distinctive of humans from other (at any rate terrestrial) creatures and objects. It would have been understandable, even, that he should have been somewhat awestruck by this remarkable and seemingly unique phenomenon. But the fact is that, to beat no further about the bush, this simply is not the conclusion that he wanted to reach; he really wanted to display as the proper object of veneration not Reason, but Virtue; and the fatal difficulty was that his own theory of morals precluded him in effect from distinguishing relevantly between the two.

It is interesting, but perhaps not surprising, to observe that Kant was apparently not always unmoved by that more general, as it were Aristotelian, respect for reason which was, I have suggested, the natural outcome of his theoretical position. In a note written probably in the 1760s, he says: 'By inclination I am an inquirer. I feel a consuming thirst for knowledge, the unrest which goes with the desire to progress in it, and satisfaction at every advance in it. There was a time when I believed this constituted the honour of humanity, and I despised the people who know nothing.'[1] This attitude—which, discounting a certain romanticism of expression, is indeed sufficiently Aristotelian—is one which, Kant implies even

[1] Beck, op. cit., p. 7.

at that relatively early date, he had decisively abandoned. But we find him again, in an essay published some twenty years later, speaking of reason as 'the highest good on earth'—and not, in this context, as being the ground of virtue and the Moral Law, but rather as being 'the ultimate touchstone of truth'.[1] But now, if, as no doubt was natural enough, he was disposed at one time to regard as 'the highest good' reason in its specifically intellectual, non-moral employment, what led him eventually, and with such fervour, to embrace the alternative view—to accord the 'primacy' to *practical* reason, and to consciousness of the Moral Law as its peculiarly awe-striking expression? Was he in fact moved by the arguments which we have considered, and have found to be, in my submission, by no means adequate to their intended purpose? I believe that it is clear that he was actually not moved by those arguments. In the note of the 1760s which I have just mentioned, he attributes his conversion from the 'blinding prejudice' of veneration for the theoretical intellect to Rousseau; and what he learned from Rousseau, what actually brought about his conversion, was surely not those arguments which he later deployed in the second *Critique*. Rousseau's gospel was of the sanctity of uncorrupted natural feeling, of the holiness of the heart's affections, of man as a sensitive —some would say, sentimental—rather than a rational being. It was, it seems to me clear, from this Romanticist source—combined, no doubt, with the persistent influences of a Pietist upbringing— that Kant's awestruck veneration for Virtue was actually derived; such were the grounds on which (with occasional lapses) he came to abstain from speaking in such reverential terms of Reason in general. The trouble is, though, that his later ethical theory is itself unbendingly rationalistic; and thus we find him in search, albeit somewhat perfunctorily in search, of some sort of philosophical grounds for a conviction which it does not occur to him to question, but to which his theory, I believe, can actually offer no support.

Is there anything of more general philosophical interest to be extracted from this brief scrutiny of Kant's dilemmas? I believe that there is something to be learned, if only from the circumstance that, so far as I know, this particular aspect of Kant's moral theory has been so seldom considered. Kant wished to assign to moral

---

[1] Beck, op. cit., p. 305.

virtues a special pre-eminence among human characteristics, to moral 'imperatives' an authority predominant over any other practical considerations. Though much in his moral theory has been exhaustively and critically examined, this feature of it has, I believe, too often been accepted without any examination at all. But even if one supposes that Kant was obviously right here, should there not be some statable reason *why* he was right? And if the reasons he offers seem insufficient for the purpose, should one not raise the question whether better reasons are to be found? It is, I think, a just criticism of much recent moral philosophy that from this issue it seems determined positively to avert its gaze.

I would myself be inclined to venture somewhat further than this, and to draw from Kant's example the further supposition that, if the 'worth' of moral virtue is to be effectively argued for, then the argument will surely have to bring in considerations of a type which he was determined to exclude. One will surely have to raise the question: what good does it do? Kant himself, I believe, falls into a not uncommon trap here. When, towards the close of his second *Critique*, he asks 'what pure morality really is', what is 'the distinctive mark of pure virtue', he proceeds at once to describe an extreme example of devotion to duty at a terrible price— specifically, of steadfast refusal to bear false witness, with disastrous consequences to the virtuous man himself and also, along with him, to all his family and friends. In this he presents us, no doubt, with an instance of 'pure virtue'; but do we find here its 'distinctive mark', what pure virtue 'really is'? Is it distinctive of virtue that its practice has disastrous consequences? Is morality 'really' a way of bringing catastrophe upon yourself, your family and your friends? Is this what we are supposed to learn from this dramatic example? Well, of course, it is not; what Kant wishes his example to teach us is that 'pure virtue' is to be valued *without regard* to its consequences. But then it is not clear that the example shows any such thing; for it is by no means impossible, surely, to derive from it the moral that virtue is to be valued even if sometimes the consequences of its practice are disastrous, on the understanding of course that usually they are highly desirable. Kant feels, no doubt rightly, that unswerving devotion to virtue is most admirable, most striking, when the cost to the virtuous man is great; but it is surely fallacious, though perhaps not uncommon, to infer from this that the 'worth' of virtue has *no* connection *ever* with the question what comes of its practice. To take thus, as seems often to be done, as the typical, representative, central case of virtuous action that case in which no good, and perhaps much harm, comes of it, is indeed to limit very severely the grounds on which it can thereafter be urged that the practice of virtue is to be valued above all things. Perhaps our consideration of the case of Kant may further the suggestion that that limitation cannot sensibly be accepted at all. If we eschew the question what good comes of being virtuous, then awe in contemplation of virtue is hard indeed to explain.

Index

PRINTED IN GREAT BRITAIN
AT THE UNIVERSITY PRESS, OXFORD
BY VIVIAN RIDLER
PRINTER TO THE UNIVERSITY